World Scientific Series on Public Policy and Technological Innovation – Vol. 2

Urban Economics, Real Estate, Transportation and Public Policy

World Scientific Series on Public Policy and Technological Innovation

Series Editor-in-Chief: Donald Siegel (*Arizona State University*)

Published

Vol. 2   *Urban Economics, Real Estate, Transportation and Public Policy*
edited by Jeffrey P. Cohen

Vol. 1   *Student Start-Ups: The New Landscape of Academic Entrepreneurship*
by Mike Wright, Philippe Mustar & Donald Siegel

World Scientific Series on Public Policy and Technological Innovation – Vol. 2

Urban Economics, Real Estate, Transportation and Public Policy

Editor

Jeffrey P. Cohen
University of Connecticut, USA

World Scientific

W JERSEY · LONDON · SINGAPORE · BEIJING · SHANGHAI · HONG KONG · TAIPEI · CHENNAI · TOKYO

Published by

World Scientific Publishing Co. Pte. Ltd.

5 Toh Tuck Link, Singapore 596224

USA office: 27 Warren Street, Suite 401-402, Hackensack, NJ 07601

UK office: 57 Shelton Street, Covent Garden, London WC2H 9HE

Library of Congress Cataloging-in-Publication Data
Names: Cohen, Jeffrey P., editor.
Title: Urban economics, real estate, transportation and public policy /
    [edited by] Jeffrey P. Cohen, University of Connecticut, USA.
Description: Hackensack, NJ : World Scientific, [2024] |
    Series: World scientific series on public policy and technological innovation,
    2661-4502 ; Vol. 2 | Includes bibliographical references and index.
Identifiers: LCCN 2023000834 | ISBN 9789811271656 (hardcover) |
    ISBN 9789811271663 (ebook) | ISBN 9789811271670 (ebook other)
Subjects: LCSH: Urban economics. | Real property. | Transportation. |
    Political planning. | Econometric models.
Classification: LCC HT321 .U323 2024 | DDC 330.9173/2--dc23/eng/20230109
LC record available at https://lccn.loc.gov/2023000834

British Library Cataloguing-in-Publication Data
A catalogue record for this book is available from the British Library.

For any available supplementary material, please visit
https://www.worldscientific.com/worldscibooks/10.1142/13288#t=suppl

Desk Editor: Kura Sunaina

Typeset by Stallion Press
Email: enquiries@stallionpress.com

Printed in Singapore

About the Editor

Jeffrey P. Cohen, PhD, is a Professor and the Kinnard Scholar in Real Estate at the University of Connecticut's School of Business. His research interests include transit oriented development; whether the real estate wealth associated with highway construction has been distributed equitably across residents; the impact of airports and airport noise on commercial and residential property values; equitable approaches to property taxation; land value estimation; housing price spillovers across jurisdictions; and the relationships between substance use treatment provider operating costs and urban economic issues (such as transit and affordable housing). Among approximately 50 peer-reviewed journal publications, he has published his research in several top journals, including: *Review of Economics and Statistics, Journal of Urban Economics, Journal of Regional Science, Regional Science and Urban Economics, Journal of Real Estate Finance and Economics, Real Estate Economics, Federal Reserve Bank of St. Louis Review*, and others.

Contents

Chapter 1

Motorcycle Fatalities Revisited: A Classical and Bayesian Analysis

Richard Fowles

Department of Economics, University of Utah, USA

Peter D. Loeb

Department of Economics, Rutgers University, USA

This paper examines the determinants of motorcycle fatality rates using panel data and classical and Bayesian statistical methods. It focuses on five variables in particular: universal helmet laws, partial helmet laws, cell phone use, suicidal propensities and beer consumption. Universal helmet laws are found to be favored over partial helmet laws to reduce motorcycle fatality rates while cell phone use is found to be a significant contributor to motorcycle fatalities as is alcohol consumption. Suicidal propensities are also shown to contribute to these crashes.

1. Introduction

Motorcycle fatalities continue to be of concern to public health officials, economists and policy makers. It is estimated that motorcyclists have a risk of death in a crash (measured as fatalities per vehicle-mile) which is 34 times higher than experienced in other motor vehicles.[i] In 2006, motorcycles (two–three wheel vehicles) accounted for 3 percent of the all motor vehicles registered in the US. However, motorcycle crashes accounted for 11 percent of motor vehicle crashes that same year.[ii] Looking at national trends, one can see that motorcycle fatalities trended downward from 5,144

---

[i] See Lin and Kraus (2009).

[ii] See National Highway Traffic Safety Administration (2008).

in 1980 to 2,116 in 1997. The trend then reversed, increasing to 5,312 in 2008. In 2009, fatalities decreased to 4,469 but then started increasing again. By 2011, the number of cyclists killed was 4,612.[iii] The changes in motorcycle fatality rates from 1980 to 2010 are provided in Appendix 3 which not only portrays changes in the trend but allows for observing similarities among the states.

The causes of motorcycle fatalities have been attributed to the avoidance of the use of helmets and the lack of universal or partial helmet laws, speeding, alcohol and poor body protection, among others. A great deal of research has gone into estimating the marginal contributions of these factors. However, the results of these studies have not always been convincing or have resulted in significant different estimates of the marginal effects of these factors.[iv]

This paper examines the determinants of motorcycle fatalities using econometric models and two Bayesian techniques. The analysis employs a rich panel data set by state for the period 1980 through 2010. The models examined not only consider the traditional factors found in many econometric studies but this paper extends those earlier models to include the effects of cell phone usage and suicidal propensities. Both of these factors are recent additions to variables which are thought to influence motor vehicle crashes and have been found significant in explaining motor vehicle crashes overall as seen, for example in Blattenberger *et al.* (2012, 2013) but have not been investigated regarding motorcycle fatality rates alone with the exception of one paper, i.e., Fowles and Loeb (2016).[v] In addition, unlike other studies, this paper differentiates between the effects of universal helmet laws and partial laws.[vi]

From a Bayesian perspective, we focus on the effects of five determinants of motorcycle fatality rates after normalizing for other

---

[iii]See National Highway Traffic Safety Administration (2011).

[iv]An early review of the causes of motorcycle crashes along with other transportation related crashes can be found in Loeb *et al.* (1994).

[v]The general form of the models estimated and the independent variables included in the models are based on the general work dealing with regulations suggested by Peltzman (1975), French *et al.* (2009) and Lin and Kraus (2009).

[vi]Unlike Fowles and Loeb (2016), which made use of sturdy-values, this paper examines the issue using extreme bounds analysis and Bayesian model averaging.

factors, i.e.: universal helmet laws, partial helmet laws, cell phone use, suicidal propensities and beer consumption.

2. Background

2.1. *The Focus Variables*

The 1966 Highway Safety Act attempted to address safety conditions on the US roadways. The act required states to implement a universal helmet law by imposing the risk of reducing up to 10 percent of their federal highway construction funds for noncompliance. The imposition of a helmet law was expected to increase helmet usage in that head injuries are the most common cause of motorcyclist deaths. The act resulted in 48 states adopting some measure of the law by 1976. However, there was strong opposition to this law by such groups as the American Motorcycle Association. They argued that the act violated a citizen's right of choice. Alternative arguments against requiring the use of helmets were that they were heavy for the riders, impaired vision and limited hearing. The outcome of these disagreements was the passage of the 1976 Federal Highway Safety Act which revised the requirement that all riders wear helmets to requiring only those under the age of 18 to wear helmets. Approximately 25 percent of the states then either abolished or reduced the requirements of the universal helmet law by 1980. Another attempt to increase helmet usage was through the Intermodal Surface Transportation Act of 1991 which provided grants to states that imposed helmet and seatbelt laws. However, this law was repealed in 1995.[vii]

Research efforts to establish the efficacy of helmet laws were generally of two types. One method was to compare motorcycle fatalities (and injuries) before and after a state imposed some form of helmet law or, alternatively, the use of regression models to estimate the effect of helmet laws on fatalities. Table 1 reviews a sample of these results. Although there is evidence that helmet laws reduce

---

[vii]See National Highway Traffic Safety Administration (2003) for a review of legislative history.

Table 1. Literature review of the effect of focus variables on crashes.

Focus Variable	References	Effect on Fatality Rate
Helmet Laws[a]	Hartunian *et al.* (1983)	−
	Graham and Lee (1986)	−/+(risk-compensation behavior over time)
	Sass and Zimmerman (2000)	−
	Weiss (51)	− (head injuries)
	French *et al.* (2009)	− (universal =laws)
	Sass and Leigh (1991)	? (less than 1% effect)
Alcohol	French *et al.* (2009) − motorcycle Fatalities	+
	Loeb *et al.* (2005) − motor vehicle Fatalities	+
	Blattenberger *et al.* (2012) − motor vehicle fatalities	+
BAC	Loeb and Clark (2009) − motor vehicle fatalities	+
	French *et al.* (2009) − motorcycle fatalities	not significant
MLDA	Lin and Kraus (2009) − motorcycle fatalities	no studies reported
	Sommers (1985) − motor vehicle fatalities	−
	Blattenberger *et al.* (2012) − motor vehicle fatalities	fragile results
	Fowles *et al.* (2010) − motor vehicle fatalities	fragile results

Table 1. (*Continued*)

Focus Variable	References	Effect on Fatality Rate
Cell Phones	Redelmeier and Tibshirani (1997)	+(on property damage)
	Violanti (1998)	+
	McEvoy et al. (2005)	+
	Neymens and Boyle (2007)	+
	Sampaio (2014)	+
	Consiglio et al. (2003)	+
	Beede and Kaas (2006)	+
	Laberge-Nadeau et al. (2003)	varied with size of model
	Chapman and Schoefield (1998)	−
	Sullman and Baas (2004)	not significant
	Pöysti et al. (2005)	No increase vis-à-vis the growth of the cell phone industry
	Loeb et al. (2009)	+ and −
	Fowles et al. (2010)	+ and −
	Blattenberger et al. (2012, 2013)	+
Suicide	Porkorny et al. (1972)	+
	Porterfield (1960)	+
	Murray and de Leo (2007)	+(collisions)
	Connolly et al. (1995)	+
	Huffine (1971)	+
	Phillips (1979)	+
	Souetre (1988)	+
	Etzerdorfer (1995)	?
	Blattenberger et al. (2012)	+

[a]Note that prior studies pertaining to the effect of helmet laws did not differentiate between universal and partial laws.

fatalities and head injuries, not all studies are as convincing as others. More importantly from our perspective, the above studies did not attempt to determine the trade-off in potential life-saving effects of universal helmet laws from partial helmet laws vis-a-vis a situation where there are no such laws. Rather, the emphasis is placed on the general viability of helmet laws on motorcycle fatality measures. The present study separates these effects.

Alcohol consumption has almost uniformly been found to have a significant deleterious effect on motor vehicle safety in general. Although this is not a new factor for consideration, it is of such importance that it deserves to be focused on, i.e., as a focus variable from a Bayesian perspective and one which most certainly should be, at the very least, selected as a control variable in econometric models dealing with crashes. Table 1 reviews some of the results found in other studies, both pertaining to motorcycle crashes and motor vehicle crashes in general.[viii]

Studies have been conducted to evaluate the effect of Blood Alcohol Concentration (BAC) thresholds on crashes. Most of these studies, e.g., Loeb *et al.* (2009), have addressed BAC effects on motor vehicle crashes in general and found that reducing the acceptable limits on BAC to designate driving while impaired reduced vehicle fatalities. Motorcycle fatalities seem to correlate similarly with alcohol usage and BAC measures found in general transportation studies. French *et al.* (2009, p. 831) note that, "An estimated 34 percent of all motorcyclists who were fatally injured in 2006 had BAC levels above 0.01 g/dL (NHTSA, 2008). In addition, it has been demonstrated that motorcycle riders have a lower helmet usage rate if they were drinking as compared to non-drinkers."[ix] However, French *et al.* (2009) did not find a significant effect on motorcycle fatalities when evaluating a BAC limit equal to or less than 0.08.

In addition, studies to address the effects of alcohol on safety, have examined the effect of the minimum legal drinking age on motor vehicle crashes. The results from these studies have not been consistent. Lin and Kraus (2009, p. 716) indicate that such an intervention has not yet been examined with regard to motorcycle riders. Yet others, as noted in Table 1, have not found consistent

---

[viii]See Loeb *et al.* (1994) for additional reviews, some showing opposite or insignificant results.

[ix]See Lin and Kraus (2009, p. 712–713) for a review of this literature.

results when examining the effect of the minimum legal drinking age on motor vehicle fatalities in general.[x]

Recently there have been two additional factors which have been examined for their influence on motor vehicle related fatalities. They are the effects of cell phones and suicidal propensities.[xi]

It is argued that cell phone usage contributes to motor vehicle fatalities due to its distracting effect on the driver, the reduction of attention spans and its propensity to increase reaction time. Cell phone subscriptions have increased exponentially since 1985 when there were 340 thousand subscribers to over 310 million in 2010.[xii] Not only has the number of cell phones available to the public increased, but so has the propensity to use them for both phone use and texting. Glassbrenner (2005) has estimated that approximately 10 percent of all drivers are on their cell phone while driving during daylight hours. Given the apparent danger of using cell phones while driving, 16 states plus the District of Columbia had banned their use by drivers at the time of this study (California, Connecticut, Delaware, Georgia, Hawaii, Illinois, Maryland, Nevada, New Hampshire, New Jersey, New York, Oregon, Rhode Island, Vermont, Washington and West Virginia).[xiii]

Given the above, numerous studies have been conducted regarding the effect of cell phone usage on motor vehicle crash rates. However, the effect of cell phone use on motorcycle crashes has not been well studied. Hence, the "prior" one regarding the impact of cell phone usage on motorcycle fatalities would been based on the general effect they have on motor vehicle crashes over-all.

The statistical evidence regarding the ban of cell phone use by drivers has generally been in support of such bans, but not

---

[x]See Loeb *et al.* (1994) for additional reviews.

[xi]See Blattenberger *et al.* (2012, 2013) for a discussion of these two factors with regard to overall motor vehicle fatality rates.

[xii]See CTIA (2011).

[xiii]See Governors Highway Safety Association (2019) for the list of states banning cell phone use. By April 2021, this list expanded to 24 states and DC which had a primary hand-held cellphone ban. These additional states were Arizona, Idaho, Indiana, Maine, Massachusetts, Minnesota, Tennessee, and Virginia. See Governors Highway Safety Association (2021).

consistently. Redelmeier and Tibshirani (1997) find that cell phones are linked to a four-fold increase in property damage while Violanti (1998) finds that cell phones are responsible for a nine-fold increase in fatalities. McEvoy *et al.* (2005) also finds evidence linking cell phone use with motor vehicle crashes as well as Neyens and Boyle (2007) and Sampaio (2014) find that a cell phone ban in New York led to a reduction in fatality rates of about 9 percent. Consiglio *et al.* (2003) using a laboratory environment finds that both hand-held and hands-free devices increase brake reaction time while Beede and Kaas (2006) find that hand-held devices adversely affected driver performance. However, other researchers found results inconsistent with those above.

Laberge-Nadeau *et al.* (2003) find a relation between phone use by drivers and crashes, but this relation diminished as their models were expanded. Chapman and Schoefield (1998) argue that cell phones were life-saving due to the "golden hour rule" allowing victims of crashes or onlookers to call for help and get quick medical responses. The probability of surviving an accident increases with the speed that aid can be obtained for the victim and sufficient cell phones in the hands of the public (and possibly by victims themselves) increases the likelihood of a timely medical response. Sullman and Baas (2004) add to these findings with their investigation which did not find a significant correlation between cell phone use and crash involvement. Similarly, Pöysti *et al.* (2005) find that, "phone-related accidents have not increased in line with the growth of the mobile phone industry."[xiv]

These inconsistent results led to a study by Loeb *et al.* (2009) using classical econometrics and specification error tests where cell phones were found to have a non-linear effect on motor vehicle fatalities. Cell phone usage among the population was first associated with increasing fatalities when there was a low volume of cell phones in use among the public followed by a life-saving effect on net with the growth of cell phone subscribers in the US until slightly fewer than 100 million were in use, after which they were associated with

---

[xiv]See Pöysti *et al.* (2005, p. 50).

increases in fatalities on net. Since, there are over 300 million cell phone subscriptions in the US, one anticipates a life-taking effect of cell phones. Blattenberger *et al.* (2012, 2013) and Fowles *et al.* (2010) have also demonstrated a relationship between cell phones and motor vehicle fatalities using Bayesian methods.

Motorcycle drivers have access to cell phones as do all other motor vehicle drivers. They can accommodate their cell phone activities directly through their helmets (if worn) as well as using devices to attach their cell phones to their bikes. One would anticipate a similar distracting effect and reaction time effect due to cell phone use on motorcyclists as found in the general motor vehicle driving population. In addition, cell phone using drivers in other types of motor vehicles may put motorcyclists at risk as well. The present study evaluates the cell phone effect on motorcycle fatalities using two Bayesian methods to address model and parameter uncertainty.

Suicides and suicide rates have rarely been used as determinants in motor vehicle fatality models. However, there is some statistical evidence that suicides and motor vehicle fatality rates are related. For example, Phillips (1979) examines the importance of imitation and found a 31 percent increase in automobile fatalities three days following a publicized suicide. Pokorny *et al.* (1972) and Porterfield (1960) also find a relation between suicides and motor vehicle fatalities. Murray and de Leo (2007) using Australian data also find a relation between suicidal propensity and motor vehicle collisions. One can make a case for this association based on economic grounds in that suicide via automobile may dismiss the stigma to the victim's family and there may be an insurance component to the decision in that death due to an accident may leave the victim's estate with an asset, i.e., a life-insurance policy. In addition, as argued in Blattenberger *et al.* (2012), suicide rates may account for changes in societal characteristics over time. Further, they may serve as a companion variable to account for factors not included in a model and not picked up by traditional proxies such as a time trend as presented by Loeb (1995).

However, the association between suicides and automobile crashes is not consistent among studies. For example, Connolly *et al.* (1995),

Huffine (1971), and Souetre (1988) find strong support for this relationship, while others, e.g., Etzerdorfer (1995), question the ability to determine if the victim of the crash was indeed a suicide. Most recently, Blattenberger *et al.* (2012) using a large panel data set and Bayesian and classical econometric methods, found a strong statistically significant and non-fragile effect of suicides on motor vehicle fatalities. This leads one to consider whether suicidal propensities may have an effect on motorcycle fatalities.

2.2. *Other Normalizing Variables*

A set of normalizing factors are usually included in models of motorcycle crashes and/or motor vehicle crashes in general. The deterministic propensities of these factors have been reviewed in many papers as outlined in Table 2. Their exclusion would potentially result in biased estimates of those variables which are focused on in the present study.

Motor vehicle speed and speed variance were considered as potentially important determinants of motor vehicle crashes and fatalities in general. Speed adds utility by diminishing travel time and by providing, at least for some, thrills and excitement. Yet speed is associated with an increase in the probability of crashes and deaths. Peltzman (1975) and others find evidence of the life-taking property of speed while Lave (1985) and others contribute the life-taking effect of speed to its variance. Others, for example Fowles and Loeb (1989) find evidence that both speed and the variance of speed contributed to motor vehicle fatalities. As with the case of motor vehicles in general, speed has been found to have an impact on motorcycle fatalities.[xv]

The effect of speed limits on fatality rates pertaining to the general motor vehicle fleet has been examined in the past. These statistical results have provided varying conclusions depending on model specification and data used, as seen in Table 2. French *et al.* (2009) investigates the effect of speed limits on rural interstates and found no significant effect on various measures of motorcycle fatalities

---

[xv]See Lin and Kraus (2009) and Shankar (2001).

Table 2. Literature review of the effect of normalizing variables on crashes.

Normalizing Variable	References	Effect on Fatality Rate
Speed (motorcycle crashes)	Lin and Kraus (2009)	+
	Shankar (2001)	+
Speed (all vehicles)	Peltzman (1975)	+
	Forester *et al.* (1984)	+
	Zlatoper (1984)	+
	Sommers (1985)	+
	Loeb (1987, 1988)	+
	Lave (1985)	+(re. speed variance)
	Levy and Asch (1989)	+
	Snyder (1989)	+
	Fowles and Loeb (1989)	+
Speed Limits (motorcycles)	French *et al.* (2009)	no effect on fatalities but - on non-fatal injuries
Speed Limits (all vehicles)	Forester *et al.* (1984)	+
	Garbacz and Kelly (1987)	−
	Loeb (1990)	−
	Keeler (1994)	varying results
	Blattenberger *et al.* (2012, 2013)	varying results
	Fowles *et al.* (2010)	varying results
Measures of Income Experience and Age	Peltzman (1975)	?
	Asch and Levy (1987)	+
	Garbacz (1990)	+
	Loeb (1990)	+
	Saffer and Grossman (1987a, 1987b)	+
	McCarthy (1992)	−
	Loeb (1985)	−
Education	Blattenberger *et al.* (2012)	−

although they did find a negative and significant effect on measures of non-fatal injuries. As such, it appears as if speed limits affect motorcycle fatalities similarly to that in the general motor vehicle population based on this limited comparison.

Measures of income are of particular interest to economists when studying motor vehicle crashes. Assuming that driving intensity and safety are normal goods, then the demand for each should increase with income. Peltzman (1975) argues that income would have an ambiguous effect on crashes given its offsetting effects. The net effect of income would depend on the relative strengths of these offsetting effects. In addition, Peltzman argues that transitory income would have a smaller life-saving effect than permanent income. Furthermore, one might notice a different effect using time series data in an analysis, possibly portraying short-run effects, as opposed to models using cross-sectional data which would possibly portray long-run effects. One would anticipate that income might also affect motorcycle purchases and then crashes. Higher incomes might induce affluent and older members of society to purchase large motorcycles which might be used infrequently and thus exacerbate motorcycle fatality rates. Similarly, low levels of income and high measures of unemployment rates might result in substitutions from automobiles to lower powered (less expensive) motorcycles and thus increase the number of motorcycle crashes.

Additional socio-economic factors used to normalize model specifications have been incorporated in the past. These include measures of poverty, measures of education and the distribution of the population among different age categories. One might expect young drivers to have less experience than older ones and thus take more risks while driving. Asch and Levy (1990), Garbacz (1990), Loeb (1990), and Saffer and Grossman (1987a, 1987b) find such a relationship. However, McCarthy (1992) and Loeb (1985) find a significant negative association between youthful drivers, and fatality and injury measures. One might expect either of these to occur with motorcycle crashes given the number of older individuals purchasing motorcycles in the last two decades.[xvi]

Higher levels of education might be associated with greater stocks of human capital which would then be expected to be inversely related with risky behavior. At the overall motor vehicle level,

---

[xvi]Between 1985 and 2003, the percentage of motorcycle owners who are 50 or older steadily grew from 8.1 to 25.1 percent. See Morris (2009).

Blattenberger *et al.* (2012) did indeed find some evidence on this. One might expect the same relationship when one only examines motorcycle fatalities. However, higher levels of education are also associated with higher levels of income and there may be some confounding effects if higher income individuals over the age of, for example 50, use motorcycles infrequently and, as such, fail to gain significant experience riding motorcycles.

3. Data

We utilize a rich set of data collected on 50 states and Washington, D.C. over the period from 1980 to 2010. The total number of motorcycle fatalities per billion vehicle-miles traveled is our dependent variable. Our choice of explanatory variables is based on literature reviewed in Section 2 that highlights the importance of policy, safety, demographic and economic determinants of fatality rates. Issues related to the choice of these variables, as well as the general form of the models, are well described in Blattenberger *et al.* (2012, 2013) Fowles *et al.* (2010) Loeb *et al.* (2009) and Loeb and Clark (2009). Our data cover years during which there were significant changes in several important variables that are "*a priori*" plausible predictors of motorcycle fatalities. Notably, the data record the complex and changing pattern of helmet laws across states and over time. The data also capture the explosive growth in cell phone subscriptions from effectively zero to over 300 million. Annual subscription data at the state level were only available beginning from year 2000. For the earlier years, we used national level data and imputed state level subscriptions to be proportional to state population proportions for the prior years.[xvii] We anticipate that increases in cell phone subscriptions are positively correlated with their use. This is the same assumption used in studies analyzing their effect on the total motor vehicle fatality rate as seen, for example, in Fowles *et al.* (2010).

Another major change observed in the data relates to changes in Federal law that allowed individual states to modify the 55 mile

---

[xvii] Our method of imputing cell phone subscriptions correlates with the actual data with a correlation coefficient of 0.9943.

per hour speed limit on their interstate highways. Our data records the highest posted urban interstate speed limit that was in effect during the years for each state. Within the data, per se Blood Alcohol Concentration (BAC) laws vary widely, even though by 2005 all states and the District of Columbia had mandated a 0.08 BAC illegal per se law.[xviii] BAC thresholds for addressing issues of driving under the influence of alcohol have previously been found to have an effect on motor vehicle crashes in general, but it has not shown to be significant with respect to motorcycle crashes. However, alcohol consumption and helmet laws have generally been found to be significant, or of interest, as determinants of motorcycle fatalities. These factors are of particular interest given the review of the literature in Section 2.

We investigate the effect of suicides on motorcycle crashes as well, in that, individuals may use motorcycles as the instrument in such actions so as to minimize stigma and for a possible insurance/economic benefit to the estate. In addition, suicide in the model may measure to some extent changes in societal risk taking or life preferences. Also, measures of the percent of young males in the population, the minimum legal drinking age, a measure of poverty, the unemployment rate, education levels, the crime rate, and real income are included in the model as normalizing factors. In addition, a time trend is included to adjust for changes over time not specifically picked up by the other regressors in the model. However, we focus in particular on five variables: cell phones, suicidal propensities, alcohol consumption, and the two helmet factors.[xix]

The data are organized by the geographical coding of states into 11 regions.[xx] The variables are defined and described in Table 3 along

---

[xviii]The per se law refers to legislation that makes it illegal to drive a vehicle at a blood alcohol level at or above the specified BAC level.

[xix]We are interested not only in the effects of universal helmet laws and partial helmet laws, but which has a stronger and less uncertain effect on motorcycle fatality rates.

[xx]The use of regions mirrors the US standard federal regions, but we isolate Alaska and Hawaii since they are non-contiguous. In all analyses the regional variables are included but results are not presented.

Table 3. Explanatory Variables[a] Cross Sectional–Time Series Analysis of Motorcycle Fatality Rates For 50 States and DC from 1980 to 2010.

	Description	Expected Sign
YEAR	A time trend.	−
PERSELAW	Dummy variable indicating the existence of a law defining intoxication of a driver in terms of Blood Alcohol Concentration (BAC) of 0.1 or lower. PERSELAW=1 indicates the existence of such a law and PERSELAW=0 indicates the absence of such a law.	−
SPEED	Maximum posted speed limit, urban interstate highways, in miles per hour.	+
REGION	Dummy for Regional Fixed Effects (geographical coding from north to south and east to west).	?
BEER	Per capita beer consumption (in gal) per year.	+
MLDA21	Dummy variable indicating the minimum legal drinking age is 21.	−
YOUNG	Proportion of males (16–24) relative to population of age 16 and over.	?
CELLPOP	Number of cell phone subscriptions per 10,000 population.	+
POVERTY	Poverty rate (percentage).	+
UNPLOY	Unemployment rate (percentage).	−
INCOME	Real per household income in 2000 dollars.	?
ED_HS	Percent of persons with a high school diploma.	−
ED_COL	Percent of persons with a college degree.	−
CRIME	Violent crime rate (crimes per million persons).	+
SUICIDE	Suicide rate (suicides per 100,000 population).	?
GINI	The Gini coefficient. An index measuring income inequality (0 as complete equality and 1 as complete inequality).	+
PARTIAL	Dummy variable indicating the presence of a partial helmet law in a given state for a given year.	−
UNIVERSAL	Dummy variable indicating the presence of a universal helmet law in a given state for a given year.	−

[a]For data sources, see Appendix 1.

Table 4. Descriptive Statistics.

	Median	Mean	Range
Fatality Rate	1.468	1.654	6.753
YEAR	1995	1995	30
PERSELAW	1	0.8937	1
SPEED	65	64.32	25
BEER	1.3	1.308	1.52
MLDA21	1	0.8684	1
YOUNG	0.19	0.1849	0.19
CELLPOP	12.856	28.221	207.571
POVERTY	12.5	13.05	24.3
UNPLOY	5.6	6.012	15.8
INCOME	22321	23749	64037
ED_HS	81.9	80.54	39.7
ED_COL	22.3	22.82	39.7
CRIME	4455	4586	10383
SUICIDE	12.4	12.8	24.16
GINI	0.4053	0.4102	0.261
NO LAW	0	0.09614	1
UNIVERSAL	0	0.4314	1
PARTIAL	0	0.4605	1

with their expected effects (prior) on fatality rates.[xxi] Descriptive statistics are provided in Table 4.

4. Classical Econometric Results

Various specifications of the standard form:

(1) $Y = X\beta + \mu$ are estimated using Ordinary Least Squares. The Full Ideal Conditions[xxii] are assumed to be upheld where:

(2) $b = (X^T X)^{-1} X^T Y$ and

(3) $\mu \sim N(0, \sigma^2 I)$ and

[xxi]The anticipated sign for YEAR as a time trend is negative because it proxies advances in technology and possibly permanent income. Poverty is anticipated to have a positive effect serving as a proxy for infrastructure such as improved highways and faster emergency response. Income inequality and crime are anticipated to have positive signs that may reflect social malaise or risky behaviors (see Blattenberger *et al.* (2013)). Mixed results in previous literature are associated with young riders, so we are uncertain as to the anticipated sign of this variable.

[xxii]See Ramsey (1974) and Ramsey and Zarembka (1971).

with Y as the vector of fatality rates, X is a matrix of explanatory variables whose composition conceivably varies across specified models, β is a vector of unknown slope parameters, μ is a vector of disturbance terms, σ^2 is a scalar variance parameter, and b is the OLS estimator.

Table 5 presents a sample of regression results starting from a fully inclusive model using all of the variables from Table 3 to a simpler model using our focus variables along with a trend, a minimum legal drinking age dummy, an intercept, and regional dummies.[xxiii] The results are generally in compliance with our *a priori* expectations.[xxiv] Most notably, with regard to our focus variables, all five (cell phones, suicides, helmet laws and alcohol) are stable in terms of the sign of their respective coefficients and all are statistically significant at a 1 percent significance level.[xxv] Of particular interest are the consistent effects of both the universal and partial helmet laws.[xxvi]

[xxiii]Similar models for total motor vehicle fatality rates have been investigated in prior research for specification errors of omission of variables, misspecification of the structural form of the regressors, simultaneous equation bias, serial correlation, and non-normality of the error term and found to be in compliance with the Full Ideal Conditions. See, for example, Loeb, *et al.* (2009). In addition, see Fowles *et al.* (2013) and Loeb and Clarke (2009).

[xxiv]Regional dummy variables were included in the regressions, all are estimated as negative and mostly significant given that the region including Hawaii was the reference region. Hawaii has the highest motorcycle fatality rate. The reference group for helmet laws is NO LAW.

[xxv]The inclusion of these variables in the models is based on many other classical models starting with Peltzman (1975). See, for example, Loeb *et al.* (2009), Fowles *et al.* (2010), and Loeb *et al.* (1994) for a further discussion of these factors. The selected models we present in Table 5 include only five possible specifications and show that the results associated with our focus variables are stable for this small group of specifications. One might be concerned that these results are due to data mining. However, they are presented not as the for sure true potential set of specifications, but rather to give a sense of possible results and as a set of Bayesian "priors". The Bayesian techniques we employ can examine these variables for stability and fragility across millions of models and provide some insight into the uncertainty which we may entertain regarding our results. As such, stability or fragility of results are not due to traditional data mining. This is not within the traditional methods employed with classical econometric techniques, i.e., examining virtually all possible specifications, given the variables considered as potential contributors to the explanation of the dependent variable.

Note that model uncertainty is implicit in Table 5 and thus the standard notion of significance level testing, assuming any given model is true (the sampling distribution is known), must be relaxed. This issue is addressed in the following section.

5. Bayesian Model Averaging (BMA)

Although it is common, as in Table 5 above, to report regression results for a handful of model specifications (here 5 out of over 268 million specifications), the reported t- and F-statistics are valid only on the presumption of one model's truth. Without model certainty, characteristics of the sampling distribution are unknown, and thus, classical inference is fraught with difficulty.[xxvii] Bayesian theory, however, can directly address model uncertainty and in this paper, we utilize advances in Bayesian research regarding model choice as discussed, for example, in Key *et al.* (1999), and Clyde (1999). An early investigator in model uncertainty was Leamer (1978, 1982, 1983, and 1985) who, in a book and series of articles, dealt with specification searches and problems that arise when inferences are based on non-experimental data. Bayesian Model Averaging (BMA) was a product of this work and is discussed in depth by Raftery *et al.* (1997).

By averaging across many model specifications, BMA is able to explicitly account for model uncertainty as it relates to parameter estimation. As presented in Hoeting *et al.* (1999), BMA provides a straightforward method to summarize the effects of explanatory variables as measured by their regression coefficients as they are manifested in assorted models.

Table 6 summarizes BMA analysis for the full model presented above (in Table 5), regressing fatality rates on the core set of

---

[xxvi]Some additional insight on the relative importance of the focus variables (as well as other explanatory variables) from a classical perspective can be obtained using standardized data and our OLS regression results. Appendix 2 provides these standardized OLS Regression Coefficients for the classical full model specification. The focus variables ranked in order of importance using this technique are: cell phones, universal helmet laws, partial helmet laws, alcohol, and suicides.

[xxvii]See, for example, Leamer (1978) and Hill (1985).

Table 5. OLS Motorcycle Fatality Rate Models for the US states from 1980 to 2010 estimates and t-values.

	Full Model	Model 2	Model 3	Model 4	Model 5
(Intercept)	212.000	218.300	193.100	195.600	263.100
	(13.622)	(14.259)	(13.789)	(15.560)	(25.824)
YEAR	−0.106	−0.109	−0.095	−0.096	−0.132
	(−13.225)	(−13.873)	(−13.342)	(−15.011)	(−25.638)
PERSELAW	0.027	0.010	0.060		
	(0.489)	(0.179)	(1.111)		
SPEED	−0.004	−0.004	−0.005		
	(−1.051)	(−1.017)	(−1.245)		
BEER	0.409	0.410	0.421	0.422	0.501
	(5.156)	(5.166)	(5.314)	(5.349)	(6.480)
MLDA21	−0.262	−0.258	−0.274	−0.272	−0.253
	(−4.574)	(−4.510)	(−4.808)	(−4.802)	(−4.363)
YOUNG	−0.035	0.118	0.209		
	(−0.048)	(0.161)	(0.293)		
CELLPOP	0.029	0.029	0.028	0.028	0.030
	(15.944)	(16.010)	(18.969)	(21.060)	(23.628)
POVERTY	−0.013				
	(−2.191)				
UNPLOY	−0.008	−0.013			
	(−0.932)	(−1.646)			
INCOME[a]	0.0001	0.0001			
	(−1.282)	(−0.838)			
ED_HS	−0.016	−0.014	−0.025	−0.025	
	(−2.985)	(−2.582)	(−5.444)	(−5.441)	
ED_COL	−0.033	−0.032	−0.023	−0.023	
	(−5.198)	(−4.984)	(−4.370)	(−4.354)	
CRIME[a]	0.0001	0.0001	0.0001	0.0001	
	(2.809)	(3.095)	(4.854)	(5.129)	
SUICIDE	0.023	0.024	0.021	0.021	0.031
	(2.838)	(2.926)	(2.606)	(2.638)	(4.391)
GINI	4.899	4.346			
	(5.321)	(4.902)			
UNIVERSAL	−0.812	−0.815	−0.762	−0.773	−0.668
	(−14.171)	(−14.205)	(−13.441)	(−13.761)	(−11.789)
PARTIAL	−0.275	−0.286	−0.252	−0.256	−0.168
	(−5.108)	(−5.313)	(−4.695)	(−4.792)	(−3.113)
Adjusted R²	0.619	0.618	0.612	0.6125	0.588
F-stat[b]	96.210	99.480	109.500	125.900	133.800

[a]Coefficients on income and crime < 0.00001 but coded as 0.0001
[b]n = 1581

Table 6. Bayesian Model Averaging for Motorcycle Fatality Rate Models for the US states from 1980 to 2010.

	p!=0	EV	SD	model 1	model 2	model 3	model 4	model 5
(Intercept)	100	235.400	14.440	237.200	242.100	220.400	239.600	236.600
YEAR	100	−0.118	0.007	−0.119	−0.122	−0.110	−0.120	−0.119
PERSELAW	0	0.000	0.000	.	.	.	.	.
SPEED	0	0.000	0.000	.	.	.	.	.
BEER	100	0.443	0.086	0.465	0.396	0.400	0.440	0.498
MLDA21	100	−0.263	0.057	−0.260	−0.271	−0.271	−0.253	−0.269
YOUNG	0	0.000	0.000	.	.	.	.	.
CELLPOP	100	0.029	0.001	0.029	0.029	0.028	0.029	0.029
POVERTY	9.8	−0.001	0.003	.	.	.	.	.
UNPLOY	2.1	0.000	0.002	.	.	.	.	.
INCOME[a]	0	0.000	0.000	.	.	.	.	.
ED_HS	24.8	−0.003	0.006	.	.	−0.013	.	.
ED_COL	100	−0.041	0.006	−0.044	−0.041	−0.033	−0.044	−0.043
CRIME[a]	90.4	0.000	0.000	0.000	0.000	0.000	0.000	0.000
SUICIDE	47.1	0.011	0.013	.	0.023	0.028	.	.
GINI	100	4.549	0.891	4.265	5.006	4.024	4.653	4.412
UNIVERSAL	100	−0.813	0.059	−0.803	−0.833	−0.834	−0.786	−0.803
PARTIAL	100	−0.279	0.054	−0.280	−0.291	−0.284	−0.282	−0.265
Number of Variables				14	16	17	15	15
R2				0.618	0.621	0.623	0.619	0.619
Posterior Probability				0.179	0.173	0.14	0.072	0.054

[a]Coefficients on CRIME and INCOME < 0.00001 but EV and SD coded as 0.000

explanatory variables.[xxviii] Millions of models are considered and the top models, ranked in terms of highest posterior probability, are retained.[xxix] From among these, the top five are shown in Table 6. The column headed "p! = 0" gives the posterior probability that the particular variable is included in the model. The "EV" column shows the weighted average posterior mean for that variable's coefficient, with weights calculated from the model's posterior probability. The "SD" column is the average posterior standard deviation for that variable's coefficient. Over all retained models, BMA never chooses to include PERSELAW, SPEED, YOUNG, and INCOME, and rarely chooses to include UNPLOY (2.1 percent). The procedure always includes YEAR, BEER, MLDA21, CELLPOP, ED_COL, GINI, UNIVERSAL, and PARTIAL. In addition, CRIME is included in 90.4 percent of the top models, SUICIDE in 47.1 percent, and ED_HS in 24.8 percent. POVERTY is included in just under 10 percent of the models. One might note that OLS and BMA results are in complete agreement in the sense that all variables that are always included in BMA have extraordinarily high t-values (absolute values > 4.5) in Table 5 (Full Model). Once again, as with the OLS results, both the universal and partial helmet laws appear to be important in diminishing motorcycle fatality rates.

6. Extreme Bounds Analysis

As a final test of inferential stability, we examine the motorcycle fatality model using Bayesian Extreme Bounds Analysis (EBA) developed by Leamer (1978). It is a methodology of global sensitivity analysis that computes the maximum and minimum values for Bayesian posterior means in the context of linear regression models. Global sensitivity analysis is especially important in order to address the myriad of issues that arise when dealing with specification uncertainty that include problems of variable selection, identification,

---

[xxviii]BMA results were obtained using the bicreg procedure. See Raftery *et al.* (2009). Regional variables were included, but results are not reported.

[xxix]Here, we chose to retain models with a posterior odds ratio greater than 20 to 1.

collinearity, heterogeneity, and endogeneity.[xxx] These issues are especially problematic when dealing with non-experimental data.

We can visualize how EBA works using a two-dimensional simplification. The standard Bayesian model is illustrated in Figure 1. The likelihood contours implied by the data are shown along with the maximum likelihood (MLE) or OLS estimate. In addition, typical iso-prior contours implied by the prior location vector and the fully defined prior precision matrix are shown.[xxxi]

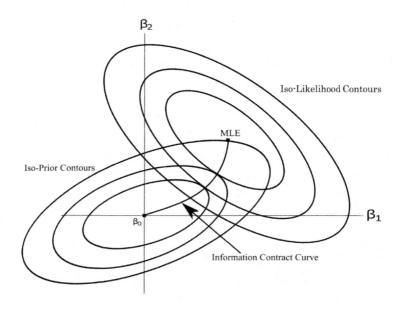

Figure 1. Likelihood/Prior Contours & Information Contract Curve.

[xxx]Leamer (2010) advocates the use of sensitivity analysis, e.g., Extreme Bounds Analysis, as a way of dealing with uncertainty and ambiguity in econometric models. The approach is argued to be useful when concerned with confounding factors, heterogeneity, instrumental variable selection and endogeneity as well as making inferences from one domain to another.

[xxxi]As is common in Bayesian statistics, we use Σ_0^{-1} as prior precision, the inverse of the prior variance/covariance matrix for the vector β. The precision parameters associated with the gamma distribution for the prior distribution are accounted for in EBA where prior precision is allowed to vary from zero to infinity.

The potential set of posterior means for this prior and likelihood are indicated by the relation labeled the "information contract curve" which is comprised of the locus of tangencies between the "iso-likelihood contours" and the "iso-prior contours". The exact position of the posterior mean along this curve is a function of the relative sample and prior precisions. With strong priors, the posterior mean is pulled closer to the prior mean and with strong data, the posterior mean is closer to the MLE estimate.[xxxii]

The analysis depicted in Figure 1 requires specifying both a prior mean vector, β_0, and a prior precision matrix, Σ_0^{-1}. These prior parameters determine the center and the shape of the iso-prior ellipses. Specification of these parameters is an almost impossible task and particular results are likely to be too dependent on the chosen prior.

In considering the prior location, a sensible solution is to define a subset of explanatory variables that have a well specified prior mean at zero. Such variables are called doubtful variables since a researcher would be comfortable including or excluding such variables. Sets of variables that would not be excluded are called free variables and there are no priors associated to them.[xxxiii]

For the prior variance, a remarkable result of Chamberlain and Leamer (1976), demonstrates that there exists a relatively small ellipse that contains the set of posterior means for both doubtful and free variables. This feasible ellipse requires only minimal assumptions regarding the nature of the precision matrix. The feasible ellipse is illustrated in Figure 2 along with an example of a confidence ellipse, from which the feasible ellipse takes its shape. As indicated by this

---

[xxxii]Mathematical developments are discussed in Leamer (1978) and further discussion of EBA in the context of automobile fatalities is presented in Blattenberger, *et al.* (2013).

[xxxiii]Priors that are completely uninformative (or diffuse) are associated with free variables. Because proper prior information is required for some parameters for meaningful EBA, we select variables that one might be comfortable dropping from a model specification. From a Bayesian perspective, dropping a variable is exactly the same as imposing a proper prior on that variable with a prior mean of zero and perfect precision (the prior variance also zero). In this sense, EBA results reflect the free/doubtful mix of variables.

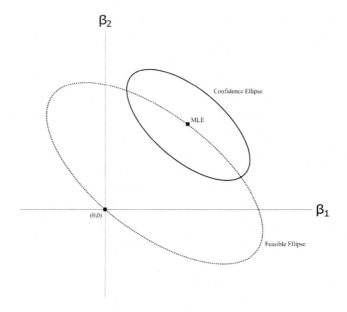

Figure 2. Feasible ellipse.

figure, the range of potential posterior values associated with the feasible ellipse, called global bounds, necessarily encompasses zero. In terms of priors, these bounds are associated with prior precisions swept from zero to infinity. Without further restrictions all variables are necessarily fragile with global bounds covering zero.

Because global bounds are necessarily wide when all variables are doubtful, we can focus attention to values of bounds that are highly likely, for example those falling within the 95 percent confidence ellipsoid. Bounds within the 95 percent ellipsoid are referred to as being data favored. Figure 3 illustrates the implication of this restriction for the extreme bounds on the parameter values. In this illustration, the extreme bounds on β_2 are positive and X_2 is not a fragile variable while bounds on β_1 cover zero and thus X_1 is fragile.

Another solution to the issue of wide bounds is to specify the doubtful/free mix. In Figure 4, we illustrate EBA bounds when X_2 is set as a doubtful variable and X_1 is considered as a free variable. As shown here, bounds on β_1 do not cover zero, and thus X_1 is not considered fragile.

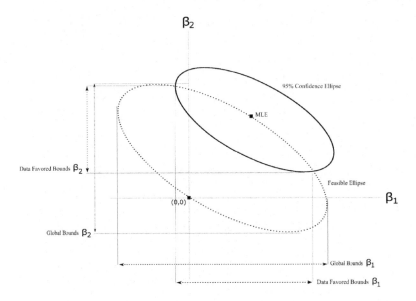

Figure 3. Extreme global and data favored bounds within 95 percent likelihood contour with X_1 and X_2 doubtful.

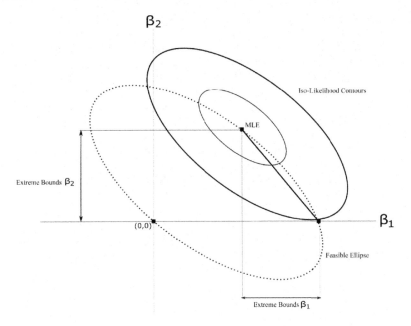

Figure 4. Extreme global bounds with X_1 free and X_2 doubtful.

Empirical results for data favored bounds when 17 explanatory variables are set to be doubtful are presented in Table 7.[xxxiv] With this very agnostic specification, the three variables YEAR, CELLPOP, and UNIVERSAL are shown to be non-fragile. In Table 8, data favored and global bounds are shown when our five focus variables, BEER, CELLPOP, SUICIDE, UNIVERSAL, and PARTIAL are set as free variables (and the other 12 are set as doubtful).[xxxv] In this specification, YEAR, BEER, CELLPOP, UNIVERSAL, and PARTIAL are seen to be non-fragile within 95 percent data favored bounds. Further, Table 8 shows that UNIVERSAL is non-fragile globally and is the only variable with this characteristic. For these data, no matter what other variables

Table 7. Maximum likelihood and EBA upper and lower bounds within 95 percent confidence ellipsoids. All variables considered are doubtful. Non-fragile bounds are shaded.

Variable	MLE	Upper 95%	Lower 95%
YEAR	−0.1055	−0.0541	−0.1524
PERSELAW	0.0270	0.3783	−0.3253
SPEED	−0.0039	0.0197	−0.0272
BEER	0.4086	0.9036	−0.1014
MLDA21	−0.2616	0.1064	−0.6201
YOUNG	−0.0352	4.6824	−4.7515
CELLPOP	0.0287	0.0390	0.0171
POVERTY	−0.0131	0.0252	−0.0508
UNPLOY	−0.0077	0.0449	−0.0599
INCOME	0.0000	0.0000	−0.0001
ED_HS	−0.0161	0.0185	−0.0501
ED_COL	−0.0331	0.0079	−0.0728
CRIME	0.0000	0.0001	−0.0001
SUICIDE	0.0228	0.0736	−0.0288
GINI	4.8996	10.6471	−1.0271
UNIVERSAL	−0.8118	−0.4430	−1.1459
PARTIAL	−0.2752	0.0716	−0.6120

[xxxiv] Regional variables and a constant were designated as free variables; results are not shown.

[xxxv] Regional variables and a constant were included but results are not shown.

Table 8. Maximum likelihood, EBA upper and lower bounds within 95 percent confidence ellipsoids, and EBA global bounds with BEER, CELLPOP, SUICIDE, UNIVERSAL, and PARTIAL as free variables. Non-fragile bounds are shaded.

Variable	MLE	Upper 95%	Lower 95%	Global Upper	Global Lower
YEAR	−0.1055	−0.0541	−0.1510	0.1132	−0.2187
PERSELAW	0.0270	0.3771	−0.3244	1.1612	−1.1342
SPEED	−0.0039	0.0196	−0.0272	0.0746	−0.0784
BEER	0.4086	0.6612	0.1816	1.4577	−0.1631
MLDA21	−0.2616	0.1063	−0.6171	1.0598	−1.3214
YOUNG	−0.0352	4.6690	−4.7378	15.3707	−15.4059
CELLPOP	0.0287	0.0377	0.0174	0.0481	−0.0237
POVERTY	−0.0131	0.0251	−0.0506	0.1176	−0.1306
UNPLOY	−0.0077	0.0448	−0.0597	0.1671	−0.1748
INCOME	0.0000	0.0000	−0.0001	0.0001	−0.0001
ED_HS	−0.0161	0.0185	−0.0499	0.1041	−0.1202
ED_COL	−0.0331	0.0079	−0.0724	0.1159	−0.1490
CRIME	0.0000	0.0001	−0.0001	0.0004	−0.0003
SUICIDE	0.0228	0.0648	−0.0194	0.1569	−0.1171
GINI	4.8996	10.5912	−1.0266	21.6122	−16.7127
UNIVERSAL	−0.8118	−0.6115	−1.001	−0.0448	−1.350
PARTIAL	−0.2752	−0.1159	−0.4277	0.3056	−0.7168

are included or excluded (or even all possible linear combination of the other variables), the posterior mean for UNIVERSAL is always negative.

7. Discussion

Table 9 summarizes and compares results from our classical and Bayesian methods.[xxxvi] OLS estimates, t-values, and standard significance stars are shown in columns 2, 3, and 4; BMA inclusion probabilities are shown in column 5; EBA bounds that are non-fragile (NF) when all variables are considered doubtful are shaded in column 6 (from Table 7); and EBA non-fragile bounds (data-favored and

---

[xxxvi] A constant and the regional variables were included, but results are not shown.

Table 9. Summary of OLS, BMA, and EBA results for Motorcycle Fatality Rate Models for the US states from 1980 to 2010.

	OLS	t-value	sig	BMA	EBA1	EBA2	EBA2 Global
YEAR	−0.1055	−13.225	***	100	NF	NF	
PERSELAW	0.0270	0.489		0.8			
SPEED	−0.0039	−1.051		1.9			
BEER	0.4086	5.156	***	100		NF	
MLDA21	−0.2616	−4.574	***	100			
YOUNG	−0.0351	−0.048		1.3			
CELLPOP	0.0287	15.944	***	100	NF	NF	
POVERTY	−0.0131	−2.191	*	10.9			
UNPLOY	−0.0077	−0.932		2.3			
INCOME	0.0001	−1.282		1.7			
ED_HS	−0.0161	−2.985	**	24.6			
ED_COL	−0.0331	−5.198	***	100			
CRIME	0.0001	2.809	**	88.6			
SUICIDE	0.0228	2.838	**	47.9			
GINI	4.8990	5.321	***	100			
UNIVERSAL	−0.8118	−14.171	***	100	NF	NF	NF
PARTIAL	−0.2752	−5.108	***	100		NF	

Significance codes: 0 '***', 0.001 '**', 0.01 '*'.

global) when the five focus variables are considered free are shaded as non-fragile (NF) in columns 7 and 8 (from Table 8).

The classical and Bayesian Model Average results, as mentioned above, are in strong agreement with one-another. Estimated marginal effects from all procedures are very similar. When p-values are less than 0.001, BMA inclusion is 100 percent; there are eight variables that pass this criterion: YEAR, BEER, MLDA21, CELLPOP, ED_COL, GINI, and both UNIVERSAL and PARTIAL helmet laws. For EBA, when all variables are doubtful, non-fragile data-favored bounds are indicated for only three variables: YEAR, CELLPOP, and for the UNIVERSAL helmet law (column 6 — EBA1). When our five focus variables are not set as being doubtful, EBA data-favored bounds are non-fragile for YEAR, BEER, CELLPOP, and both UNIVERSAL and PARTIAL helmet laws (column 7 — EBA2). The final column in Table 9 highlights the unique characteristic of the UNIVERSAL helmet law — it is the only variable that has non-fragile global bounds in addition to being data-favored, always included in BMA, and statistically significant.[xxxvii]

7.1. *The Focus Variables*

There is an impressive cellphone effect (CELLPOP) as shown by its significant outcome depicted by the classical methods and 100 percent inclusion by BMA. It also proves to be non-fragile in two of the three EBA specifications which entail between 2^{17} to 2^{23} different models. These results are consistent with that found by Loeb *et al.* (2009), Fowles *et al.* (2010) and Blattenberger *et al.* (2012, 2013) for motor vehicle fatalities in general. One can conclude that the distracting effect of cell phones impinges on motorcyclists directly or through their interaction with other vehicles, or both. This would lead to a recommendation that cell phone bans be extended beyond the 24 states and D.C., which have currently enacted such laws. In addition, such laws might be expanded to include hands-free devices and that stricter policing of the laws and more viable fine structures be put in place for violation of the law.

Universal Helmet Laws are found to be statistically significant and are always included in the models by BMA. The Partial Helmet Law is also always significant by classical analysis and is always included in the BMA analysis. However, of great interest are the EBA results which add particularly strong reason to recognize the importance of the Universal Helmet Law in reducing motorcycle fatality rates over that of the Partial Helmet Law given the non-fragile results associated with all three EBA criteria. This draconian procedure considers up to 2^{23} specifications, all non-fragile. This is a very strong policy finding that supports legislation for universal helmet laws as opposed to either partial or no helmet laws.

[xxxvii]Wasserstein and Lazar (2016) caution on the use of p-values (alone) in statistical analysis based on the recent American Statistical Association's statement on this issue. Bayesian methods are suggested by some to supplement or replace p-values. See Wasserstein and Lazar (2016, p. 11). This provides additional support for the use of BMA and EBA with classical methods as used in the present study.

Alcohol has been generally found to be a significant cause of motor vehicle fatalities and crashes in general. The results found here with respect to motorcycle fatality rates are consistent with those found in general. Both BEER and MLDA21 are indicative of the risk imposed on motorcyclists from a classical perspective as well as from a Bayesian Model Average perspective. In addition, the BEER effect proves non-fragile with our data-favored EBA analysis when using our focus variables as free. These results suggest that imposing stricter sanctions against driving while under the influence along with stricter policing and perhaps the use of expenditures on substance abuse treatment centers are worthy of further investigation.[xxxviii]

The SUICIDE effect is similar to that found by Blattenberger *et al.* (2013) Although this factor is included in only 47.9 percent of the models via BMA, it proves always to be statistically significant from a classical perspective. It should be noted that high suicide states are also high motor vehicle fatality states.[xxxix] In addition, suicides are a leading cause of death among young people in the United States, making it an important factor from a public health perspective.[xl] It may be that suicidal propensities are measuring, changes in risk taking propensities by individuals or society in general. A potential avenue of future research may be investigating the effectiveness of posting phone numbers/help lines for those suffering from emotional or psychiatric issues who might benefit from this and/or the investment of public monies to reduce reckless or violent behaviors while driving.[xli] However, it seems that suicidal propensities are not as pronounced for motorcycle fatalities as they are for automobile fatalities.

7.2. *The Normalizing Variables*

The variable, YEAR, i.e., the time trend, is found to be highly significant, always included by BMA. Furthermore, it proves to be

---

[xxxviii]See Chaloupka *et al.* (1993) and Freeborn and McManus (2007).

[xxxix]See Blattenberger *et al.* (2013).

[xl]See Centers for Disease Control and Prevention.

[xli]See Conner *et al.* (2001).

non-fragile in two of the three EBA specifications. YEAR picks up the influence of potentially omitted factors in the model as well as serving as a proxy for technology advances and possibly permanent income.[xlii]

Crime rates may also be measuring the effects of economic wellbeing along with differing tolerances for risk in society over time. Although the coefficient associated with crime is always significant (although small in absolute value) and included by BMA in 88.6 percent of the time, it is considered fragile from an EBA perspective.

The effect of the maximum speed limit on urban interstate highways was never significant in the classical analysis and was never included by Bayesian Model Averaging and was found fragile by EBA. As such, the results here are similar to those reported by French *et al.* (2009).

The effects of education and income distribution are what we expect *a priori*. Investment in a college education is an investment in human capital and might be expected to lead to higher income over the life of the individual. With a higher life-time income, safety while driving may be preferred over the utility from the thrills of speed.[xliii] The GINI coefficient is always significant and included in all models by BMA. As one would expect, greater income inequality is associated with higher fatality rates with all else equal. This may argue for greater income equality.

8. Concluding Remarks

One of the most important statistical problems today is the task of inference in the context of model uncertainty.[xliv] Dealing with both parameter and model uncertainty is a challenging endeavor due to the sheer magnitude of the number of models that need to be considered. In this paper, we have looked at intuitive Bayesian methods along

---

[xlii]See Loeb (1993, 2001) and Peltzman (1975).

[xliii]The effect of permanent income might be picked up by the trend variable as suggested by Peltzman (1975).

[xliv]See Breiman (2001).

with Ordinary Least Squares. With our data, there are millions of possible model specifications. Bayesian procedures are nicely suited to explore this high dimensional model space. These procedures are not model mining but are based on solid probability and statistical theory, and provide researchers with inferential tools that are not a part of the non-Bayesian toolkit.

Our results find a strong relationship between our focus variables and motorcycle fatality rates using both classical and two Bayesian methods. The Bayesian methods, in particular, are quite draconian and lend strong reason to recognize the impact of alcohol, helmet laws, and cell phone usage on motorcycle fatality rates. The evidence regarding the importance of suicidal propensities on motorcycle fatality rates from a Bayesian perspective is not as strong as found in the general motor vehicle fatality rate literature, such as in Blattenberger *et al.* (2012). Nonetheless, we find classical estimates and BMA to be supportive of inclusion of this factor and it still warrants additional study.

Previous studies have found a link between alcohol and motorcycle fatality rates, as we have. However, prior studies on the effect of helmet laws did not disentangle the effects of universal laws from partial helmet laws. We have been able to do so and have found strong Bayesian evidence favoring universal helmet laws over partial helmet laws as a way of reducing motorcycle fatality rates, although helmet laws in general save lives.[xlv] This can be seen in Table 9 and Appendix 2 which graphically portrays the magnitude effect and advantage of universal helmet laws over partial helmet laws using standardized data. In any case, universal helmet laws were most impressively supported by all Bayesian methods as well as OLS. As mentioned above, this would lead to considering a policy recommendation of imposing universal helmet laws in place of partial or no helmet laws. At the very least, this deserves further study given the resistance cyclists may have towards this.

[xlv]See Fowles and Loeb (2021) for some additional evidence based on an alternative Bayesian approach, i.e., s-values.

Cell phone effects on motorcycle fatality rates is a new factor we examine. Our study shows a very strong detrimental effect of cell phone usage on motorcycle fatality rates. This is seen in virtually all of the EBA analyses other than the global results as well as the classical estimates. It can be seen quite imposingly in the graphical portrayal found in Appendix 2 where it has the greatest effect on motorcycle fatality rates of all variables considered other than the time trend (marginally) using standardized data. As such, we can conclude with little uncertainty that the net effect of cell phones on such fatality rates is detrimental. This suggests that public policy should be designed to diminish the probability of using distracting devices such as cell phones by motorcycle drivers.[xlvi]

Suicides, as mentioned above, have been shown to be related to motorcycle fatality rates using classical methods as well as Bayesian Model Averaging. The BMA results are not as strong as those associated with the other focus variables. Nonetheless, given the rise in suicides over the last decade, especially among young people, they may warrant additional study from a public health position. If warranted, additional funds might be allocated for mental health and emotional health services along with expenditures in the media providing information for support services.

An exciting additional avenue of exploration will be unfolding with the advent of the popular use of driverless cars. Clearly, such vehicles will have benefits and risks associated with them, one of which will be concerned with safety issues. The Bayesian methods suggested here should prove helpful in considering these matters.

[xlvi]There is an argument that cell phone availability via Bluetooth, which may be accessible in motorcycle helmets, increases the likelihood of motorcyclist wearing helmets. Banning Bluetooth of phone use by motorcycle drivers may result in a reduction in helmet use. Nevertheless, based on the data at hand, cell phone use can be shown to have a deleterious effect of motorcycle fatality rates.

Appendix 1: Data Sources

Name	Data Source
MCFATAL	Highway Statistics (various years), Federal Highway Administration, Traffic Safety Facts (various years), National Highway Traffic Safety Administration
PERSELAW	Digest of State Alcohol-Highway Safety Related Legislation (various years), Traffic Laws Annotated 1979, Alcohol and Highway Safety Laws: A National Overview 1980, National Highway Traffic Safety Administration
SPEED	Highway Statistics (various years), Federal Highway Administration
BEER	U.S. Census Bureau, National Institute on Alcohol Abuse and Alcoholism
MLDA21	A Digest of State Alcohol-Highway Safety Related Legislation (various years), Traffic Laws Annotated 1979, Alcohol and Highway Safety Laws: A National Overview of 1980, National Highway Traffic Safety Administration, U.S. Census Bureau
YOUNG	State Population Estimates (various years), U.S. Census Bureau http://www.census.gov/population/www/estimates/statepop.html
CELLPOP	Cellular Telecommunication and Internet Association Wireless Industry Survey, International Association for the Wireless Telecommunications Industry.
POVERTY	Statistical Abstract of the United States (various years), U.S. Census Bureau website http://www.census.gov/hhes/poverty/histpov19.html

Name	Data Source
UNPLOY	Statistical Abstract of the United States (various years), U.S. Census Bureau
INCOME	State Personal Income (various years), Bureau of Economic Analysis website http://www. bea.doc.gov/bea/regional/spi/dpcpi.htm
ED_HS	Digest of Education Statistics (various years), National Center for Education Statistics, Educational Attainment in the United States (various years), U.S. Census Bureau
ED_COL	Digest of Education Statistics (various years), National Center for Education Statistics, Educational Attainment in the United States (various years), U.S. Census Bureau
CRIME	FBI Uniform Crime Reporting Statistics website http://www.ucrdatatool.gov
SUICIDE	Statistical Abstract of the United States (various years), U.S. Census Bureau
GINI	University of Texas Inequality Project website http://utip.gov.utexas.edu
UNIVERSAL PARTIAL	Governors Highway Safety Association http://www.ghsa.org/html/stateinfo/laws/ helmet_laws.html (accessed 4/13/2019)
REGION	US States 1: ME, NH, VT; 2: MA, RI, CT; 3: NY, NJ, PA; 4: OH, IN, IL, MI, WI, MN, IA, MO; 5: ND, SD, NE, KS; 6: DE, MD, DC, VA, WV; 7: NC, SC, GA, FL; 8: KY, TN, AL, MS, AR, LA, OK, TX; 9: MT, ID, WY, CO, NM, AZ, UT, NV; 10: WA, OR, CA; 11: AK, HI

Appendix 2: Plot of Standardized OLS Regression Coefficients for the Fatality Model Specification

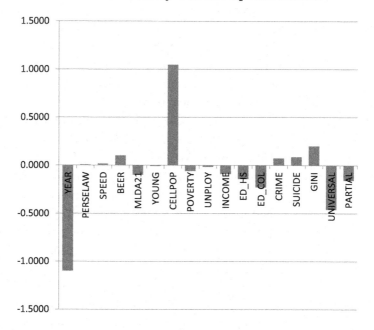

Figure A.1. Standardized OLS regression coefficients for the Fatality Model Specification.[xlvii].

[xlvii]See Table 3, Full Model, for the basis for this specification using raw data. All variables are standardized to mean 0 and variance 1 so as to allow unit-free comparisons.

Appendix 3: Plot of the US State Motorcycle Fatality Rates

Figure A.2. [xlviii].

References

Asch, P., and Levy, D.T. (1987). Does the Minimum Drinking Age Affect Traffic Fatalities? *Journal of Policy Analysis and Management, 6,* 180–192.

Asch, P., and Levy, D.T. (1990). Young Driver Fatalities: The Roles of Drinking Age and Drinking Experience. *Southern Economic Journal, 57*(2), 512–520.

Beede, K.E., and Kass, S.J. (2006). Engrossed in Conversation: The Impact of Cell Phones on Simulated Driving Performance. *Accident Analysis and Prevention, 38*(2), 415–421.

[xlviii]Each line represents a different state.

Blattenberger, G., Fowles, R., and Loeb, P.D. (2013). Determinants of Motor Vehicle Crash Fatalities Using Bayesian Model Selection Methods. *Research in Transportation Economics*, *43*(1), 112–122.

Blattenberger, G., Fowles, R., Loeb, P.D., and Clarke, Wm.A. (2012). Understanding the Cell Phone Effect on Vehicle Fatalities: A Bayesian View. *Applied Economics*, *44*(14), 1823–1835.

Breiman, L. (2001). Statistical Modeling: The Two Cultures. *Statistical Science*, *16*(3), 199–231.

Centers for Disease Control and Prevention, National Center for Injury Prevention and Control. *Web-based Injury Statistics Query and Reporting System (WISQARS)*. [online] http://www.cdc.gov/injury/wisqars/ [Accessed 7 July 2012].

Chaloupka, F.J., Saffer, H., and Grossman, M. (1993). Alcohol-control Policies and Motor Vehicle Fatalities. *Journal of Legal Studies*, *22*(1), 161–186.

Chamberlain, G., and Leamer, E.E. (1976). Matrix Weighted Averages and Posterior Bounds. *Journal of the Royal Statistical Society, Series B*, *38*(1), 73–84.

Chapman, S., and Schoefield, W.N. (1998). Lifesavers and Samaritans: Emergency Use of Cellular (Mobile) Phones in Australia. *Accident Analysis and Prevention*, *30*(6), 815–819.

Clyde, M.A. (1999). Bayesian Model Averaging and Model Search Strategies. *Bayesian Statistics*, *6*, 157–185.

Conner, K.R., Cox, C., Duberstein, P.R., Tian, L., Nisbet, P.A., and Conwell, Y. (2001). Violence, Alcohol, and Completed Suicide: A Case-control Study. *The American Journal of Psychiatry*, *158*(10), 1701–1705.

Connolly, J.F., Cullen, A., and McTigue, O. (1995). Single Road Traffic Deaths: Accident or Suicide? *Crisis: The Journal of Crisis Intervention and Suicide Prevention*, *16*(2), 85–89.

Consiglio, W., Driscoll, P., Witte, M., and Berg, W.P. (2003). Effect of Cellular Telephone Conversations and Other Potential Interference on Reaction Time in Braking Responses. *Accident Analysis and Prevention*, *35*(4), 494–500.

CTIA — *The Wireless Association (2011)*. [online] Available at: http://www.ctia.org [accessed 10 February 2011].

Etzerdorfer, E. (1995). Single Road Traffic Deaths: Accidents or Suicide? Comment. *Crisis: The Journal of Crisis Intervention and Suicide Prevention*, *16*(4), 188–189.

Forester, T.H., McNown, R.F., and Singell, L.D. (1984). A Cost Benefit Analysis of the 55 MPH Speed Limit. *Southern Economic Journal*, *50*(3), 631–641.

Fowles, R., and Loeb, P.D. (1989). Speeding, Coordination, and the 55-MPH Limit: Comment. *The American Economic Review, 79*(4), 916–921.

Fowles, R., and Loeb, P.D. (2016). Sturdy Inference: A Bayesian Analysis of U.S. Motorcycle Helmet Laws. *Journal of the Transportation Research Forum, 55*(3), 41–63.

Fowles, R., and Loeb, P.D. (2021). A Sturdy Values Analysis of Motor Vehicle Fatalities. *Empirical Economics, 60*(4), 2063–2081.

Fowles, R., Loeb, P.D., and Clarke, Wm.A. (2010). The Cell Phone Effect on Motor Vehicle Fatality Rates: A Bayesian and Classical Econometric Evaluation. *Transportation Research Part E, 46*(6), 1140–1147.

Fowles, R., Loeb, P.D., and Clarke, Wm. A. (2013). The Cell Phone Effect on Truck Accidents: A Specification Error Approach. *Transportation Research Part E: Logistics and Transportation Review, 50*, 18–28.

Freeborn, B.A., and McManus, B. (2007). Substance Abuse Treatment and Motor Vehicle Fatalities. Working Paper Number 66. Department of Economics, College of William and Mary, VA.

French, M.T., Gumus, G., and Homer, J.F. (2009). Public Policies and Motorcycle Safety. *Journal of Health Economics, 28*(4), 831–838.

Garbacz, C. (1990). How Effective is Automobile Safety Regulation? *Applied Economics, 22*(12), 1705–1714.

Garbacz, C., and Kelly, J.G. (1987). Automobile Safety Inspection: New Econometric and Benefit/Cost Estimates. *Applied Economics, 19*(6), 763–771.

Glassbrenner, D. (2005). Driver Cell Phone Use in 2005 — Overall Results. *Traffic Safety Facts: Research Note,* NHTSA, DOT HS 809967. [online] Available at: http://www-nrd.nhtsa.dot.gov/Pubs/809967.PDF [Accessed 11 February 2011].

Governors Highway Safety Association (2019). [online] Available at https://www.ghsa.org/ [Accessed 14 March 2019].

Governors Highway Safety Association (2021). [online] Available at https://www.ghsa.org [Accessed 16 April 2021].

Graham, J.D., and Lee, Y. (1986). Behavioral Response in Safety Regulation: The Case of Motorcycle Helmet Wearing Legislation. *Policy Sciences,19*(3), 253–279.

Hartunian, N.S., Smart, C.N., Willemain, T.R., and Zador, P.L. (1983). The Economics of Safety Deregulation: Lives and Dollars Lost Due to Repeal of Motorcycle Laws. *Journal of Health Politics, Policy and Law, 8*(1), 78–98.

Hill, B.M. (1985). Some Subjective Bayesian Considerations in the Selection of Models. *Econometric Reviews, 4*(2), 191–246.

Hoeting, J., Madigan, D., Raftery, A., and Volinsky, C. (1999). Bayesian Model Averaging: A Tutorial. *Statistical Science*, *14*(4), 382–417.

Huffine, C.L. (1971). Equivocal Single-Auto Traffic Fatalities. *Life-Threatening Behavior*, *1*(2), 83–95.

Keeler, T.E. (1994). Highway Safety, Economic Behavior, and Driving Environment. *The American Economic Review*, *84*(3), 684–693.

Key, J.T., Pericchi, L., and Smith, A.F.M. (1999). Bayesian Model Choice: What and Why? *Bayesian Statistics*, *6*, 343–370.

Laberge-Nadeau, C., Maag, U., Bellavance, F., Lapiere, S.D., Desjardins, D., Messier, S., Saidi, A. (2003). Wireless Telephones and Risk of Road Crashes. *Accident Analysis and Prevention*, *35*(5), 649–660.

Lave, C.A. (1985). Speeding, Coordination and the 55 MPH Limit. *American Economic Review*, *75*(5), 1159–1164.

Leamer, E.E. (1978). *Specification Searches: Ad Hoc Inference with Non-Experimental Data*. Wiley & Sons, New York.

Leamer, E.E. (1982). Sets of Posterior Means with Bounded Variance Priors," *Econometrica*, *50*(3), 725–736.

Leamer, E.E. (1983). Let's Take the Con Out of Econometrics. *American Economic Review*, *73*(1), 31–43.

Leamer, E.E. (1985). Sensitivity Analyses Would Help. *American Economic Review*, *75*(3), 308–313.

Leamer, E.E. (2010). Tantalus on the Road to Asymptopia. *Journal of Economics Perspectives*, *24*(2), 31–46.

Levy, D.T., and Asch, P. (1989). Speeding, Coordination, and the 55-MPH Limit: Comment. *The American Economic Review*, *79*(4), 913–915.

Lin, M.R. and Kraus, J.F. (2009). A Review of Risk Factors and Patterns of Motorcycle Injuries. *Accident Analysis and Prevention*, *41*(4), 710–722.

Loeb, P.D. (1985). The Efficacy and Cost-effectiveness of Motor Vehicle Inspection Using Cross-sectional Data — An Econometric Analysis. *Southern Economic Journal*, *52*(2), 500–509.

Loeb, P.D. (1987). The Determinants of Motor Vehicle Accidents with Special Consideration to Policy Variables. *Journal of Transport Economics and Policy*, *21*(3), 279–287.

Loeb, P.D. (1988). The Determinants of Motor Vehicle Accidents: A Specification Error Analysis. *Logistics and Transportation Review*, *24*(1), 33–48.

Loeb, P.D. (1990). Automobile Safety Inspection: Further Econometric Evidence. *Applied Economics*, *22*(12), 1697–1704.

Loeb, P.D. (1993). The Effectiveness of Seat Belt Legislation in Reducing Various Driver-Involved Injury Rates in California. *Accident Analysis and Prevention*, *25*(2), 189–197.

Loeb, P.D. (1995), The Effectiveness of Seat Belt Legislation in Reducing Injury Rates in Texas. *The American Economic Review: Paper and Proceedings*, *85*(2), 81–84.

Loeb, P.D. (2001). The Effectiveness of Seat Belt Legislation in Reducing Driver-Involved Injury Rates in Maryland. *Transportation Research Part E: Logistics and Transportation Review*, *37*(4), 297–310.

Loeb, P.D. and Clarke, Wm.A. (2009). The Cell Phone Effect on Pedestrian Fatalities. *Transportation Research Part E: Logistics and Transportation Review*, *45*(1), 284–290.

Loeb, P.D., Clarke, Wm.A., and Anderson, R. (2009). The Impact of Cell Phones on Motor Vehicle Fatalities. *Applied Economics*, *41*(22), 2905–2914.

Loeb, P.D., Talley, W., and Zlatoper, J. (1994). *Causes and Deterrents of Transportation Accidents: An Analysis by Mode.* Quorum Books, Westport, CT.

McCarthy, P. (1992). Highway Safety Implications of Expanded Use of Longer Combination Variables (LCVs). Paper presented at the 6th World Conference on Transport Research, Lyon, France.

McEvoy, S.P., Stevenson, M.R., McCartt, A.T., Woodward, M., Haworth, C., Palamara, P., and Cercarelli, R. (2005). Role of Mobile Phones in Motor Vehicle Crashes Resulting in Hospital Attendance: A Case-Crossover Study. *British Medical Journal*, *331*, 428–435.

Morris, C.C. (2009). *Motorcycle Trends in the United States.* Bureau of Transportation Statistics, U.S. Department of Transportation, Washington, DC. http://www.rita.dot.gov/bts/sites/rita.dot.gov.bts/files/publications/special_report_and issue briefs/special_report/2009_05_14/html/entire.html [Accessed June 4, 2015].

Murray, D., and de Leo, D. (2007). Suicidal Behavior by Motor Vehicle Collision. *Traffic Injury Prevention*, *8*(3), 244–247.

National Highway Traffic Safety Administration (NHTSA) (2003). *The Evaluation of the Repeal of Motorcycle Helmet Laws in Kentucky and Louisiana.* DOT HS 809 530, U.S. Department of Transportation, Washington, DC.

National Highway Traffic Safety Administration (NHTSA). (2008). *Traffic Safety Facts — Motorcycles 2006 Data.* DOT HS 810 806, U.S. Department of Transportation, Washington, DC.

National Highway Traffic Safety Administration (NHTSA). (2011). *Traffic Safety Facts 2011.* U.S. Department of Transportation, Washington, DC.

Neyens, D.M., and Boyle, L.N. (2007). The Effect of Distractions on the Crash Types of Teenage Drivers. *Accident Analysis and Prevention*, *39*(1), 206–212.

Peltzman, S. (1975). The Effect of Motor Vehicle Regulation. *Journal of Political Economy, 93*, 677–725.

Phillips, D.P. (1979). Suicide, Motor Vehicle Fatalities, and the Mass Media: Evidence Toward a Theory of Suggestion. *American Journal of Sociology, 84*(5), 1150–1174.

Pokorny, A.D., Smith, J.P., and Finch, J.R. (1972). Vehicular Suicides. *Life-Threatening Behavior, 2*(2), 105–119.

Porterfield, A.L. (1960). Traffic Fatalities, Suicide, and Homicide. *American Sociological Review, 25*(6), 897–901.

Pöysti, L., Rajalin, S., and Summala, H. (2005). Factors Influencing the Use of Cellular (Mobile) Phones During Driving and Hazards While Using It. *Accident Analysis and Prevention, 37*(1), 47–51.

Raftery, A.E, Hoeting, J., Volinsky, C., Painter, I., and Yeung, K.Y. (2009). *BMA: Bayesian Model Averaging. R package version 3.10.* http://CRAN.R-project.org/package=BMA [Accessed 11 February 2011].

Raftery, A.E., Madigan, D., and Hoeting, J.A. (1997). Bayesian Model Averaging for Linear Regression Models. *Journal of the American Statistical Association, 92*(437), 179–191.

Ramsey, J.B. (1974). Classical Model Selection Through Specification Error Tests. In Zarembka, P. (Ed.), *Frontiers in Econometrics* (pp. 13–47). Academic Press, New York.

Ramsey, J.B., and Zarembka, P. (1971). Specification Error Tests and the Alternative Functional Form of the Aggregate Production Function. *Journal of the American Statistical Association, Applications Section, 66*(335), 471–477.

Redelmeier, D.A., and Tibshirani, R.J. (1997). Association Between Cellular-Telephone Calls and Motor Vehicle Collisions. *The New England Journal of Medicine, 336*, 453–458.

Saffer, H., and Grossman, M. (1987a). Beer Taxes, the Legal Drinking Age, and Youthful Motor Vehicle Fatalities. *Journal of Legal Studies, 16*(2), 351–374.

Saffer, H., and Grossman, M. (1987b). Drinking Age Laws and Highway Mortality Rates: Cause and Effect. *Economic Inquiry, 25*(3), 403–417.

Sampaio, B. (2014), Identifying Peer States for Transportation Policy Analysis with an Application to New York's Handheld Cell Phone Ban. *Transportmetrica A: Transport Science, 10* (1), 1–14.

Sass, T.R., and Leigh, J.P. (1991). The Market for Safety Regulation and the Effect of Regulation on Fatalities: The Case of Motorcycle Helmet Laws. *The Review of Economics and Statistics, 73*(1), 167–172.

Sass, T.R., and Zimmerman, P.R. (2000). Motorcycle Helmet laws and Motorcyclist Fatalities. *Journal of Regulatory Economics, 18*, 195–215.

Shankar, U. (2001). Fatal Single Vehicle Motorcycle Crashes, U.S. Department of Transportation, Washington, DC, DOT HS 809 360.

Snyder, D. (1989). Speeding, Coordination, and the 55-MPH Limit: Comment. *The American Economic Review*, *79*(4), 922–925.

Sommers, P.M. (1985). Drinking Age and the 55 MPH Speed Limit. *Atlantic Economic Journal*, *13*, 43–48.

Souetre, E. (1988). Completed Suicides and Traffic Accidents: Longitudinal Analysis in France. *Acta Psychiatrica Scandiavica*, *77*(5), 530–534.

Sullman, M.J.M., and Baas, P.H. (2004). Mobile Phone Use Amongst New Zealand Drivers. *Transportation Research Part F: Traffic Psychology and Behavior*, *7*(2), 95–105.

Violanti, J.M. (1998). Cellular Phones and Fatal Traffic Collisions. *Accident Analysis and Prevention*, *30*(4), 519–524.

Wasserstein, R., and Lazar, N. (2016). The ASA's Statement on p-values: Context, Process, and Purpose. *The American Statistician*. 1–15. DOI:10.1080/00031305.2016.1154108.

Weiss, A.A. (1992). The Effects of Helmet Use on the Severity of Head Injuries in Motorcycle Accidents. *Journal of the American Statistical Association*, *87*(417), 48–56.

Zlatoper, T.J. (1984). Regression Analysis of Time Series Data on Motor Vehicle Deaths in the United States. *Journal of Transport Economics and Policy*, *18*(3), 263–274.

Chapter 2

Risk-Taking Behaviors of Young Motorcycle Drivers in Thailand

Chompoonuh K. Permpoonwiwat

Faculty of Economics, Srinakharinwirot University, Thailand

Chaturaphat Chantith

Faculty of Management Sciences, Songkhla Rajabhat University, Thailand

This study aims to examine the risky motorcycle riding behaviors among young people in Thailand. An Ordered Logit Model is used to evaluate the association between motorcycle drivers (ages 15–24 years), accident characteristics, and accident outcomes (including deaths, permanent disabilities, and injuries). The study finds that the two main characteristics of youth associated with risk-taking behaviors are driving without a helmet and being under the influence of alcohol or other drugs. Young males are significantly more likely to be driving recklessly and are involved in more severe crashes than females. In an effort to prevent road traffic accidents among youth, effective training courses must be implemented, especially motorbike-riding skills for safety. These include addressing the major risk factors, through legislation and enforcement, and by educating teenagers and young adults about the use of protective equipment.

1. Introduction

The number of road traffic fatalities in Thailand is at 36.2 deaths per 100,000 people as of 2015.[i] The group at the most significant risk in a road traffic death is teenagers and young adults, aged 15 to 24, accounting for 26.8 percent of all Road Traffic Fatalities

---

[i]See Strategy and Planning Division, Ministry of Public Health, Thailand (2017).

Table 1. Number of road traffic accident victims in teenagers in 2019.

Number of motorcycle accident victims in teenagers in 2019 classified by level of RTA severity	Person
Deaths	2,910
Permanent Disabilities	602
Serious Injuries	16,878
Slight Injuries	114,977
Total	**132,457**

Source: Thai Road Safety Collaboration (2019).

(RTF).[ii] Road accidents are also the leading cause of death for Thai teenagers.[iii] For decades, the government and related agencies have had policies to enforce laws and ongoing campaigns to prevent and reduce road traffic accidents. Unfortunately, the number of accidents and fatalities in all adolescent groups did not decrease as expected. In addition, injuries, disabilities, or premature death from traffic accidents also impose socio-economic losses upon the country in terms of productivity loss.[iv] Various studies such as the studies of Su-angka (2016) and Bates *et al.* (2014) point out that the leading cause of such loss is often the unsafe driving behavior of teenagers.

The Thai Road Safety Collaboration (2019) report the number of Road Traffic Accident (RTA) victims among young drivers and classified their severity levels, from slightly injured to death, as shown in Table 1.

Many studies confirm that cost implications associated with motorcycle accidents have laid a serious burden on victims and their families, especially those with permanent disabilities that need long-term care. Additionally, the fatalities and disabilities in teenagers caused by RTA are also future national productivity losses.[v] Permpoonwiwat *et al.* (2020) examines the economic losses from motorcycle accidents among teenagers in Thailand by using

---

[ii]See Provincial Emergency Prevention Support (2016).

[iii]See Office of Transport and Traffic Policy and Planning (2019) for a road accident situation report in Thailand.

[iv]See PIARC (2022) for socio-economic costs of road traffic crashes reviews.

[v]See Leon *et al.* (2005, p. 3186).

Table 2. Socio-economic losses caused by motorcycle accidents in teenagers (Unit: Thai baht).

	Level of RTA severities	
Lists	Deaths (2,910 people)	Permanent Disabilities (602 people)
Direct Costs	769,354,530	1,675,048,746
1) Medical Expenses	6,078,990	1,583,928,822
(1) Medical Treatment Cost	—	37,676,170
(2) Long-Term Care Cost	—	1,544,722,970
(3) Emergency Medical Service Cost	6,078,990	1,529,682
2) Property Damage Cost	662,126,850	77,501,480
3) Emergency Medical Service Cost	6,078,990	1,529,682
(1) Police Administration Cost	1,455,000	301,000
(2) Insurance Administration Cost	5,511,540	1,140,188
(3) Judicial Administration Cost	94,182,150	12,177,256
Indirect Costs (Future Income Loss)	**24,428,908,740**	**5,068,306,628**
1) Productivity Loss Due to Road Traffic Deaths	24,428,908,740	5,053,678,028
2) Productivity Loss Due to Road Traffic Disabilities	—	7,314,300
3) Productivity Loss of Careers	—	7,314,300
Intangible Cost (15% of Direct cost + Indirect cost)	**3,779,739,491**	**1,011,503,306**
Total Loss (Direct cost + Indirect cost + Intangible cost)	**28,978,002,761**	**7,754,858,680**
Average Cost per Person	**9,958,077**	**12,881,825**
Total Loss of Both Groups	**36,732,861,441**	

a human capital approach. The study finds that the value of loss incurred from motorcycle fatal accidents and permanent disabilities caused by motorcycle crashes in 2019 was approximately 36.7 billion baht (Table 2).

The study also reveals the total loss of 9.96 million baht per victim in fatal motorcycle crashes of teenagers, while the economic losses from permanent disabilities are approximately 12.9 million baht. Notice that Thailand's GDP per capita in 2019 was about 216,576 baht.[vi] This implies that *the future income loss of road traffic*

[vi]See Bank of Thailand (2021).

death per person is 46 times higher than the country's GDP per capita and is 60 times higher than the future income loss from permanent disabilities.

With enormous burdens on both, the national and individual levels, it is important to raise an awareness of motorcycle traffic accidents among teens and young adults, to prevent economic loss due to premature mortality and disability. Based on the preliminary studies, there are five main causes of road traffic accidents[vii]: (1) behavior of road users, (2) vehicles, (3) the environment, (4) enforcement, and (5) policy development. Evidently, the behavior of road users is found to be the main risk factor that results in road traffic accidents, especially among teenagers due to their inherent high-risk behavior. The Injury Data Collaboration Center (2021), Ministry of Public Health, reportes that the most motorcycle traffic fatalities in Thailand are teenagers, which comprises 25 percent of deaths among all age groups. World Health Organization (WHO, 2018a) indicates that the five main risky behaviors related to motorcycle users are driving over the speed limit, driving without wearing a helmet, drunk-driving, driving under the influence of drugs, and distracted driving (such as while using cellphones). Many studies support the WHO's report and come to the following conclusions regarding each of these five risky behaviors:

(1) Driving over the speed limit — Malyshkina and Mannering (2008) study the effect of increased speed limits on the severity of injuries sustained in accidents on US interstate highways, and their results show that higher speed limits have a high impact on severity of accident injuries.

(2) Driving without wearing a helmet — The study of Chantith *et al.* (2021) reports that one of the main risky behaviors among Thai students is driving without wearing a helmet. Moreover, the study of MacLeod *et al.* (2010) shows that not wearing a helmet leads to head injuries, the leading cause of fatality and significant trauma from motorcycle accidents.

[vii]See Sikron *et al.* (2008, p. 27–31) and WHO (2018a).

(3) Drunk-driving — The Handbook of Road Safety Measures of Elvik *et al.* (2009) determines that driving under the influence of alcohol significantly increases the risk of a crash and the severity of road traffic crashes. The global status report on alcohol and health of WHO (2018b) points out that 5 to 35 percent of all road traffic deaths worldwide are due to drinking and driving.

(4) Drug-using — Brown *et al.* (2018) evaluates driver impairment from driving under the influence of alcohol and drugs in the United States. They indicate that driving under the influence of drugs is more difficult to measure than alcohol, but illicit drugs and certain prescription drugs are linked to an increase in road accidents and deaths. Moreover, the study by Hedlund (2018) points that the risk of road traffic accidents and death also varied by the type of psychotropic drugs.

(5) Distracted driving — The Farmer *et al.* (2010) and Caird *et al.* (2008) report on cellphone-use while driving and attributable crash risk indicate that distracted driving with mobile devices such as smartphones is an increased risk factor linked to severe adverse outcomes. Cellphone-use while driving has been prevalent among young and novice drivers and has been growing among motorcyclists. As a result, these groups have been at higher risk of accidents and death. These risky behaviors are probably due to inexperience, lack of awareness of the consequences of accidents, and overestimated self-confidence.[viii]

This research has made use of the existing Injury Surveillance (IS) database in Thailand and analyzed the factors influencing the severity of road traffic accidents, to confirm the risky behaviors of teenage and young adult road users. A better comprehension of youth behavior patterns in riding motorcycles should be assessed to understand their risk perceptions. Developing policies to reduce traffic crashes in specific age groups should be examined.

[viii]See Ivers *et al.* (2009, p. 1641–1642).

2. Materials and Method

2.1. *Data Source and Selection*

This paper uses the Injury Surveillance (IS) database from the Thailand Bureau of Epidemiology, Ministry of Public Health, as an empirical analysis data source. The data is collected from the Road Accident Hospitalization Reports across 77 provinces in Thailand during the year 2015–2017. The cross-sectional data of each road traffic victim from the database are analyzed by extracting the set of national crash cases. By aiming at the risk behaviors of teenagers aged 15–18, and of young adults aged 19–24 years, 50,041 observations are obtained.[ix]

According to the WHO's (2006) "Road Traffic Injury Prevention: Training Manual", four main risk factors are identified: (1) factors influencing exposure to risk; (2) crash involvement; (3) crash severity; and (4) post-crash injury outcomes. By following the instructions of the WHO manual associated with the existing IS dataset, the factors influencing risky behaviors and causing motorcycle accidents could be characterized as being a young male, being a vulnerable road user, having youth-counterparts riding in the same vehicle, not wearing a helmet, alcohol and/or drugs use, and insufficient attention due to cellphone usage.

2.2. *Data Analysis*

For all motorcycle traffic accidents combined for young adults, this study estimates the likelihood of being involved in accidents of different severity levels by using an Ordered Logit Model (OLM).[x] The OLM is an extension of the Logistic Regression Model. Many other studies confirm that using regression models with ordered responses is an appropriate method to capture the severity of road traffic accidents and the impact of risk factors on the incidence of

---

[ix]See Injury Data Collaboration Center (2021).
[x]See Bellizzi *et al.* (2018).

crashes and injury outcomes.[xi] The data description and analysis can be explained as follows:

2.2.1. *Factors and Expected Sign*

$$Y_i^* = \sum_{j=1}^{J} \beta_j X_i + \varepsilon_i \tag{1}$$

$$Y_i^* = SRTA_i^* = \beta_1 SEX_i + \beta_2 DVP_i + \beta_3 UBR_i \tag{2}$$

$$+\beta_4 HEM_i + \beta_5 ACL_i + \beta_6 DRG_i + \beta_7 CEL_i$$

Equations (1) and (2) represent the seven variables (X_i) that cause RTAs among youths. The dependent variables (Y_i) represent the degree of accident severity in the range of moderate injury to death. The hypothesis of how each variable affects the severity level is shown in Table 3.

2.2.2. *OLM Analysis*

The $SRTA_i$ database code accident severity according to a 4-point scale from lowest to highest level: moderate injury (k = 1), serious injury (not life threatening) (k = 2), critical (life threatening/survival uncertain) (k = 3) and maximum injury/death (k = 4). The ordinal variable, $SRTA_i$, is a function of another variable, $SRTA_i^*$, that is continuous and has various threshold points. The value $SRTA_i$ of the observed variable depends on whether it crosses a particular threshold, as shown by the following formulas[xii]:

$$SRTA_i = \begin{cases} 1, \ if \ SRTA_i^* < k_1 \\ M, \ if \ k_{i=(M-1)} \leq SRTA_i^* \leq k_{i=M}, M = 2, 3 \\ 4, \ if \ SRTA_i^* > k_M \end{cases} \tag{3}$$

[xi]More detail sees Chen *et al.* (2016), Abegaz *et al.* (2014), and Kaplan and Prato (2012).
[xii]Edited from Chen *et al.* (2016).

Table 3. The factors influencing the severity of accidents and their expected sign.

Factor	Detail	Expected Sign	Reference of the hypothesis
Dependent Variable			
SRTA	Severity of RTA 1 = Moderate injury* 2 = Serious injury** 3 = Critical injury*** 4 = Maximum injury/ Death		

Independent Variables			Reference of the hypothesis
SEX	Gender (0 = Female, 1 = Male)	+	• Ulleberg and Rundmo (2003) • Bates *et al.* (2014)
DVP	Driver/Passenger (0 = Passenger, 1 = Driver)	+	• Srisawang (2018)
UBR	Location of crash (0 = Urban, 1 = Rural)	+	• Thai Road Safety Collaboration (2019) • Bureau of Epidemiology (2019)
HEM	Helmet Use (0 = Not wearing helmet, 1 = Wearing helmet)	−	• MacLeod *et al.* (2021) • Scott-Parker and Oviedo-Trespalacios (2017)
ACL	Alcohol involved (0 = Not drunk, 1 = Drunk)	+	• Scott-Parker and Oviedo-Trespalacios (2017) • Elvik *et al.* (2009)
DRG	Drug Use (0 = Not use, 1 = Use)	+	• Hedlund (2018) • WHO (2018a)
CEL	Cellphone use (0 = Not use, 1 = Use)	+	• Caird *et al.* (2008) • Horrey and Wickens (2006)

*Moderate injury means physical injury that requires medical treatment or requires hospitalization but released within one-day.
**Serious injury means an injury that requires hospitalization for more than 48 hours, commencing within seven days from the date the injury was received (not life threatening).
***Critical means an injury of a serious nature that causes life threatening/survival uncertain.

The continuous latent variable $SRTA_i^*$ is equal to:

$$SRTA_i^* = \beta_1 SEX_i + \beta_2 DVP_i + \beta_3 UBR_i + \beta_4 HEM_i$$

$$+ \beta_5 ACL_i + \beta_6 DRG_i + \beta_7 CEL_i + \varepsilon_i$$

$$= \sum_{j=1}^{7} \beta_j X_i + \varepsilon_i$$

$$= Z_i + \varepsilon_i \tag{4}$$

where $SRTA_i^*$ is a severity category, X_i accounts for the included explanatory variables in the model estimation, β_j is a vector of the corresponding coefficient that is estimated, and ε_i is the error term, assumed to follow a logistic distribution.

This study simulates the risk factors for road accidents into four models as follows:

Model I: The model includes risk factors — difference in behavior between male and female youth (male/female), the geographic area of the accident in relation to the access to post-crash treatment (urban/rural), and motorcycle user's position (driver/passenger). More importantly, the model included whether users wear helmets, which directly relates to the severity of motorcycle accidents.

Model II: This model is developed from the first model with the addition of co-risk behaviors that may increase the severity of accidents involving alcohol consumption. (This is due to drunk-driving behavior being the number one cause of death in RTA in Thailand[xiii]).

Model III: This model is developed from Model II and the WHO (2018a) report, which states that in addition to alcohol, drug use is another risky behavior that could impair motorcyclists' awareness, leading to road traffic accidents as well.

Model IV: This model is developed from Model III, noting that distraction from driving is a typical risk behavior that leads to road accidents.[xiv] Therefore, this model includes behavioral variables like using mobile phones while driving.

3. Results

The results are divided into two stages. First, the descriptive statistics of variables used in OLM. Second, the confirmation of the significant causes of road traffic accidents among teenagers in Thailand.

[xiii]See Center for Prevention and Reduction of Road Accidents (2020).
[xiv]See WHO (2018a), Farmer *et al.* (2010), and Caird *et al.* (2008).

3.1. Part 1: Descriptive Results

This part explaines the characteristics of motorcycle RTA in Thailand (as shown in Table 4 below).

In Table 4, the moderate injury (victims who are hospitalized but released within one-day) severity of motorcycle accidents group is found to be the most common consequence of RTA among teenagers, with 68.31 percent. This is followed by serious injury (not life-threatening) at 23.11 percent, life-threatening/survival uncertain at 7.69 percent, and death at 0.89 percent. The no injury/minor injury group is not reported.

The results of the factors influencing RTA show that the RTAs are strongly reported in males at 74.92 percent, which is much more than females, regardless of whether they are drivers or passengers.

Table 4. Variable definitions and descriptive statistics.

Variable	Codes/Values	Number of cases	Percentage
Severity of RTAs	Moderate injury	34,184	68.31
	Serious injury	11,564	23.11

Table 4 (a).

	Life threatening	3,847	7.69
	Death	446	0.89
Gender	Female	12,551	25.08
	Male	37,490	74.92
Driver/Passenger	Passenger	7,503	14.99
	Driver	42,538	85.01
Location of Crash	Urban	23,018	46.00
	Rural	27,023	54.00
Helmet Used	Not wearing helmet	43,072	86.07
	Wearing helmet	6,969	13.93
Alcohol Involved	Not drunk	36,243	72.43
	Drunk	13,798	27.57
Drug Used	Not used	49,935	99.79
	Used	106	0.21
Cellphone Used	Not used	49,918	99.75
	Used	123	0.25

Note: 50,041 observations were used.

However, the data also show that drivers are the main group of youth road traffic victims at 85.01 percent, while passengers are at 14.99 percent. The areas of crash location from the report of motorcycle victims in Thailand show that 54 percent of motorcycle accidents occur in rural areas while 46 percent are in urban areas.

For risky behaviors, the helmet-use rate among young motorcyclists is low, at 13.93 percent. And the statistic also points out that the drunk-driving rate is high, at 72.43 percent in this age group, while the number of cases with drug and cellphone-use is low, at 0.21 percent and 0.25 percent, respectively.

3.2. Part 2: Regression Results

From the cutting points in Table 5, the results can be interpreted as in Table 6 below:

The results of OLM analysis in all models indicate that all independent factors are significantly related to the severity of RTA (see Tables 5 and 6). The discussions of each model are as follows:

Model I: These independent variables have the anticipated signs, based on the hypotheses: (1) the gender variable is related to the severity of motorcycle accidents in a positive direction. This model finds that the likelihood of accident severity in male youths is significant. (2) The accidents that occur in urban/rural areas are positively related to the severity of road traffic accidents. The trend is statistically significant in rural areas. (3) Non-helmet use is a risky behavior directly related to the severity of motorcycle accidents, with a negative correlation. In other words, if the motorcycle user wears a helmet, it significantly reduces the severity of a motorcycle accident. However, the sign of the driver/passenger variable is the opposite of the hypothesis. We find a negative correlation, with a statistically significant trend for motorcycle passengers. Moreover, this model can predict the severity of motorcycle accidents of each case by using the cutting points (see Table 6) to interpret the results, as follows: (1) if the value of a continuous latent variable $(SRTA_i^*)$ is less than 1.00642, this results in moderate injury; (2) if in between 1.00642 and 2.62012, this results in serious injury; (3) between 2.62012 and

Table 5. The factors influencing the severity of RTA resulting from OLM.

	Model I	Model II	Model III	Model IV
SEX	0.227309***	0.217571***	0.2172000***	0.217173***
	(0.0233127)	(0.0238323)	(0.0238290)	(0.0238261)
DVP	−0.192394***	−0.192736***	−0.191799***	−0.191977***
	(0.0272904)	(0.0273022)	(0.0272923)	(0.0272632)
UBR	0.447200***	0.449786***	0.449111***	0.449266***
	(0.0193989)	(0.0194426)	(0.0194471)	(0.0194463)
HEM	−0.164124***	−0.158499***	−0.161481***	−0.162214***
	(0.0283129)	(0.0284504)	(0.0284769)	(0.0284790)
ACL	—	0.0446008**	0.0434877**	0.0427383*
		(0.0218397)	(0.0218515)	(0.0284790)
DRG	—	—	0.569981***	0.511078***
			(0.194354)	(0.195382)
CEL	—	—	—	0.476306***
				(0.178916)
Cut 1[a]	1.00642***	1.01329***	1.0394***	1.01467***
	(0.0288736)	(0.0290487)	(0.0290506)	(0.0290554)
Cut 2[b]	2.62012***	2.62714***	2.62799***	2.62891***
	(0.0317665)	(0.0319380)	(0.0319412)	(0.0319473)
Cut 3[c]	4.96984***	4.97699***	4.97802***	4.97905***
	(0.0549632)	(0.0550674)	(0.0550703)	(0.0550743)
Mean dependent Var	1.411583	1.411583	1.411583	1.411583
S.D. dependent Var	0.670389	0.670389	0.670389	0.670389
Log-likelihood	−41580.71	−41578.63	−41574.53	−41571.14
Akaike criterion	83175.42	83173.26	83167.07	83162.29
Schwarz criterion	83237.16	83243.82	83246.45	83250.50
Hannan-Quinn	83194.76	83195.36	83191.93	83189.92
Likelihood ratio test:	8187.56	8191.72	8199.9	8206.68
Chi-square	(0.0000)	(0.0000)	(0.0000)	(0.0000)

Notes: 50,041 observations were used, *significant at level of 90 percent;
**95 percent; ***99 percent;
(n.s.) not significant.
[a,b,c] the Ordered Logit Models of this study fit three parallel lines (four groups, minus a baseline) with different intercepts, and the cut points are precisely those intercepts.

4.96984 results in life-threatening; and (4) if the value is over 4.96984 the results suggest death.

Model II: The correlation direction between independent variables (gender, drivers or passengers, crash location, helmet use) and the motorcycle accident severities are similar to Model I. For the additional regressor variable, drunk-driving, the results show that there is a positive relationship with the accident severities, thus drinking

Table 6. The interpretations of each cutting point from OLM.

Interpretations	Cutting Points ($SRTA^*$ or Y^*)			
	Model I	Model II	Model III	Model IV
Moderate injury	$Y^* < 1.00642$	$Y^* < 1.01329$	$Y^* < 1.0394$	$Y^* < 1.01467$
Serious injury	$1.00642 \leq Y^* \leq 2.62012$	$1.01329 \leq Y^* \leq 2.62714$	$1.0394 \leq Y^* \leq 2.62799$	$1.01467 \leq Y^* 2.62891$
Life threatening	$2.62012 \leq Y^* \leq 4.96984$	$2.62714 \leq Y^* 4.97699$	$2.62799 \leq Y^* 4.97802$	$2.62891 \leq Y^* \leq 4.97905$
Death	$Y^* > 4.96984$	$Y^* > 4.97699$	$Y^* > 4.97802$	$Y^* > 4.97905$

alcohol before driving could raise the severity levels significantly. The interpretations of cutting points of this model (see Table 6) are as follows: (1) if the continuous latent variable is less than 1.01329, this results in moderate injury; (2) if in between 1.01329 and 2.62714, this results in serious injury; (3) between 2.62714 and 4.97699 results in life-threatening; and (4) if the value is over 4.97699, the results suggest death.

Model III: This model is extended Model II and has the exact correlation directions between the severity of accidents with the same regressors. The sign of drug use, an additional explanatory variable, is positively correlated with road traffic severity levels, confirming our hypothesis. This relationship is statistically significant. This model predictes the severity of motorcycle accidents of each case by using the cutting points (see Table 6) to interpret the results as follows: (1) if the value of a continuous latent variable is less than 1.0394, this results in moderate injury; (2) if in between 1.0394 and 2.62799, this results in serious injury; (3) between 2.62799 and 4.97802 results in life-threatening; and (4) if the value is over 4.97802, the results suggest death.

Model IV: This model is the full model (see Model II), which includes all independent variables from all previous models, in addition to cellphone-use while driving. The results find a positive correlation with road traffic severity levels, which follow the anticipated sign of our hypothesis. The relationship is also statistically significant. The interpretations of cutting points of this model (see Table 6) are as follows: (1) if the continuous latent variable is less than 1.01467, the results suggest moderate injury; (2) if in between 1.01467 and 2.62891, the results suggest serious injury; (3) between 2.62891 and 4.97905 suggest life-threatening; and (4) if the value is over 4.97905, the results suggest death.

4. Conclusions

The conclusions of this study can be summarized as follows. The severity of road accidents is higher if the motorcyclists are male, since young males are naturally prone to risk-taking behaviors. Motorcycle crashes tend to increase in rural areas and roads. When motorcycle accidents occur, most passengers seem to have severe injuries. This is consistent with the Global Status on RTA Report,[xv] which states that in Thailand, the proportion of motorcycle passengers wearing helmets is as low as 20 percent, leading to increase in injury severities and fatality rates. The main risky driving behaviors among teenagers are not wearing helmets and drunk-driving, while drug use and distracted driving with mobile devices make up a few cases. The results are in line with Permpoonwiwat *et al.* (2020). Their study uses the same data as this paper and points out that the main risky driving behaviors found among teenagers are not wearing helmets and driving while drunk. Motorcycle driving under the influence of alcohol is mostly found among males. The critical level of injury severity is lower among helmet wearers than non-helmet wearers. Furthermore, the survival rate among helmet wearers is higher than those not wearing helmets. Our policy recommendations are similar to Permpoonwiwat *et al.* (2020), specifically: knowledge and training on safe driving and using protective equipment by central and local authorities should start at school, as well as conducting an orientations on safe driving measures prior to obtaining a driver's license. Penalties and fines for teenage road users may be imposed at higher rates.

References

Abegaz, T., Berhane, Y., Worku, A., Assrat, A., and Assefa, A. (2014). Effects of Excessive Speeding and Falling Asleep While Driving on Crash Injury Severity in Ethiopia: A Generalized Ordered Logit Model analysis. *Accident Analysis & Prevention, 71*, 15–21.

Bank of Thailand. (2021). *GDP per Capita in 2019, Thailand.* Retrieved from https://www.bot.or.th/App/BTWS_STAT/statistics/ BOTWEBSTAT.aspx?reportID=409&language=TH

Bates, L.J., Davey, J., Watson, B., King, M.J., and Armstrong, K. (2014). Factors Contributing to Crashes Among Young Drivers. *Sultan Qaboos University Medical Journal, 14*(3), 297–305.

Bellizzi, M.G., Eboli, L., Forciniti, C., and Mazzulla, G. (2018). Air Transport Passengers' Satisfaction: An Ordered Logit Model. *Transportation Research Procedia, 33*, 147–154.

[xv]See WHO (2018a).

Brown, T., Milavetz, G., and Murry, D.J. (2013). Alcohol, Drugs and Driving: Implications for Evaluating Driver Impairment. *Annals of Advances in Automotive Medicine, 57*, 23–32.

Bureau of Epidemiology. (2019). *Injury Surveillance — IS Database, 2015–2017.* Unpublished raw data.

Caird, J.K., Willness, C.R., Steel, P., and Scialfa, C. (2008). A Meta-Analysis of the Effects of Cell Phones on Driver Performance. *Accident Analysis & Prevention, 40*(4), 1282–1293.

Center for Prevention and Reduction of Road Accidents. (2020). *Summarized Report on Prevention and Reduction of Road Accidents During New Year Festival 2020.* Retrieved from: http://www.roadsafety thailand.com/

Chantith, C., Permpoonwiwat, C.K., and Fowles, R. (2021). Cost-Effectiveness of Road Safety Policy for Preventing and Reducing Road Traffic Fatalities in Thailand. *Thailand and The World Economy, 39*(2), 1–17.

Chen, C., Zhang, G., Huang, H., Wang, J., and Tarefder, R.A. (2016). Examining Driver Injury Severity Outcomes in Rural Non-Interstate Roadway Crashes Using a Hierarchical Ordered Logit Model. *Accident Analysis & Prevention, 96*, 79–87.

Elvik, R., Høye, A., Vaa, T., and Sørensen, M. (Eds.). (2009). *The Handbook of Road Safety Measures* (2nd Edn.). Emerald Group Publishing Limited, Bingley, UK.

Farmer, C.M., Braitman, K.A., and Lund, A.K. (2010). Cell Phone Use while Driving and Attributable Crash Risk. *Traffic injury prevention, 11*(5), 466–470.

Hedlund, J. (2018). *Drug-Impaired Driving: Marijuana and Opioids Raise Critical Issues for States.* Governors Highway Safety Association. Retrieved from: https://www.ghsa.org/sites/default/files/2018-05/ GHSA_DrugImpairedDriving_FINAL.pdf

Horrey, W.J., and Wickens, C.D. (2006). Examining the Impact of Cell Phone Conversations on Driving Using Meta-Analytic Techniques. *Human factors, 48*(1), 196–205.

Injury Data Collaboration Center. (2021). *Road Traffic Fatalities Situation in Thailand (2019–2021): Report by Age Group.* Retrieved from: https://dip.ddc.moph.go.th/new/บริการ/3base_status_new.

Ivers, R., Senserrick, T., Boufous, S., Stevenson, M., Chen, H.Y., Woodward, M., and Norton, R. (2009). Novice Drivers' Risky Driving Behavior, Risk Perception, and Crash Risk: Findings from the DRIVE Study. *American Journal of Public Health, 99*(9), 1638–1644. DOI: 10.2105/AJPH.2008.150367.

Kaplan, S., and Prato, C.G. (2012). Risk Factors Associated With Bus Accident Severity in the United States: A Generalized Ordered Logit Model. *Journal of Safety Research, 43*(3), 171–180.

Leon, M.R., Cal, P.C., and Sigua, R.D. (2005). Estimation of Socio-Economic Cost of Road Accidents in Metro Manila. *Journal of the Eastern Asia Society for Transportation Studies, 6*, 3183–3198.

MacLeod, J.B., DiGiacomo, J.C., and Tinkoff, G. (2010). An Evidence-Based Review: Helmet Efficacy to Reduce Head Injury and Mortality in Motorcycle Crashes: EAST Practice Management Guidelines. *Journal of Trauma and Acute Care Surgery, 69*(5), 1101–1111.

Malyshkina, N.V., and Mannering, F. (2008). Effect of Increases in Speed Limits on Severities of Injuries in Accidents. *Transportation Research Record, 2083*(1), 122–127.

Office of Transport and Traffic Policy and Planning, Ministry of Transport. (2019). *Road Accident Situation Analysis Report of the Ministry of Transport, 2018.*

Permanent International Association of Road Congresses (PIARC). (2022). *Socio-Economic Costs of Road Traffic Crashes.* Retrieved from: https://roadsafety.piarc.org/en/strategic-global-perspective-scope-road-safety-problem/socio-economic-costs.

Permpoonwiwat, C.K., Kleepbua, C., and Chanthit, C. (2020). *Road Traffic Accidents among Young and Reckless Drivers With Risk-Taking Behaviors.* Thai Health Promotion Foundation, Bangkok.

Provincial Emergency Prevention Support, Office of Health Promotion., and Khon Kaen Limited Partnership. (2016). *Thailand Road Safety Report 2014.*

Scott-Parker, B., and Oviedo-Trespalacios, O. (2017) Young Driver Risky Behavior and Predictors of Crash Risk in Australia, New Zealand, and Colombia: Same but Different? *Accident Analysis & Prevention, 99*(Part A), 30–38. DOI: 10.1016/j.aap.2016.11.001.

Sikron, F., Baron-Epel, O., and Linn, S. (2008). The Voice of Lay Experts: Content Analysis of Traffic Accident "Talk-Backs". *Transportation Research Part F: Traffic Psychology and Behaviour, 11*(1), 24–36.

Srisawang, B. (2018). Trends in Road Accidents and their Associated Risk Factors in Sichon District, Nakhon Si Thammarat, Thailand. *Region 11 Medical Journal, 32*(4), 1451–1462.

Strategy and Planning Division, Ministry of Public Health. (2017). *Public Health Statistics A.D.2017.* Retrieved from: http://bps.moph.go.th/new_bps/sites/default/files/statistics60.pdf.

Su-angka, K. (2016). *A Study of Young Driver Behavior that Affect the Risk of Accidents from the Motorcycle.* Suranaree University of Technology, Nakhon Ratchasima.

Thai Road Safety Collaboration. (2019). *Statistic of Injuries and Deaths all Provinces.* Retrieved from http://www.thairsc.com/.

Ulleberg, P., and Rundmo, T. (2003). Personality, Attitudes, and Risk Perception as Predictors of Risky Driving Behavior Among Young Drivers. *Safety Science,* *41*(5), 427–443. https://doi.org/10.1016/S0925-7535(01)00077-7.

World Health Organization, Geneva. (2006). *Road Traffic Injury Prevention: Training Manual.*

World Health Organization, Geneva. (2018a). *Global Status Report on Road Safety 2018.*

World Health Organization, Geneva. (2018b). *Global Status Report on Alcohol and Health 2018.* Retrieved from: https://www.who.int/substance_abuse/publications/global_alcohol_report/en/.

https://doi.org/10.1142/9789811271663_0003

Chapter 3

Inverse Probability Tilting with Heterogeneous Average Treatment Effects

Jeffrey P. Cohen

School of Business, University of Connecticut, USA

Ke Yang

Barney School of Business, University of Hartford, USA

There are many applied empirical studies, including those in health, development and real estate, that have data that are "missing at random". We extend the Inverse Probability Tilting (IPT) estimator by developing a nonparametric, geographic estimator that allows for average treatment effect (ATE) heterogeneity and addresses "missing data" problems. We propose a new estimator, Geographic Inverse Probability Tilting (GIPT) that re-weights twice: using propensity scores that equate moments across treated (and untreated) sub-samples with the entire sample, as in IPT; and also, down-weighting observations far from each target point. This allows for heterogeneous ATE estimates. In large samples, the ATE surface is smooth with GIPT, whereas using IPT in several different locations would result in discrete jumps in such a surface. Monte Carlo simulations validate the strong small sample performance of GIPT. Among many possible applications of GIPT, we demonstrate how a severe storm leading to an extended water-boil advisory, imposed much longer on sub-sections of Metro-Vancouver Canada (the "treatment"), impacted individual commercial property prices (the ATEs) differently.

1. Introduction

Two increasingly popular areas of focus in recent applied econometrics research are average treatment effect (ATE) heterogeneity, and missing data problems. Our methodology extends an existing approach, intended to be a useful tool in a specific applied setting. Our approach addresses both ATE heterogeneity and missing data problem in one framework.

One set of approaches to missing data problems in general settings is propensity score approaches. There is an extensive body of literature on Inverse Probability Weighting (IPW), as in Rosenbaum and Rubin (1983) and followed by Imbens (2004) and Wooldridge (2007). More recently, Graham *et al.* (2012) developed an approach called Inverse Probability Tilting (IPT), which imposes a balance between the treated and control groups while estimating the ATE.

Some recent research has focused on specific types of missing data problems and some have addressed them with propensity score approaches. For instance, Abrevaya and Donald (2017) consider a situation where some observations on an explanatory variable are missing, and they develop an estimator to handle this problem.

One objective of this paper is to incorporate a second adjustment for missing data problems as a part of the estimation strategy in our specific application.[i] Specifically, we extend the IPT estimator to allow for re-weighting based on heterogeneity, in addition to a propensity score approach for the missing data problem. The attractive features of IPT that we describe below have prompted us to explore this geographic IPT. This type of additional adjustment is important in the context of many treatment effect problems, because the ATEs can be different across various target points. While it would be possible to estimate IPT in various neighborhoods, doing so discards potentially useful data from observations that are further apart. This allows for heterogeneous ATE estimates. In large samples, the ATE surface is smooth with GIPT, as can be seen in our Monte Carlo simulations. In contrast, using IPT in one location results in an

---

[i]This specific application differs from the application in Graham *et al.* (2012) in terms of the structure of the data and type of problem considered. Our approach would not be possible to implement for the application in Graham *et al.* (2012) unless more information were available on the geographic locations of the observations.

ATE surface that is a "plane", and IPT estimates at several different locations would result in discrete jumps in such a surface.

In particular, the issue of ATE heterogeneity has received some recent attention. While one advantage of IPT is that it leads to a unique treatment effect for each observation, it may also be useful to consider heterogeneity in a nonparametric framework that could lead to different ATEs across individual observations or target points. In such situations, an approach to deal with the missing data problem while allowing for heterogeneity in ATEs across target points could be desirable in certain contexts. Thus, we demonstrate how a geographic version of the IPT approach that considers heterogeneity in the data can address the missing data problem while at the same time allowing for ATEs to vary across observations.

One potential application of our estimator is property sales, where a treatment is imposed on some properties in a geographic region, but neither on others in the same region nor upon any properties in a neighboring region. With this particular missing data problem, the researcher knows what price a treated property is sold for but does not know how much the same property would have sold for if it had been untreated. The ATEs might vary across different locations. While this is the specific application that we consider in this paper in order to demonstrate the implementation of our estimator, there are many other potential applications, in contexts where there is heterogeneity in the data and a treatment is imposed on units at some target points, but not in others.

A health and development economics application of IPT is described in Graham *et al.* (2011). The application considers the impact of a cash transfer program, which was provided to some households but not others, on household calorie consumption in 42 rural Nicaraguan communities in the early 2000s. This type of application would be an excellent candidate for our geographic IPT that would allow for heterogeneous average treatment effects in different villages.

In the remainder of this paper, we first motivate one type of missing data problem (although our estimator can be applicable to other missing data problems). Next, we explain the extension to the

IPT estimator that allow for ATE heterogeneity, and the adjustments to the propensity score weights made to allow for more distant observations to be down-weighted relative to more close observations. We call this new method the GIPT estimator (representing "Geographic Inverse Probability Tilting"). We prove consistency and asymptotic normality of GIPT in Appendix.[ii] We describe the computation process of the GIPT estimator, then provide some Monte Carlo evidence to demonstrate that the estimator performs well in one particular context. We apply this GIPT estimator to the case of how commercial property prices in the metro-Vancouver, BC Canada region may be impacted differently, shortly before versus after a storm leading to an extended water-boil advisory that is imposed on some parts of the region for much longer than other areas. A key feature of this example is that we know the geographic locations of the problems. Also, this is not a panel data set; some properties sold before the storm and others sold after, but none sold shortly before and after. In other words, we do not have any repeat sales observations. Finally, we discuss potential future extensions to this approach and summarize our findings.

2. Motivation

Consider the following problem as one particular type of missing data problem. First, suppose one is interested in analyzing a data set on units that are in various locations throughout a particular geographic region, to determine the ATEs at each location in the region shortly after versus shortly before a random "event". The treatment area may be confined to specific parts of a particular metro area, for instance, which we call the subject area. The "untreated" observations are a set of units that are in some parts of the metro area, before and after the "event" as well as a set of different units within the subject area before the "event". Then, we can estimate

---

[ii]Graham *et al.* (2012) prove local efficiency of IPT. While the proof of local efficiency of GIPT would be non-trivial, it is not necessarily the case that local efficiency does not hold. This proof would be a potential topic for future research.

the effect of being in the treatment sub-sample opposed to the non-treated sub-sample.

But in this type of empirical application, the researcher does not know what the treatment outcome would have been if a particular unit had been untreated. Also, the researcher does not observe the outcome for units in the treated group if each unit had been untreated. These two situations are the missing data problem that we consider in this paper. In these cases, in order to obtain valid treatment effects, one can re-weight the data with propensity scores. There are several approaches to accomplishing this. One is an Inverse Probability Weighting (IPW) approach, which has received extensive attention in the literature (see, e.g., Rosenbaum and Rubin (1983), and Imbens (2004), among others). An attractive alternative is the IPT approach, as in Graham *et al.* (2012), which generates separate tilting parameter estimates for the treated and untreated samples, and imposes a balance between the treated and control groups when estimating the ATE. There are alternative missing data approaches that have been proposed by others, such as random forests (Wager and Athey, 2018), and some methods closely related to IPT (e.g., Imai and Ratkovic, 2014, and Hainmueller, 2012), among others. A comparison of many of these approaches is presented in Frolich *et al.* (2017), however there is no known analysis of GIPT in the literature. Allowing for ATE heterogeneity in missing data problems in the context of IPT is one contribution of our paper.[iii]

Specifically, the IPT and IPW approaches do not allow for heterogeneity in the ATEs and the tilting parameters. If the target points of observations are varied, this could be an important consideration in many but not all applications. It may be helpful to re-weight a second time, to consider heterogeneity across target points. This is common in the nonparametric estimation literature, specifically, with an approach called Locally Weighted Regressions (LWR), also commonly referred to as Geographically Weighted Regressions (GWR), as in Brunsdon *et al.* (1996). McMillen and Redfearn (2010)

[iii]Other recent contributions to the ATE heterogeneity literature include Allcott (2015), Hsu *et al.* (2018), and Hotz *et al.* (2005).

describe LWR and present an application. However, no known work has incorporated this type of estimation into an IPT framework.

In a recent research, Abrevaya *et al.* (2015) consider a Conditional Average Treatment Effect estimation (CATE). Meanwhile, Lee *et al.* (2017) consider a Conditional Average Treatment Effect Function (CATEF) estimation. While both procedures can be conceptually extended to estimate ATE heterogeneity across geographical locations, the procedure proposed in this paper differs from the existing procedures in two important ways. First, we propose a procedure based on inverse probability tilting while Abrevaya *et al.* (2015) consider a procedure based on inverse probability weighting (IPW) and Lee *et al.* (2017) consider a procedure based on Augmented Inverse Probability Weighting (AIPW). As argued in Graham *et al.* (2012), we expect some of the advantages of IPT over existing IPW estimation (including augmented IPW), in terms of robustness and higher-order bias, to carry over to our procedure. Second, in our proposed procedure, the propensity score function is estimated with a geographically weighted regression, which is a semiparametric procedure tailored for geographical data. Abrevaya *et al.* (2015) consider a fully nonparametric local linear regression for the propensity score function estimation. Lee *et al.* (2017) consider a fully parametric logit regression for the propensity score function estimation. The local linear regression approaches have clear strengths, but they could suffer from the curse of dimensionality when there are large number of confounders.

3. Approach

3.1. *Model*

Suppose that there are N units, indexed by $i = 1, \ldots, N$, viewed as drawn randomly from a large population. We postulate the existence for each unit of a pair of potential outcomes, $Y_i(0)$ for the outcome under the control treatment and $Y_i(1)$ for the outcome under the active treatment. Let $X_i = \{X_i^1, L_i\}$. Each unit has a vector of covariates, pretreatment variables or exogenous variables, X_i^1, and vector of covariates L_i that may consist of a subset of X_i^1 and/or a set of variables not included as part of $X_i{}^1$ (such as geographic coordinates). Each unit is exposed to a single treatment; $D_i = 0$ if unit i is untreated and $D_i = 1$ if unit i receives the active treatment. We therefore observe for each unit the triple (D_i, Y_i, X_i), where Y_i is the realized outcome:

$$Y_i \equiv Y_i(D_i) = \begin{cases} Y_i(0) & if \quad D_i = 0, \\ Y_i(1) & if \quad D_i = 1. \end{cases}$$

Assuming the existence of potential outcomes, $Y(1)$ and $Y(0)$ correspond to the outcome the subject at a specific target point would have experienced with or without treatment, respectively.

Then we can define the average treatment effect (ATE) at l as

$$\gamma(l) = \mathbb{E}[Y(1) - Y(0)|L = l].$$

In practice, however, one only observes

$$Y_i = (1 - D_i)Y_i(0) + D_i Y_i(1)$$

i.e., only $Y_i(1)$ for actively treated units or $Y_i(0)$ for untreated units are observed at any given target point. First, we make the following assumption:

Assumption 1. (Un-confoundedness): $\{Y(1), Y(0)\} \perp D|X$.

This assumption effectively implies that we can treat the nearby observations as having come from a randomized experiment. It follows immediately that the ATE at target point l, $\gamma(l)$, is given as:

$$\gamma(L = l) = E[E[Y|D = 1, X] - E[Y|D = 0, X]|L = l]$$

or equivalently

$$\gamma(L = l) = E\left[\frac{DY}{p(X)} - \frac{(1 - D)Y}{1 - p(X)}|L = l\right] \tag{1}$$

where $p(X) = P[D = 1|X = x] = E[D_i|X_i = x]$ is the propensity score function that prescribes the conditional probability of receiving treatment at x (which is a generalization of the setup in Rosenbaum and Rubin, 1983). As this propensity score function is generally unknown, many earlier methods on average treatment effect (ATE) estimation differ in how they estimate $p(X)$ using, e.g., variants of maximum likelihood approaches, such as the Inverse Probability Weighting (IPW) estimator that we describe in the next section, and then the estimate of $p(X)$ implies an ATE.

3.2. *Geographic Inverse Probability Tilting Estimator (GIPT)*

Rosenbaum and Rubin (1983) proposed the Inverse Probability Weighting ATE estimator by first replacing the $p(X)$ with a maximum likelihood estimator, then averaging over sample points. The Rosenbaum and Rubin (1983) setup implicitly assumes no variation in the ATE across observations. Graham *et al.* (2012) proposed an alternative method by estimating the propensity score function that imposes a balance across the treated and control groups with a particular estimator consisting of two separate tilting parameters, one for each observation in the treatment group and another for observations in the control group. We incorporate target point specific weights into the IPT estimator from Graham *et al.* (2012), in the following way: Our method of estimating the target point specific average treatment effects is based on an extension of the IPT estimator proposed by Graham *et al.* (2012) and relies upon the following Assumptions 2 through 9 below, in addition to Assumption 1 above (the un-confoundedness assumption).

Assumption 2. (Random Sampling): $\{D_i, X_i, Y_i\}_{i=1}^N$ is an independently and identically distributed random sequence. We observe D, X, and $Y = DY(1) + (1 - D)Y(0)$ for each sampled unit.

Assumption 3. (Identification): For some known $K \times 1$ vector of functions $\Phi(Y, X, \gamma(l))$,

$$E(\Phi(Y, X, \gamma(l))) = 0$$

with (i) $E(\Phi(Y, X, \gamma(l))) \neq 0$ for all $\gamma(l) \neq \gamma_0(l)$, $\gamma(l) \in \Theta \subset \mathbb{R}^K$, and Θ compact with $\gamma_{0(l)} \in int(\Theta)$; (ii) $|\Phi(Y, X, \gamma(l))| \leq c(Y, X)$ for all Y, X with $c(\cdot)$ a non-negative function and $\mathbb{E}(c(Y, X)) < \infty$; (iii) $\Phi(Y, X, \gamma(l))$ is continuous on Θ for each Y, X and continuously differentiable in a neighborhood of $\gamma_0(l)$, (iv) $\mathbb{E}[\| \Phi(Y, X, \gamma(l)) \|^2] < \infty$, and (v) $\mathbb{E}[sup_{\gamma(l) \in \Theta} \| \nabla_{\gamma(l)} \Phi(Y, X, \gamma(l)) \|] < \infty$.

Assumption 4. (Strong Overlap): $p(X) = P[D = 1|X = x]$ is bounded away from 0 and 1 over $\aleph$, the support of X.

Assumption 5. There is a continuous function $\delta_0(\cdot)$ and compact, known vector $r(X)$ of linearly independent functions of X, and known function $G(\cdot)$ such that (i) $G(\cdot)$ is strictly increasing, continuously differentiable, and maps into the unit interval with $\lim_{\nu \to -\infty} G(\nu) = 0$ and $\lim_{\nu \to \infty} G(\nu) = 1$; (ii) $p(x) = G(r(w(l)x^1)'\delta_0(l))$ for all $x \in \aleph$; and (iii) $G(r(w(l)x^1)'\delta_0(l))$ is bounded away from 0 and 1 for $\delta_0(\cdot)$ and $x \in \aleph$.

GIPT is a kernel based estimator.[iv] The following additional regularity assumptions are needed for the GIPT estimator to have desirable large sample properties. Assumptions 6 through 8 are analogous to assumptions made by Abrevaya and Donald (2017).

Assumption 6. (Distribution of X): the Support χ of the k-dimensional covariate X is a Cartesian product of compact intervals, and the density of X, $f(X)$ are p-times continuously differentiable over χ.

Assumption 7. (Kernels): $K(\cdot)$ is a kernel of order s, is symmetric around zero, is equal to zero outside $\prod_{i=1}^{k}[-1, 1]$, integrate to 1 and is continuously differentiable.

Assumption 8. (Bandwidths): The bandwidth b satisfies the following conditions as $N \to \infty : b \to 0$ and $log(N)/(Nb^{k+s}) \to 0$.

[iv]There is a large literature on locally weighted regressions (LWR), which is essentially a form of weighted least squares and is a commonly used kernel estimator in spatial studies to allow for geographic heterogeneity in regression parameters. In other words, this approach leads to the possibility of different marginal effects at each target point. The basic idea behind LWR is to assign higher weights to observations near the target point when calculating a point specific estimate. The measure of distance between observations has a natural geographic interpretation in spatial modeling. The GWR approach is readily extended to Maximum-Likelihood Estimation (MLE) methods as well. While a typical MLE procedure chooses estimates to maximize the log-likelihood function, the geographically weighted version of MLE estimates a pseudo log-likelihood function, where the log-likelihood function depends on the functional form of the regression model. See McMillen and McDonald (2004), for more details.

Assumption 8 implies that b is a nuisance parameter.[v]

In developing the GIPT estimator, we modify Equation (A.22) in Graham *et al.* (2012)[vi] by incorporating kernel weights and a bandwidth parameter. If the researcher believes that the potential outcome function $G(\cdot)$ is a nonparametric function, then we could transform both $t(\cdot)$ and D_i with some kernel weights.[vii] More specifically, suppose one is interested in the first m moments (however, the choice of number of moments to be included is described in more detail in footnote vii below). Then, we denote $\tau(\hat{w}_i(l)x_i^1) = [1, \hat{w}_i(l)x_i^1, (\hat{w}_i(l)x_i^1)^2, \ldots (\hat{w}_i(l)x_i^1)^m,]'$, as a column vector where the weight $\hat{w}_i(l) = \left[K\left(\frac{d_i(l)}{b}\right)\right]^{1/2}$, with $K(\cdot)$ being the Gaussian kernel, b being the bandwidth parameter, m is the number of moments included, and $d_i(l)$ being the distance between observations i and target point $L = l$. This setup amounts to a nonparametric specification of the tilting parameters, $\delta^0(l)$ and $\delta^1(l)$, as defined in the following Assumption 9 below.

---

[v]There is a large literature on kernel and bandwidth selection in nonparametric estimation. For kernel selection, McMillen and Redfearn (2010) indicate that the results tend to be robust with respect to the specific functional form of the kernel, but more sensitive to the bandwidth. Silverman (1986) proposes a "rule of thumb" bandwidth, while others such as McMillen and Redfearn (2010) propose variations of cross validation techniques. In the context of GIPT, we describe our bandwidth selection process below, which was somewhat different in the Monte Carlo simulations than with the empirical application of GIPT.

[vi]In Graham *et al.* (2012), they compute separate tilting parameters for the treatment and control groups by solving an optimization problem that imposes a balance between the two groups. Among their assumptions includes variants of our Assumptions 1 through 5, but the location variable, l, is not included in their vector of X. See our Assumption 5 below for more details.

[vii]In the case, $G(\cdot)$ is a non-parametric function. A naive way to estimate treatment effect heterogeneity is to estimate, e.g., using IPT, the conditional effects for each different location, $L = l$. Our proposed method is conceptually more appealing because $G(\cdot)$ at $L = l$ is estimated using observations not only at location l, but also observation in the surroundings. In addition, with our method, researchers can control how to use nearby observations through the choice of kernel function and bandwidth. Furthermore, the spatial dependence is also accounted for in our proposed method, through assigning higher weights to observations closer to the target location and lower weights further away.

Assumption 9. (Moment Conditional Expectation Function Model): For some unique matrix Π^* and vector of linear independent functions $\tau^*(w_i(l)x_i^1)$ with a constant in the first row, we have

$$E(\Phi(y, \gamma_0(l)|X) = \Pi^*\tau^*(w_i(l)x_i^1))$$

Graham *et al.* (2012) describe the implications for over-fitting the propensity score depending on the requirements of their Assumption 3.1 (analogous to our Assumption 9).[viii]

Analogous to Equation (5) and (6) in Graham *et al.* (2012), when our Assumptions 1 through 8 hold, then at each target point l we have the following just-identified unconditional moment problem:

$$\mathbb{E}\left[\frac{\hat{w}_i(l) \cdot D_i}{G(\tau(\hat{w}_i(l) \cdot x_i^1)'\delta_0(l))}\Phi(X, Y, \gamma_0(l))\right] = 0, \tag{2}$$

$$\mathbb{E}\left[\left(\frac{\hat{w}_i(l) \cdot D_i}{G(\tau(\hat{w}_i(l) \cdot x_i^1)'\delta_0(l))}-1\right)\tau(\hat{w}_i(l) \cdot x_i^1)\right] = 0. \tag{3}$$

Our GIPT estimator chooses $\hat{\beta}_{GIPT}(l) = \left[\hat{\gamma}'(l), \hat{\delta}_{GIPT}'(l)\right]'$ at each target point l to solve the sample analogue of the above two equations, i.e.,

$$\frac{1}{N}\sum_{i=1}^{N}\left[\frac{\hat{w}_i(l) \cdot D_i}{G\left(\tau(\hat{w}_i(l) \cdot x^1{}_i)'\hat{\delta}_{GIPT}(l)\right)}\Phi(X_i, Y_i, \hat{\gamma}_{GIPT}(l))\right] = 0, \tag{4}$$

$$\frac{1}{N}\sum_{i=1}^{N}\left[\left(\frac{\hat{w}_i(l) \cdot D_i}{G\left(\tau(\hat{w}_i(l) \cdot x_i^1)'\hat{\delta}_{GIPT}(l)\right)} - 1\right)\tau(\hat{w}_i(l) \cdot x_i^1)\right] = 0. \tag{5}$$

[viii]Graham *et al.* (2012) indicate that their Assumption 3.1 has implications for whether the propensity score needs to include additional moments (when r(X) is contained within t*(X)) or when the opposite is true where a replacement is made to "eliminate any over-identifying restrictions." In other words, IPT "over-fits the propensity score if Assumption 3.1 requires us to do so..." (Graham *et al.*, 2012). In our problem with GIPT, the analogous carries through to GIPT, depending on what Assumption 9 requires us to do.

Theorem 1. *Given the missing data model defined by Assumptions 1 through 8, then at each target point l for $\hat{\gamma}_{GIPT}(l)$, the solution to Equation (4) (i) $\hat{\gamma}_{GIPT}(l)$ is a consistent estimator of $\gamma_0(l)$ and (ii) $\sqrt{N}(\hat{\gamma}_{GIPT}(l) - \gamma_0(l)) \xrightarrow{D} \mathcal{N}(0, \mathcal{I}(\gamma_0(l))^{-1})$.*
Proof: See Appendix A.

Equation (5) is solved first, separately for each target point l, and the resulting tilting parameter estimates for each target point l are plugged into Equation (4) for each target point l to obtain the estimate of the ATE at each target point, l.[ix]

For computational simplicity, G is often assumed to take the Logit functional form, that is, $G(v) = exp(v)/[1+exp(v)]$, and $\phi_v = 1/G(v)$.

Let $h = 0, 1$ denote the treatment status of each individual with "1" for treatment group and "0" for control group. Then to compute $\tilde{\delta}^h(l)$, for each target point the GIPT estimator solves the following optimization problem separately for each target point l, adapted from Equation (A.22) of Graham *et al.* (2012) to incorporate multiple target points[x]:

For each target point, l, choose $\delta^h(l)$ to $\max L(\delta^h(l)) = (1/N)\sum_i D_i^h \hat{w}_i(l)\phi^h(\tau(\hat{w}_i(l)x_i^1)'\delta^h(l)) - (1/N)\sum_i \tau(\hat{w}_i(l)x_i^1)'\delta^h(l)$

where D_i^h is the treatment dummy for group h and ϕ^h is specific to group h. In this case, where there is one control group and one treatment group, the notation for these dummies can equivalently be reduced to $(1 - D)$ and (D), respectively.

The first order condition for this optimization problem is:

$$\partial(L(\delta^h(l)))/\partial\delta^h(l) = (1/N)\sum_i D_i^h \hat{w}_i(l)\tau(\hat{w}_i(l)x_i^1)'\phi_\delta^h(\cdot)$$

$$- (1/N)\sum_i \tau(\hat{w}_i(l)x_i^1)' = 0,$$

[ix]While it might be desirable to test restrictions among the ATEs, this is not a straightforward issue to implement.

[x]While there is no required minimum number of target points, the problem is only interesting when there is more than one target point, as otherwise there will not be any ATE heterogeneity.

and the second order condition is:

$$\partial^2(\mathrm{L}(\delta^h(l)))/(\partial\delta^h(l))^2 = (1/N)\sum_i D_i^h \hat{w}_i(l)\tau(\hat{w}_i(l)x_i^1)'' \phi_{\delta\delta}^h(\cdot)$$

Graham *et al.* (2012) show for IPT that $\phi_{\delta\delta}^h(\cdot) < 0$ (see their Equation (A.21)), so that (L) is strictly concave. It follows here that concavity holds for GIPT at each target point, l.

When the treatment status is denoted by h, where $h = 0$ is the control group and $h = 1$ is the treatment group, it is reasonably straightforward to solve the optimization problem above (analogous to Equation (A.22) in Graham *et al.*, 2012) for $\tilde{\delta}^h(l)$ for all l. The GIPT estimator will lead to separate parameter estimates of $\tilde{\delta}^h(l)$, $l = 1, \ldots, N$. In contrast, the IPT estimator includes a single estimate of $\tilde{\delta}^h(l)$, for all l.

Our GIPT discussion below closely parallels parts of the IPT approach of Graham *et al.* (2012). When there is one treatment group and one control group, then let N_1 and N_0 denote the number of treated units and untreated units, respectively. First, for the unit at target point $L = l$ in the treatment group, the GIPT estimator of δ, denoted by $\tilde{\delta}^1$, is a solution to:

$$\frac{1}{N}\sum_{i=1}^{N}\left\{\frac{\hat{w}_i(l)\cdot D_i}{G\left(\tau(\hat{w}_i(l)\cdot x_i^1)'\tilde{\delta}^1(l) - 1\right)}\right\}\tau(\hat{w}_i(l)\cdot x_i^1) = 0, \qquad (6)$$

where, given Assumptions 5 and 9, $G\left(\tau(\hat{w}_i(l)\cdot x_i^1)'\tilde{\delta}^1(l)\right) = p(x)$ for all $x \in \mathbb{X}$ and some δ_1, $\tau(\hat{w}_i(l)\cdot x_i^1)$ is a $1 + M$ column vector of known functions of X with a constant as its first element, and $\tilde{\delta}^1$ is a vector of estimates of δ_1. Following the logic of Graham *et al.* (2012), the propensity score for the ith unit in the treated sample can be written as:

$$\tilde{\pi}_i^1(l) = \frac{1}{N}\frac{\hat{w}_i(l)}{G\left(\tau(\hat{w}_i(l)\cdot x_i^1)'\tilde{\delta}^1(l)\right)}, \quad i = N_0 + 1, N_0 + 2, \ldots, N. \quad (7)$$

These two equations imply:

$$\sum_{i=N_0+1}^{N_1} \tilde{\pi}_i^1(l) \cdot \tau(\hat{w}_i(l) \cdot x_i^1) = \frac{1}{N}\sum_{i=1}^{N} \tau(\hat{w}_i(l) \cdot x_i^1). \qquad (8)$$

Second, for the target point $L = l$ in the untreated group, the GIPT estimator of δ^0, denoted as $\tilde{\delta}^0(l)$, is the solution to:

$$\frac{1}{N}\sum_{i=1}^{N} \left\{ \frac{\hat{w}_i(l) \cdot (1 - D_i)}{1 - G\left(\tau(\hat{w}_i(l) \cdot x_i{}^1)\tilde{\delta}^0(l)\right)} | - 1 \right\} \tau(\hat{w}_i(l) \cdot x_i{}^1) = 0,$$

$$i = 1, \ldots, N_0. \qquad (9)$$

Similarly, the propensity score for the ith unit in the control sample can be written as:

$$\tilde{\pi}_i^0(l) = \frac{1}{N}\frac{\hat{w}_i(l)}{1 - G\left(\tau(\hat{w}_i(l) \cdot x_i^1)'\tilde{\delta}^0(l)\right)}. \qquad (10)$$

These two equations imply:

$$\sum_{i=1}^{N_0} \tilde{\pi}_i^0(l) \cdot \tau(\hat{w}_i(l) \cdot x_i^1) = \frac{1}{N}\sum_{i=1}^{N} \tau(\hat{w}_i(1) \cdot x_i^1). \qquad (11)$$

In words, Equation (8) states that after twice re-weighting the moments of x_i^1 across treated units, once with the propensity score parameters and once with the kernel weights, this equals the (kernel weighted) moments of x_i^1 over the entire sample. An analogous relationship for the untreated sample and the entire sample is in Equation (11).

The GIPT ATE estimate for the unit at target point $L = l$ is given by

$$\tilde{\gamma}^{GIPT}(l) = \sum_{i=N_0+1}^{N} \tilde{\pi}_i^1(1)Y_i - \sum_{i=1}^{N_0} \tilde{\pi}_i^0(l) \cdot Y_i \qquad (12)$$

where $\tilde{\pi}_i^1(l)$ and $\tilde{\pi}_i^0(l)$ are target point dependent and defined by Equations (7) and (10).

With GIPT, we estimate an ATE for each target observation. In footnote 21 of the Appendix of Graham *et al.* (2012), they describe the process for obtaining the overall ATE that is based on the single treatment effect for each observation. Our approach to obtaining the ATE for each target observation is similar to the overall ATE generation process outlined by Graham *et al.* (2012), but we modify the moments condition using $\tau(\hat{w}_i(l)x_i^1)$ instead of $t(x)$. With GIPT, we obtain a very representative estimate of the ATE by generating an ATE estimate for each target point, rather than generating one treatment effect for each target point and using these to calculate one overall ATE. Assumptions 1 through 8 are satisfied in our Monte Carlo study below, and in many applications that consist of randomized treatments. In applications where there are multiple target points, we expect that GIPT would lead to a precise estimate of the ATE at each target point, and in turn, the overall average of the ATEs may have lower bias than the estimated ATE from IPT. On the other hand, in applications where the dimension of l is large, the performance of estimates of ATE might be affected negatively, as we can expect from any nonparametric estimator, especially when the sample size is small.

We next perform Monte Carlo simulations to demonstrate that the GIPT estimator performs well in small samples.

4. Monte Carlo Study

In our specific Monte Carlo study, we consider a model with heterogeneity in the geographic locations of observations.[xi] We first denote the two-dimensional vector, $l_i = \begin{bmatrix} l_i^1, l_i^2 \end{bmatrix}$.[xii] In this Monte Carlo

---

[xi]We base our Monte Carlo study on a setup that mirrors our specific empirical application that we present later. It is not clear to what extent GIPT's performance would withstand an alternative application and/or dramatically different Monte Carlo setup.

[xii]We looked into a possibility of including the CATE procedure in Abrevaya *et al.* (2015) and the CATEF procedure in Lee *et al.* (2016) in our Monte Carlo study. However, both of those procedures are conditioned on one confounder in their applications, while our GIPT procedure is conditioned on both longitude and latitude variables. Even though the extension of CATE and CATEF to two-dimensional data is possible conceptually, the task of applying these estimators on our geographical data is much less straightforward. Therefore, we did not include CATE or CATEF in this Monte Carlo study.

study, we generate our response variables, y_i, from the following causal model and selection model:

$$y_i = \beta_0(l_i) + DT_i \cdot DS_i \cdot \beta_1(l_i) + x \cdot \beta_2(l_i) + u_i, \tag{13}$$

$$DS_i = \begin{cases} 1 & for \quad l_i^1 + 0.25 \times l_i^2 > 1.25 \\ 0 & for \quad l_i^1 + 0.25 \times l_i^2 \leq 1.25. \end{cases}, i = 1, \ldots, N \tag{14}$$

$$DT_i = \begin{cases} 1 & for \quad i > N/2 \\ 0 & for \quad i \leq N/2 \end{cases}, i = 1, \ldots, N \tag{15}$$

where Equation (13) is the causal model that produces the response variable y_i, Equations (14) and (15) are the selection model that produces the treatment group. If DS_i equals 1, this indicates that the unit is in the location where some observations are treated and units with 0 will be in the control group. Also, DT_i is a dummy such that a value of 1 indicates an observation is only possibly treated shortly after an unexpected event. Therefore, the treated sample will be comprised of the observations for which $D_i = DT_i \times DS_i = 1$; in other words, the treated sample consists of those units for which both $DS_i = 1$ and $DT_i = 1$. The vector $l_i = \left[l_i^1, l_i^2 \right]$ is a two-dimensional location vector generated from a bi-variate uniform distribution between $[0, 2]$, u_i is i.i.d. following a standard normal distribution; x_i^1 is a random variable generated from the normal distribution $N[0, 3]$, and v_i is i.i.d from the standard normal distribution. Additionally, for simplicity we set $\beta_0(l_i) = 0$ and $\beta_2(l_i) = 0.2$, and $\beta_1(l_i)$, our main interest in the estimation, is a variant of a bi-variate standard normal density function:

$$\beta_1(l_i) = \frac{1}{2\pi} \exp\left(-\frac{(l_i^1)^2 + (l_i^2)^2}{2} \right).$$

Note that this data generating process — as given in Equations (13), (14) and (15) — is designed to meet the assumptions discussed in Section 3. First, the distribution of the outcome, Y, is independent of the treatment status ("un-confoundedness"). Second, $\{Y_i, X_i, D_i\}_{i=1}^{N}$ are i.i.d. (the "random sampling" assumption). Third, $\mathbb{P}(D_i = 1|Y, X) = \mathbb{P}(D_i = 1|X)$ (The "missing at random" assumption). Finally, $\mathbb{P}(D_i = 1|X = x) = \mathbb{P}(D_i = 1) > 0$, as

D_i and X are independent in these data generating processes (the "strong overlap" assumption). The Gaussian kernel choice satisfies the symmetry assumption and the bandwidth will be determined to satisfy Assumption 8 (it is a nuisance parameter).

We use two different sample sizes, $N = 300$ and $N = 600$, as the number of individuals. This model is estimated with a variant of difference-in-differences[xiii] (hereafter denoted quasi-DID), IPT and GIPT as defined in Section 2. For the GIPT estimator, the optimal bandwidth for each sample size is calculated through a grid search of eight different bandwidths. For a grid of b values, the average squared error, $ASE(b) = \frac{1}{N} \sum_{i=1}^{N} \left\{ \tilde{\gamma}_j(l)^{GIPT} - \gamma_j^{GIPT}(l) \right\}^2$, is computed for 100 replications and then averaged to estimate the mean ASE (MASE). The function $MASE(b)$ is then compared over the grid values of b. The optimal bandwidth, b_{MASE}, is chosen to be the value of b that yields the minimum MASE value. One optimal bandwidth is obtained for each sample size for the GIPT estimator. For the $N = 300$ sample, the optimal bandwidth is determined to be 0.85, and for the $N = 600$ sample the optimal bandwidth is 0.75. Next, using the optimal bandwidth for each sample size, we perform 500 iterations for each sample size, and then compute the average bias and ASE for each. The average bias and ASEs are reported in Table 1. In addition, in Figure 1 we also plot the distributions, with histogram and estimated density, of the ASE results from the 500 repetitions on each estimator with two different sample sizes.

Since some preliminary finite sample experimental evidence on the performance of the IPT estimator is already available (Graham *et al.*, 2012), we are primarily interested in the performance of the GIPT relative to estimators that do not account for geographic variation. There are general regularities that are evident. As expected, increases in the sample size reduce the ASE for all estimators, suggesting that the estimators under study converge with sample size. Across both

---

[xiii]We describe this as a variant of DID because we assume that we do not have multiple observations for the same target point, as is the case in many real estate applications.

Table 1. Simulation results — small sample performances for GIPT, IPT and quasi-DID.[xiv]

	GIPT	IPT	quasi-DID
		Sample Size = 600	
Bias	0.0074211	−0.0408718	−0.0408698
ASE	0.002532	0.0058796	0.0058782
		Sample Size = 300	
Bias	0.0015103	−0.0410462	−0.0410958
ASE	0.003103	0.0060545	0.0060559

sample sizes, the IPT estimator performs at least as well as the quasi-DID estimator, in both ASE and average bias. Improvement of GIPT, as measured by MASE, over IPT and quasi-DID, ranges from 49 percent for $N = 300$ to 57 percent for $N = 600$. The key implication of these results is that in situations where geographic variation is an important factor in the data, the proposed GIPT estimator provides a simple but effective way to account for it. The ASE distribution plots in Figure 1 indicate a similar pattern. For each of the three estimators, increases in the sample size from 300 to 600 generally shift the ASE distribution towards zero. When the three estimators are compared with each other for the same sample size, the ASE distribution of GIPT are much closer to zero than that of the other two estimators.

We also plot the GIPT estimated ATEs based on our simulations, in Figures 2b and 3b (separately for $N = 300$ and $N = 600$, respectively). The corresponding true ATEs for these samples are plotted in Figures 2a and 3a, respectively. In comparing the GIPT ATEs against the corresponding true ATEs, it is apparent that as the sample size increases from $N = 300$ to $N = 600$, the GIPT ATEs more closely approximate the true ATEs. This implies that GIPT is a consistent estimator of the true ATEs as the sample size increases.

[xiv]The bandwidth used for GIPT is 0.75 with N = 600 and 0.85 with N = 300. See section 4 for more details for bandwidth selection algorithm.

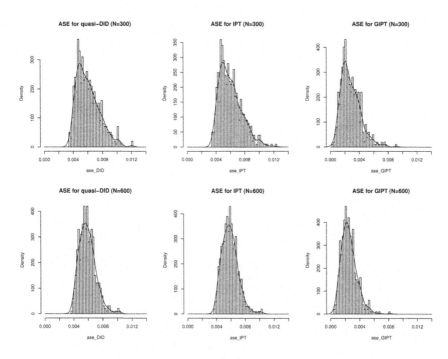

Figure 1. Simulation results on Average Squared Errors (ASE) distributions from quasi-DID, IPT and GIPT.[xv, xvi]

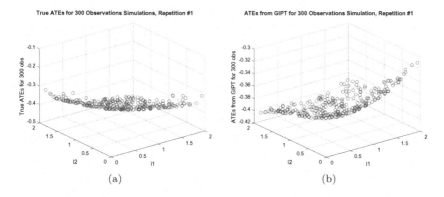

(a)   (b)

Figure 2. Simulations scatterplots — the true ATEs and the GIPT estimates.

[xv]In the ASE for GIPT (N = 300) plot, an outlier value (maximum) is dropped for the convenience of plotting.

[xvi]Observe that 1. Increases in sample sizes reduce ASE for all estimators; 2. Across both sample sizes, ASE distributions from GIPT are closer to left and narrower, compared to that of quasi-DID and IPT, suggesting that the GIPT estimator outperforms both quasi-DID and IPT.

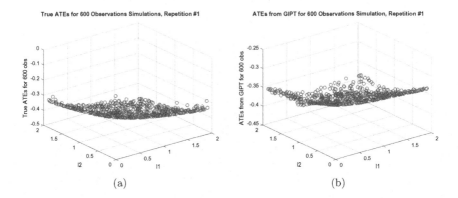

Figure 3. Simulations scatterplots — the true ATEs and the GIPT estimates.

5. Application: Commercial Real Estate Prices in Vancouver, BC Metro Area

Similar to the purpose of the IPT application in Graham *et al.* (2012), our application is intended to illustrate the GIPT method as applied to a particular data set and problem. The metro-Vancouver area was hit with a series of major storms in November 2006, which led to severe mudslides that caused contaminated storm runoff to enter the water supply (Evans, 2007). Some parts of the metro area were required to boil water for an extended period of 10 days longer (i.e., 12 days total) than the rest of the metro area (CBC News, 2006). This impacted restaurants, coffee shops, and other water-dependent businesses (Dowd, 2006). The affected area included the City of Vancouver, while the adjacent City of Richmond (and many other parts of the metro area) had the advisory lifted on the second day. This may have been a type of information shock, which could influence the probabilities of similar advisories from future storms. We examine how sale prices for properties that sold within several months after this advisory in a section of Vancouver (the treated sample) were affected differently from other properties sold in the same section of Vancouver several months before the advisory and properties that sold in nearby parts of Richmond before and after the advisory (the control sample). Thus, our identification strategy relies upon an unexpected event (the extended water boil advisory) that affects some geographic areas but not others. We have a missing data issue with this data set, because we know what properties in the control group are sold for, but we do not know what these properties would have sold for if they had been in the treatment group. Thus, a propensity score type of approach would be desirable. Meanwhile, there are clear differences in the geographic locations of properties in our sample. It is of interest to determine empirically how the effects of such a shock might be absorbed differently into property values across locations. Therefore, we consider three different approaches in this application, a variant of quasi-DID, IPT, and GIPT. Recall that we address the first of these approaches as quasi-DID approach because we do not have panel data in this particular real estate application (in other words, we do not have repeat sales observations over time).

There is a literature that examines the effects of a storm on property values, including Bin and Landry (2013), Atreya and Czajkowski (2016), and others. None of these literatures, however, consider the missing data problem in the same context or with the same approach as we are addressing it here. Also, most of the other studies in the literature focus on residential property values, while our application examines the commercial property value impacts (which is important in our context because many businesses in our sample are water dependent). Finally, we study the impacts of the storm using a quasi-experiment of the effects of a water boil advisory that was imposed on some areas of the metro area, including the City of Vancouver, for much longer than others. Therefore, we can examine the differential impacts of the water boil advisory on treated versus control areas, shortly before versus shortly after the advisory.

In the real estate finance and investments literature (e.g., Ling and Archer, 2017), a commercial property's value or sale price can be approximated by the ratio of its net operating income (NOI) to the capitalization rate (i.e., cap rate). In some cities, such as New Orleans, a major storm (i.e., a hurricane) such as Katrina led to property destruction as well as major disruption in the abilities of businesses to operate for an extended period of time. In theory, if there is an event that alters an investor's estimate of basic long-term risk, then such an event is often accompanied by an increase in the cap rate. In New Orleans, this increased risk likely led to a higher cap rate, due to the possibilities of repeat of storm events in the future, which lowered the value of commercial properties. The storm also lowered the properties' NOI due to lost revenues, etc. People may have revised their estimate of New Orleans' vulnerability because of rising sea levels, eroded barrier marshes, etc. Although the impacts of the storm in Vancouver may have been somewhat different, this 12-day extended water boil advisory in the City of Vancouver caused major disruption of some business operations, especially for those that were water-oriented such as supermarkets, restaurants, day care facilities, etc. (Dowd, 2006; CBC News, 2006). Such a disruption is expected to lead to greater long-term risk of a repeat event for all properties; and/or lost revenues or additional insurance costs, for instance, for certain businesses that are water dependent. These financial losses are expected to impact their NOI, which translates into an effect on property values and in turn, the sale prices of many properties. But other commercial property sale prices may not be affected, perhaps because they may not be as water dependent.

When we are estimating the ATE of the extended water boil advisory on the price per square foot of living area for commercial properties, the lot size (building area plus land area) of the property is expected to be negatively correlated with the NOI (and in turn, the total sale price). This is due to the fact that a larger lot size requires higher expenses for lawn maintenance and snow removal, for instance. But the effect of lot size on the price per square foot of living area may be either positive or negative. A larger lot size may or may not lead to economies of scale that are inherent in the maintenance of a commercial building. Greater economies of scale are expected to lead to higher NOI and therefore a higher price per square foot of the overall property. There may also be particularly strong price effects for older properties, or properties that have not been renovated recently. These older properties may be expected to rent for less, need more repairs, and require more to upkeep due to unanticipated issues resulting from the age of the property. This can also be expected to factor into the NOI for a property. In other words, an older property, or one that has not been renovated recently, should have a lower NOI than a similar, nearby property that has been renovated recently. Therefore, it is important to use the lot size and the effective age as proxies for NOI, especially since we do not have direct estimates of NOI in our dataset. The effective age is the number of years between the year of most recent sale and the last major renovation of a property. Properties that were renovated in the year in which they were most recently sold have an effective age of 0. Similarly, properties that have never been renovated have an effective age equal to the actual age of the property. In our model specifications, we use as the control variable the interaction term of lot size (in thousand square feet) and the effective age of the property (in years). For reasons described above, these two variables are the two best proxies for NOI that we have available to us. Also, in the IPT and GIPT specifications, when we try to include two separate quasi-DID terms for these two variables, using the first two moments of each, the model is unable to solve. We are interested in the ATE from the extended water boil advisory, and we desire to control for the lot size and effective age as proxies for NOI but are not directly interested in their marginal effects. Therefore, using the interaction term enables us to control for both of these factors as proxies for NOI. Finally, Graham *et al.* (2011) and Anderson (1982) suggest interaction terms be included in these types of propensity score models. So, for all these reasons, we use the first two moments of the interaction term in the IPT and GIPT specifications. Obviously, for consistency across specifications, we use the interaction term in the quasi-DID model as well. The impact of a change in cap rate associated with long-term risk due to the storm is reflected in the treatment effect dummy. Property owners are expected to adjust their forecasts of long-term risk after the storm, and this is reflected by the treatment effect estimate. One would expect property owners in different locations to have different forecasts of long-term risk, and therefore, we might expect heterogeneity in the ATE estimates.

Also, in these types of treatment effect studies, it is recommended to exclude observations in a buffer zone of properties that are excluded from the analysis (see, for instance, Angrist and Pischke (2009)). Therefore, we restrict our attention to a section of the metro area where some observations are in the City of Vancouver (which was subject to the water boil advisory for 12 days after the storm) and others in nearby parts of the neighboring City of Richmond (which had the water boil advisory lifted after one day). We avoid including properties outside of this buffer zone, e.g., in the central business district of Vancouver, where there are potentially many other confounding factors. Our focus on properties in the City of Richmond near the Vancouver border allows for a buffer zone consisting of properties in the western part of Richmond. We focus on a period of several months before, and several months after the 12-day water-boil advisory which occurred in the City of Vancouver in November 2006. The choice of this time period allows for a buffer in the temporal dimension. We end our sample in August 2007 because we want to avoid the effects of the recession that started in late-2007, and we begin in January 2006 because we want to avoid other events that might have impacted property values before 2006 (thus, creating a temporal buffer beyond several months around the date of the storm).

In our data set, there are 96 commercial sales observations in the selected neighborhoods between January 2006 and August 2007 for which there are also data on the sale price, square footage, lot size and the effective age. Figure 4 shows the locations of our sample of 96 commercial properties that sold (as arms-length transactions) in parts of the City of Vancouver and City of Richmond between January 2006 and August 2007. These data are from the BC Assessment database, which were purchased from Landcor Data Corporation.

Descriptive statistics are presented in Table 2. The average commercial property sold for approximately C\$ 215 per square foot, had a lot size of about 35,000 square feet, had an effective age of 38.76 years (i.e., on an average there were 38.76 years since the last major renovation), and 26 percent of the observations were in the

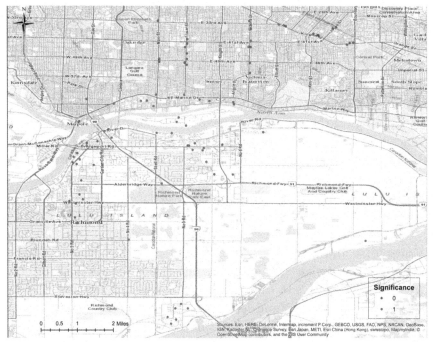

(Colour version available online)

Figure 4. Properties with statistically significant ATE from GIPT estimations.[xvii]

Table 2. Descriptive statistics, Vancouver application.

	(1) mean	sd	min	max	count
Sale price per square ft	215.9012	169.2998	20.60159	1128.099	96
Effective Age	38.76042	12.05142	9	70	96
Lotsize(thous sqft)	34.92404	49.13306	2.76459	246.88	96
Treatment Dummy	.2604167	.4411657	0	1	96

treatment group (i.e., in the City of Vancouver — opposed to the City of Richmond — and sold after the extended water boil advisory was imposed on the City of Vancouver).

[xvii]Significance = 1 if P < 0.05, Significance = 0 o.w.

We first estimate the following variant of a quasi-DID model: $Y_i = \beta_0 + \beta_1 X_i + \beta_2 D_i + e$, where Y_i is price per square foot for property i, X_i is the product of the lot size and the effective age. We assume that e is an i.i.d. error term with mean 0 and constant variance, and $E(e_i e_j) = 0$ for $i \neq j$. $D_i = 1$ for those properties in our data set that were sold between November 2006 and August 2007 (i.e., after the extended water boil advisory), inside the City of Vancouver; and $D_i = 0$ for properties that were sold in the City of Richmond before and after the advisory, and those properties that were sold in the City of Vancouver before the advisory. The regression coefficient β_2 is the "treatment effect" of locating in the City of Vancouver after the storm.

The second model we estimate is IPT. We consider the first two moments so that $t(x) = [1, X, X^2]$, and X is the product of the lot size and effective age, and Y is the sale price per square foot. We re-weight the X's so that the sample mean and variance of X in the treated sub-sample (and separately, in the untreated sub-sample) equals the entire sample mean and variance of X. We utilize the same data set as we used for the quasi-DID estimation. We calculate the ATE using IPT.

Finally, we estimate the GIPT model, with Gaussian kernel weights given as

$$\hat{w}_i(l) = [\exp(-0.5 * (d_i(l)/b)^2)]^{1/2}, \tag{16}$$

where $d_i(l)$ is the Euclidean distance between property i and location l, and b is a bandwidth parameter. We explain the bandwidth determination in more detail below. In the GIPT model, we consider the first two moments and use $\tau(\hat{w}_i(l)X) = [1, \hat{w}_i(l)X_i^1, (\hat{w})_i(l)X_i^1)^2]$ for each target point, l. In this context, we are re-weighting by including distance weights in the propensity score weighted averages of X_i^1 so that the re-weighted mean and variance of X_i^1 for the treated sample equals the re-weighted mean and variance for the entire sample.

We present the quasi-DID and IPT results in Tables 3 and 4. First, with quasi-DID the treatment dummy, D_i, has a coefficient estimate of $\beta_2 = -49.97$, implying that the typical commercial property in

Table 3. Quasi-DID model results, Vancouver application.

	(1) sale price per square ft
ATE	−49.97
	(−1.24)
[effective age]x[lotsize(thous square feet)]	−0.0467*
	(−1.69)
([effective age]x[lotsize(thous square feet)])^2	0.00000289
	(1.04)
Constant	270.3***
	(8.94)
R-sq	0.069
N	96

Note: t statistics in parentheses
*p < 0.10,** p < 0.05,*** p < 0.01

Table 4. Inverse Probability Tilting estimation results, Vancouver application.

	(1)
delta1 [effective age]x[lotsize(thous square feet)]	−0.000775**
	(−1.98)
([effective age]x[lotsize(thous square feet)])^2	9.42e-08**
	(2.21)
Constant	−0.641**
	(−1.97)
delta0	
[effective age]x[lotsize(thous square feet)]	−0.00198
	(−1.35)
([effective age]x[lotsize(thous square feet)])^2	0.000000229
	(1.43)
Constant	−0.0760
	(−0.13)
ate gamma	−50.37**
	(−2.13)
Observations	96

Note: t statistics in parentheses
*p < 0.10,** p < 0.05,*** p < 0.01

the treated sample sold for approximately C\$ 49.97 less per square foot than the typical property in the control sample. However, β_2, the ATE estimate, is highly insignificant (t-statistic= -1.24). With IPT, the ATE is C\$ -50.37 (with t-statistic $= -2.13$), indicated by the coefficient "ate gamma" in Table 4.

With the GIPT approach, first, we must determine the appropriate bandwidth. We first contemplate a "Rule of Thumb" bandwidth, as in Silverman (1986). However, this criterion requires normality of the distances data in order for it to be applicable. An informal examination of the locations of the properties in Figure 2 indicate that it is inconclusive as to whether the distances have a normal distribution. Therefore, without evidence of normality of these distances data, we perform an informal grid search to estimate bandwidths in the range of 0.03 and somewhat higher and lower, moving up and down in units of 0.01. Bandwidths smaller than 0.03 cause difficulties in the GIPT estimations that preclude it from solving for many of the target points. Therefore, we choose the smallest of these bandwidths, h = 0.03, for which the GIPT estimations solve with ease; we explain this choice as follows. This bandwidth choice allows for the maximum amount of variation in the parameter estimates. In fact, as we experimented with increasing the bandwidth above h = 0.03, the variation in the ATE estimates from GIPT across observations decreases dramatically, in general, approaching the ATE estimate from IPT for the higher bandwidths. This result is expected, as with a higher bandwidth there are more observations receiving positive weight than with a lower bandwidth, so the GIPT ATE estimates with the higher bandwidths closely approximate the IPT ATE estimate.[xviii]

In terms of the GIPT assumptions that we describe in Section 3.2 above, we propose that our data set and application satisfy these

---

[xviii]For illustrative purposes in this empirical application, we select the smallest bandwidth for which the GIPT model is still able to solve. However, a more formal approach would be to follow an algorithm for the bandwidth selection, such as bootstrap bandwidth selection or Mean Average Squared Error (MASE) methods.

assumptions.[xix] We rely on an identification strategy that considers properties that were sold inside and outside of the water boil advisory zone, in a reasonably short time frame before versus after the extended water boil advisory date. For un-confoundedness, we assume that nearby properties have come from a randomized experiment, as the treatment does not depend on the price of the property. Specifically, properties that are close to each other do not necessarily have the same treatment status, as can be seen in Figure 4. Properties on the south side of the Frasier River are in Richmond (untreated), while those just to the north are in Vancouver (some of which are treated). Also, any given pair of properties in Vancouver that are close to each other are not necessarily both treated, because some of the nearby properties in the City of Vancouver were sold shortly before the advisory and were therefore untreated. For our control variables, the interaction of effective age and lot size, it is reasonable to assume that nearby observations have no impact on the value of these two variables at a particular target point. We have data missing at random, as we know what properties sold for at their location but not what they would have sold for at other locations. We also assume, for the purpose of demonstrating how to implement the GIPT estimator, that we have strong overlap. We also postulate that Assumptions 5, 6, 8 and 9 hold, and since we use the Gaussian kernel, the symmetric kernel distribution (Assumption 7) is satisfied. We next estimate the ATEs for all target points, l, using the GIPT estimator that we have developed in this paper. Figure 5 shows the ranges of ATEs of the metro-Vancouver area with the locations of the sample of commercial properties that were sold in the period of our sample. This range is C\$ 8.08 to approximately C\$ −61.90, but the former ATE has a relatively large standard error and is statistically insignificant. Most of the larger ATEs are statistically significant (P-value ≤ 0.05). Figure 4 demonstrates the locations of properties

---

[xix]While in this specific application it may not be straightforward to demonstrate that some of the GIPT assumptions are satisfied, our purposes are primarily illustrative of an application of the GIPT technique, as was the case for the IPT application in Graham *et al.* (2012).

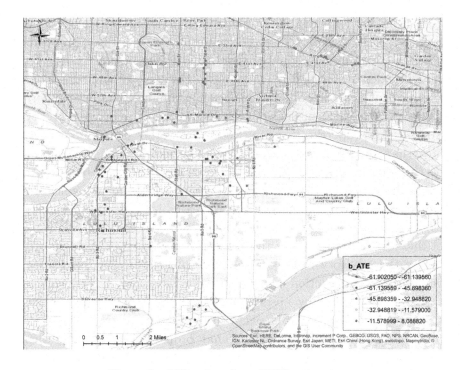

Figure 5. ATE values from GIPT estimations.

Table 5. Geographic Inverse Probability Tilting results, bandwidth = 0.03.

| | (1) | | | | |
	mean	sd	min	max	count
ATE	−38.38539	18.17553	−61.90205	8.08882	96
Standard Errors of ATE	22.54444	1.739582	18.68966	26.44306	96

with ATE that have P-value ≤ 0.05. We take the mean of all the 96 ATEs (which we denote as the "AATE"), in Table 5. The AATE equals approximately C\$ −38.38, while the mean of the standard errors is C\$ 22.54. In general, the properties with the most negative and significant ATEs are located in the central and south areas of Richmond and central Vancouver, while those with statistically insignificant ATEs are in east Vancouver.

While the ATEs from quasi-DID and IPT are statistically insignificant, with GIPT we find that most of the 96 observations have negative ATEs, but 85 out of the 96 observations have statistically significant ATEs (with P-value ≤ 0.05). Thus, using GIPT enables us to unmask which specific locations would be significantly impacted by the storm related water boil advisory and which would not. Interestingly, many of the properties with significantly negative ATEs are concentrated in five distinct neighborhoods of Richmond (which did not experience the 12-day extended water boil advisory).

Within each of these five neighborhoods of Richmond, at least one (and sometimes several) of the properties in our sample are in a water-intensive industry. For instance, in a neighborhood around Horseshoe Way in the southern part of Richmond, there is a company that manufactures liquid cleaning products and health/beauty products. Nearby there is a recycling center and a mill works production company. While we expect the ATE of the liquid product manufacturing company's property to be affected by an extended water boil advisory, the ATE of the other two companies' properties in the same neighborhood are likely to be impacted by their proximity to the liquid product manufacturing company's property. About 0.5 km south of this neighborhood is another cluster of properties with large negative, and statistically significant ATEs, including one where there is a company that processes fish products for use as fresh and preserved bait; nearby there is a produce market that undoubtedly relies on water to clean its produce; and an event planning company. In this situation, the fish products company and produce market may have a strong impact on the ATE of the event planning company due to its close proximity. Approximately 3 km north of this neighborhood (10011 Blundell Road in Richmond), there is a daycare facility with a statistically significant ATE, which was formerly a convenience market and the daycare moved into the space subsequent to the storm. The property may have had a negative, statistically significant ATE because the property relies daily on clean water for the children and staff to wash hands, dishes, etc., and if it had been in the "treated" group, this would have been expected to lower the value of the property.

On the other hand, there is a daycare facility in Vancouver (3165 Kingsway, Vancouver) with a statistically insignificant ATE, which may be somewhat surprising, although perhaps this facility relies more on hand sanitizer and other less water-intensive ways to keep its students clean. A more plausible explanation is the fact that at this address there is also a lighting store that is likely not water intensive, so the presence of this store may offset the effect on the property's overall ATE from the daycare. Approximately 2 km to the northwest of the daycare in Richmond is a restaurant/bakery, and an office building. In this case, the restaurant/bakery clearly would be impacted by an extended water boil advisory, while the ATE of the office building may be impacted due to the proximity to the restaurant/bakery. Finally, approximately 0.5 km north of the restaurant/bakery there is a cluster of four other properties that have statistically significant (negative) ATEs. These include a large shopping plaza with restaurants, a coffee shop, doctor's offices, a drug store, and other offices. Very close to this shopping plaza is an automobile repair garage, a dermatology office, and an office building. It is likely that the water dependency of many of the businesses in the shopping plaza is one explanation for a significantly negative ATE for that property, while the significantly negative ATEs for the other nearby properties may be at least in part determined by proximity to the shopping plaza.[xx]

[xx]One might conjecture that some of the differences in ATEs in the treated area (in the City of Vancouver after the boil water advisory) versus the control area (in the City of Richmond before the boil water advisory, and both Richmond and Vancouver before the advisory) may be due to differences in property tax rates in the two cities in these two years. We informally examined the property tax rates in these two cities in 2006 and 2007 and found that the 2006 base rate in Richmond for class 6 properties (commercial) was C\$ 22.38361 per thousand dollars of assessed values. There were some additional add-ons for sewer debt, which ranged between C\$ 0.23300 and C\$ 0.28300 in 2006, implying a total tax rate of approximately C\$ 22.64 per thousand dollars of assessed value. There is an additional parking tax for Richmond properties with parking, at a rate of C\$ 0.78 per square meter of parking spaces. The 2007 tax rate in Vancouver for Class 6 properties (commercial) was C\$ 24.87171. Therefore, there is a difference of approximately C\$ 2.23 per thousand dollars of assessed value. Assuming this differential is expected to persist indefinitely into the future (i.e., an infinite time

Finally, one might argue that a fuzzy regression discontinuity framework could be appropriate for this particular problem, as in Angrist and Pischke (2009). But this is not the case in our specific application. The propensity score,

$$p(x) = Pr(D_i = 1|X_i = x) = E[D_i|X_i = x],$$

does not necessarily jump at any particular value of x. There are both large and small lot sizes in our sample of properties in Richmond and Vancouver, and also there are both old and new properties in both cities as well (as required by the strong overlap assumption of IPT). Therefore, our X, the interaction term of lot size and effective age, does not have a natural jump point in the probability of treatment at any specific value of x. In future work, it may be of interest to explore how to address potential fuzzy regression discontinuity in the context of IPT and GIPT, for specific applications where at particular values of x there is a natural jump point in the propensity score.

6. Conclusion/Discussion

We develop a GIPT estimator that allows for ATE heterogeneity across target points, and we prove consistency and asymptotic normality, as well as demonstrate the desirable small sample performance with Monte Carlo simulations. We demonstrate the use of this GIPT estimator in an application of how a major storm that leads to an extended water boil advisory in some areas impacts property prices differently in a major Canadian metro area. The GIPT estimator can be a useful technique to generate ATEs for each target location, and re-weight with propensity scores when there is

---

horizon), and a discount rate of 5 percent, this implies a difference of C\$ 2.23*(1+ 0.05)/0.05 over the life of the property, or a total expected property tax differential of C\$ 46.83 per thousand dollars of assessed value. We assume the sale price of a property is highly correlated with its assessed value. Then, if the ATE is C\$ −45 for a property that sold in Richmond before the water boil advisory in 2006, for instance, then C\$ 2.10 of this C\$ −45, or less than 5 percent of the ATE, can be attributed to expected differences in property taxes in the two jurisdictions in the two years.

missing data. As we show in our application and in our simulation
study, there are several benefits, as well as some potential limitations,
of using the GIPT approach in these types of applications. One
advantage of GIPT is that we are able to generate heterogeneous
ATE estimates for each target point. These GIPT ATE estimates
approximate a smooth ATE surface in large samples. We can also test
for the statistical significance of each of the ATEs. The average of
the ATE's, or the AATE, is one way of summarizing this information
over all target points, if so desired. In our specific application,
one may be particularly interested in the ATE estimates that are
statistically significant, in order to determine where remediation
should be undertaken to try to prevent similar damage to the water
supply in the future. There are many other potential missing data
problem applications of the GIPT estimator where it would be
desirable to generate heterogeneous ATEs.

Another advantage of using GIPT in applied settings, as demonstrated by our Monte Carlo simulations, is that the bias and
average squared errors of the GIPT estimator appears to be lower
than the bias for the quasi-DID and IPT estimators. Even when
there is heterogeneity in the ATE estimates, GIPT is a more
computationally intensive procedure and in some cases this may
diminish its feasibility, especially in very large samples. However,
there are approaches to address this issue in the nonparametric
estimation literature, including limiting the number of target points
to obtain a representative sample of ATE estimates. We have also
addressed the important issue of bandwidth selection, which is crucial
for each specific context of a given empirical application and Monte
Carlo simulations when using the GIPT framework. As we have
demonstrated in our application, the GIPT approach can extract
important information about which individual observations have
statistically significant ATEs, and it allows for heterogeneity in the
magnitudes of the ATEs across space.

Clearly, there are advantages to both the IPT and GIPT
approaches to addressing the missing data problem in generating
heterogeneous estimates of ATE's. There is also evidence that
GIPT is superior to quasi-DID. GIPT performs much better than

quasi-DID in our Monte Carlo simulations, and this is to be expected, in part because quasi-DID ignores the missing data problem.

In future work, it would be of interest to consider modifying the GIPT framework to contexts where there is a balanced panel dataset (e.g., space–time), to address a broader array of applied missing data problems. Such an extension could also contribute to the literature on ATE heterogeneity by allowing for the possibility that the ATE could vary over target points and also over a long period of time. This may first necessitate extension of the regular IPT framework to a balanced panel data setting, as well as generating Monte Carlo evidence to validate the performance of the approach.

Appendix

Proof of Consistency and Asymptotic Normality of the GIPT Average Treatment Effects Estimator

First, given Assumption 8, it follows that the bandwidth b is a "nuisance parameter".[xxi] Next, given that the elements of the vector l are i.i.d., then $\hat{w}_i(l)$ is i.i.d., since a function of an i.i.d. series is i.i.d. Given that w depends only on l and b, we know that w is i.i.d. Note that since our random sampling assumption is that both X and D are i.i.d., we know that $w(l) \cdot X$ and $w(l) \cdot D$ are both i.i.d., since the product of two i.i.d. series is i.i.d. Thus, following the reasoning of Graham *et al.* (2012), who appeal to Wooldridge (2007), that $\hat{\gamma}_{GIPT}(l)$ is a consistent estimator of $\gamma_0(l)$ at any target point l.

Given the above i.i.d. discussion, the asymptotic normality of $\hat{\gamma}_{GIPT}(l)$ follows from Theorem 6.1 of Newey and McFadden (1994), as described by Graham *et al.* (2012).[xxii] Let $\beta = (\gamma(l)', \delta')'$, the

---

[xxi]We use a first stage estimator for the bandwidth that converges at the "correct rate" (to be a nuisance parameter) under the regularization assumption imposed in Assumption 8.

[xxii]Double robustness of GIPT follows from the proof of consistency in this appendix; however, it is not straightforward to prove local efficiency of GIPT.

$K + 1 + M \times 1$ moment vector and derivative matrix equal

$$m_i(\beta) = \begin{bmatrix} \frac{\hat{w}_i D_i}{G_i(\delta)} \Phi_i(\gamma(l)) \\ \left(\frac{\hat{w}_i D_i}{G_i(\delta)} - 1 \right) \tau_i \end{bmatrix},$$

where $\hat{w}_i = \hat{w}_i(l)$ and

$$M_i(\beta) = \begin{bmatrix} \frac{\hat{w}_i D_i}{G_i(\delta)} \frac{\partial \Phi_i(\gamma(l))}{\partial \gamma(l)}, & \frac{\hat{w}_i D_i}{G_i(\delta)} \frac{G_{1i}\delta}{G_i(\delta)} \Phi_i(\gamma(l))\tau_i' \\ 0, & \frac{\hat{w}_i D_i}{G_i(\delta)} \frac{G_{1i}\delta}{G_i(\delta)} \Phi_i(\gamma(l))\tau_i\tau_i' \end{bmatrix}.$$

The subscript "0" denotes the true value. First consider the case where Assumptions 1–8 hold. Let $M = \mathbf{E}[M_i(\beta_0)]$ and $\Omega = \mathrm{E}[m_i(\beta_0)m_i(\beta_0)']$, then $\sqrt{N}\left[\hat{\gamma}(l)_{GIPT}(l) - \gamma_0(l)\right] \xrightarrow{D} N(0, \Delta_o)$ for $\Delta_0 = \left\{ (M'\Omega^{-1}M)^{-1} \right\}_{1:k,1:k}$, where $A_{1:k,1:k}$ is the upper left $K \times K$ block of A.

The covariance of $m_i = m_i(\beta_0)$ equals

$$\Omega = \begin{bmatrix} \mathbb{E}\left[\hat{w}_i^2 \frac{\Phi\Phi'}{G_i} \right], & E_0 \\ E_0' & F_0 \end{bmatrix}$$

with

$$E_0 = \mathbb{E}\left[\frac{\hat{w}_i^2 \Phi \left[1 - \frac{G}{\hat{w}_i} \right] \tau'}{G} \right], \quad F_0 = \mathbb{E}\left[\frac{\hat{w}_i^2 \left[1 - \frac{2G}{\hat{w}_i} \right] \tau\tau'}{G} \right].$$

The population mean of $M_i = M_i(\beta_0)$ is

$$M = \begin{bmatrix} \mathbb{E}\left[\hat{w}_i \frac{\partial \Phi_i(\gamma(l))}{\partial \gamma(l)} \right], & -\mathbb{E}\left[\hat{w}_i \frac{G_{1i}(\delta)}{G_i(\delta)} \Phi_{\tau'} \right] \\ 0, & -\mathbb{E}\left[\hat{w}_i \frac{G_{1i}(\delta)}{G_i(\delta)} \tau\tau' \right] \end{bmatrix}.$$

So the limiting sampling variance for $\sqrt{N}[\hat{\gamma}_{GIPT}(l) - \gamma_0(l)]$ equals $M^{-1}\Omega M^{-1'}$.

When Assumption 5 does not hold, but Assumption 1–4 and 6–9 hold, let $\beta_\star = (\gamma_0(l)', \delta_\star')'$, where $\delta_\star'$ is the pseudo-true propensity score parameter.

Let $G_\star = G(\tau(w(l)x^1)'\delta_\star)$, etc. Now,

$$\Omega_\star = \left[\begin{array}{cc} \mathbb{E}\left(\frac{\hat{w}_i^2 p_0(x)\Phi\Phi'}{G_\star^2} \right), & \mathbb{E}\left[\left(\frac{\hat{w}_i^2 p_0(x)\Phi}{G_\star^2} - \frac{\hat{w}_i p_0(x)\Phi}{G_\star} \right)\tau' \right] \\ \mathbb{E}\left[\left(\frac{\hat{w}_i^2 p_0(x)\Phi'}{G_\star^2} - \frac{\hat{w}_i p_0(x)\Phi}{G_\star} \right)\tau \right], & \mathbb{E}\left[\left(\frac{\hat{w}_i^2 p_0(x)}{G_\star^2} - \frac{2\hat{w}_i p_0(x)\Phi}{G_\star} + 1 \right)\tau\tau' \right] \end{array} \right]$$

and

$$M_\star = \left[\begin{array}{cc} \mathbb{E}\left[\frac{\hat{w}_i p_0(x)}{G_\star} \frac{\partial \Phi_i(\gamma(l))}{\partial \gamma(l)} \right], & -\mathbb{E}\left[\frac{\hat{w}_i p_0(x)}{G_\star} \frac{G_{1\star}}{G_\star} \Phi'_\tau \right] \\ 0, & -\mathbb{E}\left[\frac{\hat{w}_i p_0(x)}{G_\star} \frac{G_{1\star}}{G_\star} \tau\tau' \right] \end{array} \right],$$

so that $\Delta_0 = \left\{ (M'_\star \Omega_\star^{-1} M_\star)^{-1} \right\}_{1:k,1:k}$.

Consistent variance-covariance matrix estimation. If Assumptions 1–4 and 6–8 hold, as well as either 5 or 9 hold (or both 5 and 9 hold), as well as additional regularity conditions, then the asymptotic variance at each target point l of $\hat{\gamma}(l)_{GIPT}$ may be consistently estimated by $\hat{\Delta} = \left\{ \left(\hat{M}' \hat{\Omega}^{-1} \hat{M} \right)^{-1} \right\}_{1:k,1:k}$ with $\hat{M} = \sum_{i=1}^N M_i(\hat{\beta})/N, \hat{\Omega} = \sum_{i=1}^N m_i(\hat{\beta})m_i(\hat{\beta})'/N$.

References

Abrevaya, J., and Donald, S.G. (2017). A GMM Approach for Dealing With Missing Data on Regressors and Instruments. *Review of Economics and Statistics, 99*(2), 657–662.

Abrevaya, J., Hsu, Y.C., and Lieli, R.P. (2015). Estimating Conditional Average Treatment Effects. *Journal of Business & Economic Statistics, 33*(2), 485–505.

Allcott, H. (2015). Site Selection Bias in Program Evaluation. *The Quarterly Journal of Economics, 130*(1), 1117–1165.

Anderson, J.A. (1982). 7 Logistic Discrimination. Handbook of Statistics, *2*, 169–191.

Angrist, J.D., and J.S. Pischke. (2009). *Mostly Harmless Econometrics: An Empiricist's Companion.* Princeton University Press.

Atreya, A., and Czajkowski, J. (2016). Graduated Flood Risks and Property Prices in Galveston County. *Real Estate Economics, 47*(1), 807–844.

Bin, O., and Landry, C.E. (2013). Changes in Implicit Flood Risk Premiums: Empirical Evidence from the Housing Market. *Journal of Environmental Economics and Management, 65*(1), 361–376.

Brunsdon, C., Fotheringham, A.S., and Charlton, M.E. (1996). Geographically Weighted Regression: A Method for Exploring Spatial Nonstationarity. *Geographical Analysis*, *28*(2), 281–298.

CBC News. (2006, November 27). *Greater Vancouver Boil-Water Advisory Lifted.* http://www.cbc.ca/news/canada/british-columbia/greater-vancouver-boil-water-advisory-lifted-1.584398 (accessed on 7/22/2017).

Dowd, A. (2006, November 18). *Water Warning Leaves Vancouver High and Dry.* The Star Online. http://www.thestar.com.my/news/world/2006/11/18/water-warning-leaves-vancouver-high-and-dry1/ (Accessed on 7/24/2017).

Evans, G.M. (2007). Taking Our Water Supply for Granted. *BC Medical Journal*, *49*(2), 62.

Frolich, M., Huber, M., and Wiesenfarth, M. (2017). The Finite Sample Performance of Semi-and Non-Parametric Estimators for Treatment Effects and Policy Evaluation. *Computational Statistics & Data Analysis*, *115*, 91–102.

Graham, B.S., Campos de Xavier Pinto, C., and Egel, D. (2011). Inverse Probability Tilting Estimation of Average Treatment Effects in Stata. *The Stata Journal*, *1*(1), 1–16.

Graham, B.S., Campos de Xavier Pinto, C., and Egel, D. (2012). Inverse Probability Tilting for Moment Condition Models with Missing Data. *Review of Economic Studies*, *79*, 1053–1079.

Hainmueller, J. (2012). Entropy Balancing for Causal Effects: A Multivariate Reweighting Method to Produce Balanced Samples in Observational Studies. *Political Analysis*, *20*(1), 25–46.

Hotz, V.J., Imbens, G.W., and Mortimer, J.H. (2005). Predicting the Efficacy of Future Training Programs Using Past Experiences at Other Locations. *Journal of Econometrics*, *125*(1–2), 241–270.

Hsu, Y.C., Huber, M., and Lai, T.C. (2018). Nonparametric Estimation of Natural Direct and Indirect Effects Based on Inverse Probability Weighting. *Journal of Econometric Methods*, *8*(1), 1–20.

Imai, K., and Ratkovic, M. (2014). Covariate Balancing Propensity Score. *Journal of the Royal Statistical Society: Series B (Statistical Methodology)*, *76*(1), 243–263.

Imbens, G.W. (2004). Nonparametric Estimation of Average Treatment Effects Under Exogeneity: A Review. *Review of Economics and Statistics*, *86*, 4–29.

Lee, S., Okui, R., and Whang, Y.-J. (2017). Doubly Robust Uniform Confidence Band for the Conditional Average Treatment Effect Function. *Journal of Applied Economics*, *32*, 1207–1225.

Ling, D., and Archer, W. (2017). *Real Estate Principles: A Value Approach.* 5th En. McGraw-Hill Higher Education.

McMillen, D.P., and McDonald, J.F. (2004). Locally Weighted Maximum Likelihood Estimation: Monte Carlo Evidence and an Application. In Anselin, L., Florax, R.J.G.M., and Rey, S.R. (Eds.), *Advances in Spatial Econometrics.* New York: Springer, 225–239.

McMillen, D.P., and Redfearn, C. (2010). Estimation and Hypothesis Testing for Nonparametric Hedonic House Price Functions. *Journal of Regional Science, 50,* 712–733.

Newey, W.K., and McFadden, D. (1994). Large Sample Estimation and Hypothesis Testing. *Handbook of Econometrics, 4,* 2111–2245.

Rosenbaum, P.R., and Rubin, D.B. (1983). The Central Role of the Propensity Score in Observational Studies for Causal Effects. *Biometrika, 70*(1), 41–55.

Silverman, B.W. (1986). *Density Estimation for Statistics and Data Analysis.* Monographs on Statistics and Applied Probability, London: Chapman and Hall.

Wager, S., and Athey, S. (2018). Estimation and Inference of Heterogeneous Treatment Effects Using Random Forests. *Journal of the American Statistical Association, 113*(523), 1228–1242.

Wooldridge, J.M. (2007). Inverse Probability Weighted Estimation for General Missing Data Problems. *Journal of Econometrics, 141*(2), 1281–1301.

https://doi.org/10.1142/9789811271663_0004

Chapter 4

Benefit Spillovers and a Solution with Two-Part Tariffs for Local Public Services

Yukihiro Kidokoro

National Graduate Institute for Policy Studies, Japan

Anming Zhang

Sauder School of Business, University of British Columbia, Canada

This paper examines how to correct the spillover problem for local public services, such as local public transport, by applying a two-part tariff. When the spillover problem exists, a local government charges higher prices for its public services for nonresidents, because it cannot directly capture the consumer surpluses of nonresidents. When a local government can recoup the consumer surpluses by applying a two-part tariff, the decentralized solution coincides with the centralized solution. We then focus on why uniform pricing of local public services is common in reality. Apart from the administration costs, the uniform pricing for residents and nonresidents can be justified when a local government obtains an additional gain from the demand by nonresidents, such as an increase in profits of local shops.

1. Introduction

Whether a nation adopts a centralized or decentralized fiscal system is an important characteristic of the nation, but this issue raises a controversial argument. A major advantage of fiscal decentralization is that a resident can choose public services that fit his or her preferences, as suggested by Tiebout (1956). On the contrary, a major disadvantage of fiscal decentralization is the spillover of the benefits of public services. For instance, Oates' (1972) decentralization theorem points out that fiscal decentralization is preferable under the assumption of no spillovers. He also argues that fiscal decentralization is not always desirable if spillovers are taken into account. More specifically, Besley and Coate (2003) argue that the desirability of the decentralized solution, compared with the centralized solution, depends on whether or not heterogeneity in preferences is more important than spillovers. The literature suggests that the decentralized solution is preferable to the centralized solution if the spillover problem is resolved without loss of efficiency.

To date, we have three methods to deal with the spillover problem. The first obvious method is to change the size of a jurisdiction so that no externalities arise. In reality, the supply area of a public service sometimes differs from the boundary of a legally defined locale (city/county). For example, in the US, school districts do not always coincide with city boundaries, and in Japan, water supply areas sometimes cover multiple municipalities. The second method is to apply the self-financing property (Mohring and Harwitz, 1962),[i] analyzed by De Borger and Proost (2016) and Brueckner (2015). They demonstrate that the decentralized solution coincides with the centralized solution by regulating a local government to achieve breakeven if the cost function of a public service exhibits constant returns to scale regarding quantity and capacity. Essentially, in the centralized solution, the socially optimal price is the marginal cost of providing the service. Under the assumption of a constant-returns-to-scale cost function, price equals marginal cost if the price is set to achieve breakeven. That is, the breakeven constraint makes the decentralized solution coincide with the centralized solution.

The third method is to utilize a "spillback" mechanism, advocated by Ogawa and Wildasin (2009). Their method is illustrated through a tax competition model focusing on pollution caused by capital. The essence of the argument is that spillover is fully cancelled out by "spillback," as will be described in detail below. Basically, the capital tax rate becomes, on one hand, too high under the decentralized solution, because a local government wants to move capital to other areas to reduce pollution. On the other hand, the capital tax rate

---

[i]De Palma and Lindsey (2007) name it the cost recovery theorem.

becomes too low under the decentralized solution because a local government wants to move capital in from other areas ceteris paribus so that the revenue from the capital tax increases social surplus.[ii] If the total stock of capital is fixed,[iii] the former effect, spillover, and the latter effect, spillback, are completely cancelled out by each other, and consequently the decentralized solution coincides with the centralized solution.

The purpose of this paper is to propose a method to deal with spillover that is different from the three methods mentioned above. The present paper focuses on a two-part tariff. As Oi (1971) demonstrates, a monopoly can obtain all the surpluses if it levies both a unit price, which is set at the marginal cost, and a fixed charge, which collects all the consumers' surpluses. Setting aside the distribution of surpluses, such a two-part tariff attains a socially optimal allocation, because a monopoly maximizes the total surplus. The basic idea of this paper is that the behaviors of local governments are undistorted if local governments can recoup the benefits that spill over to other areas as the fixed charge in a two-part tariff. Thus, the decentralized solution attains the social optimum, as long as a local government uses a two-part tariff. However, in the real world, uniform pricing of local public services is quite common. We then examine why uniform pricing of local public services is common in reality. Apart from administration costs, the uniform pricing for residents and nonresidents can be justified when a local government obtains an additional gain from the demand by nonresidents, such as an increase in profits of local shops.

The remainder of the paper is organized as follows. In Section 2, we analyze the case of pure public goods. Section 3 examines the case of publicly provided private goods. In Section 4, we provide a method to correct a spillover using a two-part tariff. In Section 5,

---

[ii]This is a standard result in the literature on tax competition. See Wilson (1999) for a survey. In the literature on tax competition, decentralization is usually undesirable, because competition between regions lowers the capital tax rate below the socially optimal level. See Brueckner (2004), who examines whether the effect of tax competition is larger than the Tiebout (1956) effect.

[iii]This condition is shown by Eichner and Runkel (2012).

we further demonstrate that an additional gain from the demand by nonresidents can make a two-part tariff unnecessary. Section 6 concludes the analysis.

2. Pure Public Goods

To clarify the essence of the spillover problem, we begin our analysis with the case of pure public goods. (A typical example of pure public goods is an uncongested park near the boundary of regions.) This case can be applied to the development of local transport network later. Suppose there are two regions, regions 1 and 2. The population in each region is fixed at N^1 and N^2 respectively. The residents in each region are assumed to have homogeneous preferences. To make exposition easier, the model will be explained mainly in terms of region 1 throughout the paper. The corresponding parts of the model for region 2 will have a symmetric structure.

The utility function of a consumer in region 1 is assumed to be quasi-linear, for the sake of simplicity, and is represented by

$$U^1 = z^1 + u^1(x^1, x^2), \tag{1}$$

which satisfy

$$\frac{\partial^2 u^1}{\partial (x^1)^2} < 0, \quad \frac{\partial^2 u^1}{\partial (x^2)^2} < 0, \quad \text{and}$$

$$\frac{\partial^2 u^1}{\partial (x^1)^2} \frac{\partial^2 u^1}{\partial (x^2)^2} - \left(\frac{\partial^2 u^1}{\partial x^1 \partial x^2} \right)^2 > 0, \tag{2}$$

so that $u^1(x^1, x^2)$ is strictly concave. In Equation (1), z^1 is the consumption of the numeraire good whose price is normalized at unity, x^1 is the consumption of the pure public good supplied in region 1, and x^2 is the consumption of the pure public good supplied in region 2. Throughout the paper, the superscripts denote the regions. For the sake of simplicity, we assume that the pure public goods supplied in each region are equally desirable to the residents of regions 1 and 2. We further assume that the transport costs between regions are zero. Consequently, the same amount of the pure public good supplied in each region is consumed by the residents in regions 1 and 2. That is, the benefit of the pure public good supplied in each region completely spills over to the other region.

The cost of the pure public good supplied in region 1 is assumed to be paid equally by the residents in region 1. The total demand for the pure public good supplied in region 1 is $N^1 x^1 + N^2 x^1$. The budget constraint for a consumer in region 1 is

$$z^1 + \frac{C^1(N^1 x^1 + N^2 x^1)}{N^1} = I^1 \tag{3}$$

where $C^1(N^1 x^1 + N^2 x^1)$ is the cost of the pure public good supplied in region 1 and I^1 is the income of a consumer in region 1. We assume that the cost of the pure public good supplied in region 1 is an increasing function with respect to the quantity supplied, that is, $C^{1\prime}(N^1 x^1 + N^2 x^1) > 0$.

Denoting the social surplus in region 1 as S^1, which can be represented by

$$S^1 = N^1 \left(I^1 - \frac{C^1(N^1 x^1 + N^2 x^1)}{N^1} + u^1(x^1, x^2) \right). \tag{4}$$

The social surplus in region 2, S^2, is represented similarly. Thus, the total social surplus, TS, is defined as

$$TS = \sum_{i=1}^{2} S^i$$

$$= N^1 \left(I^1 - \frac{C^1(N^1 x^1 + N^2 x^1)}{N^1} + u^1(x^1, x^2) \right)$$

$$+ N^2 \left(I^2 - \frac{C^2(N^1 x^2 + N^2 x^2)}{N^2} + u^2(x^1, x^2) \right). \tag{5}$$

We first derive the centralized solution in which the central government is assumed to maximize the total social surplus, TS. Throughout the paper, the maximization problem is assumed to have only one interior solution.[iv] Maximizing Equation (5) with respect

---

[iv]Because $u^1(x^1, x^2)$ and $u^2(x^1, x^2)$ are strictly concave by our assumption of Equation (2), $C^{1\prime\prime} > 0$ and $C^{2\prime\prime} > 0$ are sufficient for the strict concavity of Equations (4) and (5), which assures a unique interior solution.

to x^1 yields

$$N^1\frac{\partial u^{1*}}{\partial x^{1*}} + N^2\frac{\partial u^{2*}}{\partial x^{1*}} = C^{1\prime}(N^1x^{1*} + N^2x^{1*}), \qquad (6)$$

where the superscript $*$ denotes the centralized solution throughout the paper. We derive a similar result from the maximization with respect to x^2. Equation (6) represents the well-known Samuelson (1954) rule in which the centralized solution occurs when the marginal social benefits equal to the marginal (social) costs.

We next consider the decentralized solution in which the local government in region 1 is assumed to maximize the social surplus in region 1, S^1. Maximizing Equation (4) with respect to x^1 yields

$$N^1\frac{\partial u^1}{\partial x^1} = C^{1\prime}(N^1x^1 + N^2x^1), \qquad (7)$$

which leads to

$$N^1\frac{\partial u^1}{\partial x^1} + N^2\frac{\partial u^2}{\partial x^1} = C^{1\prime}(N^1x^1 + N^2x^1) + N^2\frac{\partial u^2}{\partial x^1}$$

$$> C^{1\prime}(N^1x^1 + N^2x^1). \qquad (8)$$

Equation (8) demonstrates that the pure public good in region 1 is socially undersupplied because of the spillover of the benefit to region 2.

Suppose now that the local government in region 1 can charge a per capita fixed tax, T^{21}, on a resident in region 2 equal to the amount of the utility of a resident in region 2 for the pure public good supplied in region 1. Under this setting, we derive the following proposition.

Proposition 1. *The decentralized solution coincides with the centralized solution if the local government in region 1 can charge a per capita fixed tax, $T^{21} = \int_{y^1=0}^{x^1} \frac{\partial u^2(y^1, x^2)}{\partial y^1}dx^1$, on a resident in region 2.*

The proof is shown in Appendix A.1. Proposition 1 suggests that the decentralized solution coincides with the centralized solution if a local government can collect the spillover benefit by charging a fixed tax. This result is a special case for a solution using a two-part tariff, which will be developed subsequently. In the case of the pure public good, there exists no unit price, and consequently only the fixed charge in a two-part tariff remains.

The analysis can be applied to the development of local transport network. Let us reinterpret x^1 and x^2 as the sizes of local transport network in regions 1 and 2 respectively. For the sake of simplicity, we assume that a resident in each region consumes unitary fixed demand of transport service in each region free of charge. We consider that a larger transport network in each region is preferable for residents in both regions, but the construction costs are paid only by the residents in each region. The construction cost of a transport network in each region is $C^1(x^1)$ and $C^2(x^2)$. The analysis in this section holds true if we apply $C^1(x^1)$ and $C^2(x^2)$ instead of $C^1(N^1x^1 + N^2x^1)$ and $C^2(N^1x^2 + N^2x^2)$. That is, under the decentralized solution, the development of local transport network is insufficient, but the centralized, socially optimal solution can be reached by a lump-sum transfer from nonresidents, as shown in Proposition 1.

This solution, however, would be difficult in practice, apart from the measurement problem of spillover benefits. Charging a per-capita lump-sum tax on nonresidents by a local government is almost impossible to implement. Transferring the total benefit by an inter-local-government adjustment could be more implementable, but the incentive to free ride would also make this transfer difficult.

3. Publicly Provided Private Goods

We hereafter analyze the case of a publicly provided private good. In the case of publicly provided private goods, a unit price can be charged. In the context of local transport, this case corresponds to variable demand for local transport service, given the network size. Thus, the demand and price of a publicly provided private good can be different between regions 1 and 2. In the subsequent analysis, we demonstrate that the two-part tariff solution is practically feasible in the case of publicly provided private goods.

The utility function of a consumer in region 1 is modified from Equation (1) to

$$U^1 = z^1 + u^1(x^{11}, x^{12}), \qquad (9)$$

which satisfy

$$\frac{\partial^2 u^1}{\partial (x^{11})^2} < 0, \quad \frac{\partial^2 u^1}{\partial (x^{12})^2} < 0, \quad \text{and}$$

$$\frac{\partial^2 u^1}{\partial (x^{11})^2} \frac{\partial^2 u^1}{\partial (x^{12})^2} - \left(\frac{\partial^2 u^1}{\partial x^{11} \partial x^{12}} \right)^2 > 0, \tag{10}$$

so that $u^1(x^{11}, x^{12})$ is strictly concave, as the analysis in Section 2. In Equation (9), x^{11} is the consumption of a publicly provided private good in region 1 and x^{12} is the consumption of a publicly provided private good in region 2. Hereafter, the first superscript denotes the region where a publicly provided private good is demanded and the second superscript denotes the region where a publicly provided private good is supplied. A resident in region 1 can, if he or she wants, enjoy a publicly provided private good in region 2, as well as a publicly provided private good in region 1. Transport costs to travel to another region are assumed to be zero as in Section 2.

Each region's government is assumed to charge a unit price for the publicly provided private good it supplies. The benefits that spill over to another region are consumers' surpluses enjoyed by residents in another region, which cannot be captured through the unit price. The budget constraint for a consumer in region 1 is

$$z^1 + p^{11} x^{11} + p^{12} x^{12} = I^1, \tag{11}$$

where p^{11} and p^{12}, respectively, are unit prices faced by consumers in region 1 for publicly provided private goods in regions 1 and 2.

A consumer in region 1 maximizes, by choosing x^{11} and x^{12}, utility function Equation (9), subject to the budget constraint Equation (11). This maximization yields

$$\frac{\partial u^1(x^{11}, x^{12})}{\partial x^{11}} = p^{11} \quad \text{and} \tag{12}$$

$$\frac{\partial u^1(x^{11}, x^{12})}{\partial x^{12}} = p^{12}. \tag{13}$$

Solving Equations (12) and (13), the demand functions of region 1's consumer for a publicly provided private good in regions 1 and 2, respectively, are $x^{11}(\mathbf{p}^1)$ and $x^{12}(\mathbf{p}^1)$, where $\mathbf{p}^1 \equiv \{p^{11}, p^{12}\}$.

Following the same procedure for a consumer in region 2 yields the demand functions of region 2's consumer as $x^{21}(\mathbf{p}^2)$ and $x^{22}(\mathbf{p}^2)$, where $\mathbf{p}^2 \equiv \{p^{21}, p^{22}\}$.

The cost function of a publicly provided private good for region 1's government is assumed to be

$$C^1 = C^1(X^1(\mathbf{P})), \tag{14}$$

where

$$X^1(\mathbf{P}) \equiv N^1 x^{11}(\mathbf{p}^1) + N^2 x^{21}(\mathbf{p}^2), \tag{15}$$

in which $\mathbf{P} \equiv \{\mathbf{p}^1, \mathbf{p}^2\} = \{p^{11}, p^{12}, p^{21}, p^{22}\}$. $X^1(\mathbf{P})$ represents the total demand for a publicly provided private good in region 1. We assume that $\frac{\partial C^1}{\partial X^1} > 0$ as in Section 2, that is, the cost function is increasing with respect to quantity supplied. The cost function of a publicly provided private good for region 2's government is modeled in the same way.

The social surplus in region 1, S^1, is modified as the total utility of consumers in region 1 plus the profits of the government in region 1 from a publicly provided private good. S^1 is represented by

$$S^1 = N^1(I^1 - (p^{11}x^{11}(\mathbf{p}^1) + p^{12}x^{12}(\mathbf{p}^1)) + u^1(x^{11}(\mathbf{p}^1), x^{12}(\mathbf{p}^1)))$$
$$+ p^{11}N^1 x^{11}(\mathbf{p}^1) + p^{21}N^2 x^{21}(\mathbf{p}^2) - C^1(X^1(\mathbf{P})). \tag{16}$$

The social surplus in region 2, S^2, is represented symmetrically. Thus, the total social surplus, TS, is defined as

$$TS = S^1 + S^2$$
$$= N^1(I^1 - (p^{11}x^{11}(\mathbf{p}^1) + p^{12}x^{12}(\mathbf{p}^1)) + u^1(x^{11}(\mathbf{p}^1), x^{12}(\mathbf{p}^1)))$$
$$+ p^{11}N^1 x^{11}(\mathbf{p}^1) + p^{21}N^2 x^{21}(\mathbf{p}^2) - C^1(X^1(\mathbf{P}))$$
$$+ N^2(I^2 - (p^{21}x^{21}(\mathbf{p}^2) + p^{22}x^{22}(\mathbf{p}^2)) + u^2(x^{21}(\mathbf{p}^2), x^{22}(\mathbf{p}^2)))$$
$$+ p^{12}N^1 x^{12}(\mathbf{p}^1) + p^{22}N^2 x^{22}(\mathbf{p}^2) - C^2(X^2(\mathbf{P}))$$
$$= N^1 I^1 + N^2 I^2 + N^1 u^1(x^{11}(\mathbf{p}^1), x^{12}(\mathbf{p}^1))$$
$$+ N^2 u^2(x^{21}(\mathbf{p}^2), x^{22}(\mathbf{p}^2)) - C^1(X^1(\mathbf{P})) - C^2(X^2(\mathbf{P})). \tag{17}$$

We first derive the centralized solution in which the central government maximizes the total social surplus, Equation (17), with respect to p^{11}, p^{12}, p^{21}, and p^{22}. Arranging the first-order conditions, which are shown in Appendix A.2, for a publicly provided private good in region 1, we derive

$$p^{11*} = p^{21*} = \frac{\partial C^{1*}}{\partial X^{1*}}. \tag{18}$$

Similar results are obtained for a publicly provided private good in region 2. Equation (18) shows that the social efficiency requires the prices of publicly provided private goods equal their marginal costs.

We next derive the decentralized solution and highlight a problem with this solution. The government in region 1 maximizes the social surplus in region 1, Equation (16), with respect to p^{11} and p^{21}. Arranging the first-order conditions, which are shown in Appendix A.3, for a publicly provided private good in region 1, we derive

$$p^{11} = \frac{\partial C^1}{\partial X^1}, \quad \text{and} \tag{19}$$

$$p^{21} = \frac{\partial C^1}{\partial X^1} - \frac{x^{21}}{\frac{\partial x^{21}}{\partial p^{21}}} > \frac{\partial C^1}{\partial X^1}. \tag{20}$$

Similar results are obtained for a publicly provided private good supplied in region 2 by maximizing the social surplus in region 2. The difference between the centralized solution and the decentralized solution stems from the unit price that the government in region 1 sets for the residents in region 2. Equation (18) shows that the residents in region 2 pay the same price as the residents in region 1, which is the marginal cost of a publicly provided private good in region 1, if they use a publicly provided private good in region 1. However, Equation (20) demonstrates that the residents in region 2 pay more than the marginal cost for the use of a publicly provided private good in region 1, although the residents in region 1 remain to pay the marginal cost. Rewriting Equation (20) yields

$$p^{21}\left(1 - \frac{1}{\varepsilon^{21}}\right) = \frac{\partial C^1}{\partial X^1}, \tag{21}$$

where $\varepsilon^{21} \equiv -\frac{\partial x^{21}}{\partial p^{21}}\frac{p^{21}}{x^{21}} > 1$ from $1 - \frac{1}{\varepsilon^{21}} > 0$. The left-hand side of Equation (21) shows the marginal revenue obtained by the government in region 1 from supplying a publicly provided private good for the residents in region 2. Equation (21) demonstrates that as suggested by Arnott and Grieson (1981), the government in region 1 behaves like a monopolist regarding the supply of a publicly provided private good for the residents in region 2 under this scheme. This is a natural reaction of the government in region 1 to the spillover of the benefits of a publicly provided private good to the residents in region 2.

A typical real-world example of such price discrimination is a discounted price for residents, or higher price for nonresidents. For instance, Musashino city in Tokyo sets a discounted user price for its public pool. San Francisco Botanical Garden is free for residents, although the nonresident adult admission fee is $10 (at the time of August 2021). These examples illustrate that higher user prices are imposed for nonresidents.

4. Solutions Using a Two-Part Tariff

As is apparent from the analysis in Section 3, the decentralized solution coincides with the centralized solution if the government in region 1 supplies a publicly provided private good for the residents in region 2 at the marginal cost. A natural solution would be using a Pigouvian tax (or subsidy). However, a Pigouvian tax (or subsidy) has a serious implementation problem in our context. A Pigouvian tax (or subsidy) needs to be imposed for the supplier of the public service, that is, the government in each region. For this solution, we need to assume that the central government imposes a Pigouvian tax for the local government, but we would not say that assuming an intervention by the central government is the decentralized solution. We now consider a two-part tariff, in which the government in region 1 collects the fixed charge that is equal to the consumer surplus that a resident in region 2 gains from a publicly provided private good in region 1. This two-part tariff can be implemented without the central government.

Denoting the per-capita fixed charge that the government in region 1 levies on a resident in region 2 regarding the supply of a publicly provided private good in region 1 by T^{21}, we then have the following proposition.

Proposition 2. *The decentralized solution coincides with the centralized solution under a two-part tariff, if the government in region 1 receives a per capita fixed price, $T^{21} = \int_{q^{21}=p^{21}}^{\infty} x^{21}(q^{21}, p^{22})dq^{21}$ from a resident in region 2.*

The proof is shown in Appendix A.4. This is basically the same result as Proposition 1, although T^{21} is expressed in a different way. In Proposition 1, T^{21} equals the amount of the spillover benefits, which can be expressed as the utility from the pure public good that a resident in the other region obtains. In Proposition 2, T^{21} also equals the amount of the spillover benefits, but it is expressed as a resident's consumer surplus from a publicly provided private good. In the case of a chargeable publicly provided private good, a market transaction reveals price and quantity, and consequently calculating T^{21} is relatively easier.

The basic mechanism is explained by Figure 1, in which D^{21}, MR^{21}, and MC^1 represent the demand function of a resident in region 2 for a publicly provided private good in region 1, its marginal revenue, and the marginal cost of a publicly provided private good in region 1, respectively. The initial equilibrium in

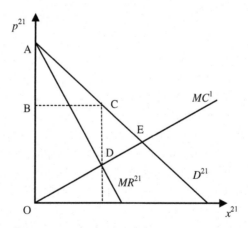

Figure 1. Monopoly pricing for nonresidents and two-part tariff.

which the government in region 1 charges the monopoly price to the residents in region 2 is point C. If the government in region 1 lowers the price marginally, it will earn the marginal profits, which are approximated by the line CD, from an increase in demand. However, at the same time, the government in region 1 will also lose the marginal profits, which are approximated by the line BC, from a decrease in price. Suppose that the government in region 1 collects consumers' surpluses, ABC, by levying the fixed charge. In this case, the government in region 1 will additionally gain the marginal increase in consumers' surpluses, which is approximated by the line BC. Thus, an increase in consumers' surpluses completely offsets a decrease in the profits. The net gain for the government in region 1 is approximated by the line CD. This effect continues up to point E, where the marginal profits, approximated by the line CD, become zero; that is, the price equals the marginal cost. In short, the government in region 1 takes into account both consumers' surpluses and its profits when it sets the price for region 2, and accordingly it sets the price for region 2 equal to the marginal cost and recovers the centralized solution.[v]

A real-world example of a two-part tariff for nonresidents is found in the one-time registration fee for prefectural universities in Japan. It is typical that prefectural universities in Japan charge higher one-time registration fees for nonresidents. For example, in Tokyo Metropolitan University, run by the Tokyo metropolitan government, the one-time registration fees for nonresidents are twice as high as those for residents. If the difference in the one-time registration fees between residents and nonresidents reflects consumers' surpluses for nonresidents from university education, we can regard this system as an example of the two-part tariff, because the marginal cost of

---

[v]This solution can also be interpreted as converting a publicly provided private good in region 1 to the club good for the residents in region 2. Important differences from the club theory are: i) the club theory does not explicitly consider spillovers by nature, and ii) the fixed charge is determined based on consumers' surpluses here, although it is based on the optimal size of the club good in the club theory. See Cornes and Sandler (1996) and Sandler and Tschirhart (1997) for the details of the club theory.

education, the tuition fee, is the same but nonresidents have to pay an additional fixed charge in the form of the one-time registration fees. Proposition 2 can be easily applied in other cases. In the aforementioned examples of Musashino public pool and San Francisco Botanical Garden in Section 3, a local government only has to charge a registration fee, which reflects a net willingness to pay, for nonresidents. Other examples are local public transport, which require a card in addition to pay-per-ride fare. For instance, in New York's subway or Atlanta's rapid transit, a rider is required to buy a pass card, MetroCard in New York and Breeze Card in Atlanta, in addition to paying pay-per-ride fare. The two-part tariff in Proposition 2 works well if nonresidents are charged higher fees for a pass card (or equivalently, residents are charged lower).[vi]

5. Why is a Two-Part Tariff Rare? — Administration Costs and Benefits by Visitors

Proposition 2 demonstrates that each region can internalize the consumer surplus of the other region by using a two-part tariff. For many public services, however, there exists no two-part tariff in reality. A possible explanation is the existence of administration costs. Implementing a two-part tariff, depending on residency, would be sometimes costly for each local government. In the aforementioned example of prefectural universities in Japan, the registration is one-time, and then administration costs are rather small, but in other public services, administration costs would be high.

With relatively high administration costs of a two-part tariff, the second-best solution for a local government is to charge a monopoly price for nonresidents. The aforementioned examples of Musashino public pool and San Francisco Botanical Garden would correspond

---

[vi]We have assumed homogeneous consumers. In fact, the Metrocard system in New York and the Breeze card system in Atlanta are more than just single two-part tariffs, since they can store different kinds of fares such as daily, weekly, or monthly unlimited-use passes, and correspond to consumers' heterogeneity. When consumers are heterogeneous, different consumers could choose different fares. See Fitzroy and Smith (1999) as well as van Vuuren and Rietveld (1999) for analyses in which these fares are taken into account.

to this. However, uniform pricing is also common in a real-world. A typical explanation would again be the existence of administration costs, but another explanation is possible. In what follows, we provide another explanation that could justify the uniform pricing for both residents and nonresidents.

Suppose that a local government in region 1 absorbs an additional gain when the residents in region 2 demand a publicly provided private good in region 1. For instance, visitors to region 1 boost up the profits of local shops in region 1 and increase their employment, which ultimately result in an increase in local income in region 1. A similar mechanism applies to airport users from outside of region 1, whose shopping at duty free shops contributes to an increase in the total profits of the airport. If we include this, the social surplus in region 1 is modified from Equation (16) to

$$S^{1''} = N^1(I^1 - (p^{11}x^{11}(\mathbf{p}^1) + p^{12}x^{12}(\mathbf{p}^1)) + u^1(x^{11}(\mathbf{p}^1), x^{12}(\mathbf{p}^1)))$$

$$+ p^{11}N^1x^{11}(\mathbf{p}^1) + p^{21}N^2x^{21}(\mathbf{p}^2) + \phi^{21}(N^2x^{21}(\mathbf{p}^2))$$

$$- C^1(X^1(\mathbf{P})) - \phi^{12}, \tag{22}$$

where $\phi^{21}(N^2x^{21}(\mathbf{p}^2))$ is an additional gain from the demand for a publicly provided private good in region 1 by the residents in region 2, which satisfy $\frac{\partial \phi^{21}}{\partial x^{21}} > 0$. In the same way, ϕ^{12} is an additional gain that a local government in region 2 obtains, which should be subtracted from the social surplus of region 1, because, for instance, region 1 loses retailer profits when the residents in region 1 go shopping in region 2. We assume that the local government in region 1 takes ϕ^{12} as given. The total social surplus, Equation (17), is unchanged, because ϕ^{21} and ϕ^{12} cancel each other out.

Under this setup, we have the following proposition.

Proposition 3. *When a local government obtains an extra gain equal to a monopoly markup, a local government charges the marginal cost for residents and nonresidents, which attains the centralized solution.*

The proof is shown in Appendix A.5. Proposition 3 demonstrates that when a local government obtains an extra gain equal to a

monopoly markup of $\frac{p^{21}}{\varepsilon^{21}}$, uniform pricing emerges and the solution
under the centralized solution is recovered. This result stems from the
complementarity between the demand for a publicly provided private
good by nonresidents and an additional gain for local government.[vii]
If the local government charges a higher user price, it can increase the
profits from a publicly provided private good, but instead it loses an
additional gain that nonresidents bring. Proposition 3 also suggests
that in an extreme case, where the extra value is sufficiently high, the
local government could charge a lower user price for nonresidents.
A discount targeted for tourists, such as a visitor transport pass,
could be considered as an example. Another example is a large
discount of landing fees at local public airports. Very low landing fees
can be justified if, the local government in charge of an airport highly
values positive effects on local economy or an increase in airport's
profits from non-aeronautical services.

6. Conclusion

This paper has examined how to correct the benefit spillover of local
public services by focusing on a two-part tariff. The main results are
summarized as follows. First, in the case of a pure public good, a
local government disregards the benefits that accrue to nonresidents.
The decentralized solution coincides with the centralized solution if
a lump-sum transfer is possible regarding the amount of benefits
derived from the pure public good. However, a lump-sum transfer in
this case would be impractical because of the difficulties in collecting
a lump-sum transfer from nonresidents, apart from the measurement
problem of spillover benefits. Second, in the case of a publicly
provided private good, a local government charges a higher price for
nonresidents because it cannot capture the benefits that accrues to
nonresidents. If a local government adopts a two-part tariff to capture

---

[vii]Kanemoto and Kiyono (1995) analyzes a pricing policy for urban railways,
considering complementarity between a railway and housing development. Airport literature also considers complementarity between aeronautical and non-
aeronautical services (e.g., Kidokoro *et al.* (2016)).

the benefits from a publicly provided private good, it charges the marginal cost for both residents and nonresidents, and consequently the decentralized solution coincides with the centralized solution. Third, the existence of administration costs could possibly make it impossible to implement a two-part tariff. The second-best solution for a local government is to charge a higher price for nonresidents. The uniform pricing for residents and nonresidents, which is common in reality, can be justified when a local government obtains an additional gain from the demand by nonresidents.

The analysis in this paper on local public services is applicable to a number of transport services with benefit spillovers. For example, an airport generates both *local* spillovers (e.g., Cantos *et al.* (2005), Zhang (2012)) and *network* spillovers (e.g., Oum *et al.* (1996), Cohen and Morrison Paul (2003, 2004), Ueda *et al.* (2005)). The local spillover refers to the benefits to the region where the airport is located, while the network spillover refers to the benefit of expanding/constructing an airport that extends to other airports in the network. For the latter, Cohen and Morrison Paul (2003) found, using the US data, that in addition to the substantive impacts of airport infrastructure on the own-state manufacturing industry's cost savings and productivity increases, the airport expansion had a comparable effect in "connected states" with hub airports and an even greater impact in other states. Basically, high congestion in passengers' destination states relative to their origin states implied greater cost and productivity effects from the own-state airport expansion. Our spillover model corresponds to both local and network spillovers because we can interpret region 2 as a surrounding area of region 1 or a connected area to region 1. In practice, the origin and destination passengers usually pay the same amount for airport facility and improvement fees. This uniform pricing may not be optimal, because local jurisdictions (e.g., state, city, county) cannot capture the consumer surplus of destination passengers. The uniform pricing could be justified, however, if we consider additional benefits by destination passengers. In an airport context, we need empirical research as to the relationship between airport pricing and additional benefits (e.g., Czerny *et al.* (2016)).

Appendix A

A.1. *Proof of Proposition 1*

Suppose that the local government in region 1 charge a per capita fixed tax,

$$T^{21} = \int_{y^1=0}^{x^1} \frac{\partial u^2(y^1, x^2)}{\partial y^1} dx^1, \tag{A.1}$$

on a resident in region 2. Under such a transfer scheme, the social surplus in region 1, Equation (4), is now modified to

$$S^1 = N^1 \left(I^1 - \frac{C^1(N^1 x^1 + N^2 x^1)}{N^1} + u^1(x^1, x^2) \right) + N^2 T^{21} - N^1 T^{12}, \tag{A.2}$$

where T^{12} is a per capita fixed tax on a resident in region 1 regarding the use of the public good in region 2. Maximizing Equation (A.2) with respect to x^1, given T^{12}, yields Equation (6), which is the centralized solution.

A.2. *Derivation of Equation (18)*

The first-order conditions are

$$\frac{\partial TS}{\partial p^{11}} = N^1 \frac{\partial u^1}{\partial x^{11}} \frac{\partial x^{11}}{\partial p^{11}} + N^1 \frac{\partial u^1}{\partial x^{12}} \frac{\partial x^{12}}{\partial p^{11}} - \frac{\partial C^1}{\partial X^1} N^1 \frac{\partial x^{11}}{\partial p^{11}}$$
$$- \frac{\partial C^2}{\partial X^2} N^1 \frac{\partial x^{12}}{\partial p^{11}} = 0, \tag{A.3}$$

$$\frac{\partial TS}{\partial p^{12}} = N^1 \frac{\partial u^1}{\partial x^{11}} \frac{\partial x^{11}}{\partial p^{12}} + N^1 \frac{\partial u^1}{\partial x^{12}} \frac{\partial x^{12}}{\partial p^{12}} - \frac{\partial C^1}{\partial X^1} N^1 \frac{\partial x^{11}}{\partial p^{12}}$$
$$- \frac{\partial C^2}{\partial X^2} N^1 \frac{\partial x^{12}}{\partial p^{12}} = 0, \tag{A.4}$$

$$\frac{\partial TS}{\partial p^{21}} = N^2 \frac{\partial u^2}{\partial x^{21}} \frac{\partial x^{21}}{\partial p^{21}} + N^2 \frac{\partial u^2}{\partial x^{22}} \frac{\partial x^{22}}{\partial p^{21}} - \frac{\partial C^1}{\partial X^1} N^2 \frac{\partial x^{21}}{\partial p^{21}}$$
$$- \frac{\partial C^2}{\partial X^2} N^2 \frac{\partial x^{22}}{\partial p^{21}} = 0, \tag{A.5}$$

$$\frac{\partial TS}{\partial p^{22}} = N^2 \frac{\partial u^2}{\partial x^{21}} \frac{\partial x^{21}}{\partial p^{22}} + N^2 \frac{\partial u^2}{\partial x^{22}} \frac{\partial x^{22}}{\partial p^{22}} - \frac{\partial C^1}{\partial X^1} N^2 \frac{\partial x^{21}}{\partial p^{22}}$$

$$- \frac{\partial C^2}{\partial X^2} N^2 \frac{\partial x^{22}}{\partial p^{22}} = 0. \tag{A.6}$$

Arranging Equations (A.3)–(A.6) using Equations (12) and (13) yields

$$A \begin{pmatrix} p^{11} - \dfrac{\partial C^1}{\partial X^1} \\ p^{12} - \dfrac{\partial C^2}{\partial X^2} \\ p^{21} - \dfrac{\partial C^1}{\partial X^1} \\ p^{22} - \dfrac{\partial C^2}{\partial X^2} \end{pmatrix} = \begin{pmatrix} 0 \\ 0 \\ 0 \\ 0 \end{pmatrix}. \tag{A.7}$$

where $A \equiv \begin{pmatrix} A^1 & O \\ O & A^2 \end{pmatrix}$, $A^1 \equiv \begin{pmatrix} \frac{\partial x^{11}}{\partial p^{11}} & \frac{\partial x^{12}}{\partial p^{11}} \\ \frac{\partial x^{11}}{\partial p^{12}} & \frac{\partial x^{12}}{\partial p^{12}} \end{pmatrix}$, $A^2 \equiv \begin{pmatrix} \frac{\partial x^{21}}{\partial p^{22}} & \frac{\partial x^{22}}{\partial p^{22}} \\ \frac{\partial x^{21}}{\partial p^{21}} & \frac{\partial x^{22}}{\partial p^{21}} \end{pmatrix}$, and $O \equiv \begin{pmatrix} 0 & 0 \\ 0 & 0 \end{pmatrix}$.

By totally differentiating Equations (12) and (13), we derive

$$\begin{pmatrix} dx^{11} \\ dx^{12} \end{pmatrix} = \frac{1}{\det A^3} \begin{pmatrix} \dfrac{\partial^2 u^1}{\partial (x^{12})^2} & -\dfrac{\partial^2 u^1}{\partial x^{11} \partial x^{12}} \\ -\dfrac{\partial^2 u^1}{\partial x^{12} \partial x^{11}} & \dfrac{\partial^2 u^1}{\partial (x^{11})^2} \end{pmatrix} \begin{pmatrix} dp^{11} \\ dp^{12} \end{pmatrix}, \tag{A.8}$$

where $A^3 \equiv \begin{pmatrix} \frac{\partial^2 u^1}{\partial (x^{11})^2} & \frac{\partial^2 u^1}{\partial x^{11} \partial x^{12}} \\ \frac{\partial^2 u^1}{\partial x^{11} \partial x^{12}} & \frac{\partial^2 u^1}{\partial (x^{12})^2} \end{pmatrix}$ and $\det A^3 = \frac{\partial^2 u^1}{\partial (x^{11})^2} \frac{\partial^2 u^1}{\partial (x^{12})^2} -$ $\frac{\partial^2 u^1}{\partial x^{11} \partial x^{12}} \frac{\partial^2 u^1}{\partial x^{12} \partial x^{11}} > 0$. We obtain $\det A^1 > 0$, from

$$\det A^1 = \frac{\partial x^{11}}{\partial p^{11}} \frac{\partial x^{12}}{\partial p^{12}} - \frac{\partial x^{12}}{\partial p^{11}} \frac{\partial x^{11}}{\partial p^{12}}$$

$$= \frac{\frac{\partial^2 u^1}{\partial (x^{12})^2} \frac{\partial^2 u^1}{\partial (x^{11})^2} - \frac{\partial^2 u^1}{\partial x^{11} \partial x^{12}} \frac{\partial^2 u^1}{\partial x^{12} \partial x^{11}}}{(\det A^3)^2}$$

$$= \frac{\det A^3}{(\det A^3)^2}$$

$$= \frac{1}{\det A^3} > 0. \tag{A.9}$$

In the same way, we derive $\det A^2 > 0$. Because $\det A = \det A^1 \det A^2$, we have $\det A > 0$.

Because $\det A > 0$ assures the existence of the inverse matrix of A, we have

$$
\begin{pmatrix}
p^{11} - \dfrac{\partial C^1}{\partial X^1} \\[2mm]
p^{12} - \dfrac{\partial C^2}{\partial X^2} \\[2mm]
p^{21} - \dfrac{\partial C^1}{\partial X^1} \\[2mm]
p^{22} - \dfrac{\partial C^2}{\partial X^2}
\end{pmatrix}
= A^{-1}
\begin{pmatrix} 0 \\ 0 \\ 0 \\ 0 \end{pmatrix}
=
\begin{pmatrix} 0 \\ 0 \\ 0 \\ 0 \end{pmatrix},
\tag{A.10}
$$

which immediately leads to Equation (18).

A.3. *Derivation of Equations (19) and (20)*

The first-order conditions are

$$
\frac{\partial S^1}{\partial p^{11}} = N^1 \left(-x^{11} - p^{11}\frac{\partial x^{11}}{\partial p^{11}} - p^{12}\frac{\partial x^{12}}{\partial p^{11}} + \frac{\partial u^1}{\partial x^{11}}\frac{\partial x^{11}}{\partial p^{11}} + \frac{\partial u^1}{\partial x^{12}}\frac{\partial x^{12}}{\partial p^{11}} \right)
$$

$$
+ N^1 x^{11} + p^{11} N^1 \frac{\partial x^{11}}{\partial p^{11}} - \frac{\partial C^1}{\partial X^1} N^1 \frac{\partial x^{11}}{\partial p^{11}} = 0,
\tag{A.11}
$$

$$
\frac{\partial S^1}{\partial p^{21}} = N^2 x^{21} + p^{21} N^2 \frac{\partial x^{21}}{\partial p^{21}} - \frac{\partial C^1}{\partial X^1} N^2 \frac{\partial x^{21}}{\partial p^{21}} = 0.
\tag{A.12}
$$

Rearranging Equation (A.11) using Equations (12) and (13) yields Equation (19). Rewriting Equation (A.12), we immediately obtain Equation (20).

A.4. *Proof of Proposition 2*

Because a per capita fixed price, T^{21}, is not larger than the per capita willingness to pay for a publicly provided private good in region 1 minus usage fees, we have

$$
T^{21} \leq \int_{q^{21}=p^{21}}^{\infty} x^{21}(q^{21}, p^{22})dq^{21} + p^{21}x^{21} - p^{21}x^{21}
$$

$$
= \int_{q^{21}=p^{21}}^{\infty} x^{21}(q^{21}, p^{22})dq^{21}.
\tag{A.13}
$$

The social surplus in region 1, S^1, is modified from Equation (16) to

$$
\begin{aligned}
S^{1\prime} = N^1(I^1 &- (p^{11}x^{11}(\mathbf{p}^1) + p^{12}x^{12}(\mathbf{p}^1)) + u^1(x^{11}(\mathbf{p}^1), x^{12}(\mathbf{p}^1))) \\
&+ p^{11}N^1x^{11}(\mathbf{p}^1) + p^{21}N^2x^{21}(\mathbf{p}^2) + N^2T^{21} \\
&- C^1(X^1(\mathbf{P})) - N^1T^{12}.
\end{aligned}
\tag{A.14}
$$

The government in region 1 maximizes Equation (A.14) subject to Equation (A.13) given the fixed payment to region 2, T^{12}. We set up the Lagrangian as

$$
\begin{aligned}
\Lambda = N^1 \big(I^1 &- (p^{11}x^{11}(\mathbf{p}^1) + p^{12}x^{12}(\mathbf{p}^1)) + u^1(x^{11}(\mathbf{p}^1), x^{12}(\mathbf{p}^1))\big) \\
&+ p^{11}N^1x^{11}(\mathbf{p}^1) + p^{21}N^2x^{21}(\mathbf{p}^2) + N^2T^{21} - C^1(X^1(\mathbf{P})) \\
&- N^1T^{12} + \lambda \left(\int_{q^{21}=p^{21}}^{\infty} x^{21}(q^{21}, p^{22})dq^{21} - T^{21} \right),
\end{aligned}
\tag{A.15}
$$

where $\lambda \geq 0$. The first-order conditions for the maximization of Equation (A.15) are

$$
\begin{aligned}
\frac{\partial S^1}{\partial p^{11}} = N^1 \left(-x^{11} - p^{11}\frac{\partial x^{11}}{\partial p^{11}} - p^{12}\frac{\partial x^{12}}{\partial p^{11}} + \frac{\partial u^1}{\partial x^{11}}\frac{\partial x^{11}}{\partial p^{11}} + \frac{\partial u^1}{\partial x^{12}}\frac{\partial x^{12}}{\partial p^{11}} \right) \\
+ N^1 x^{11} + p^{11}N^1\frac{\partial x^{11}}{\partial p^{11}} - \frac{\partial C^1}{\partial X^1}N^1\frac{\partial x^{11}}{\partial p^{11}} = 0,
\end{aligned}
\tag{A.16}
$$

$$
\frac{\partial S^1}{\partial p^{21}} = N^2 x^{21} + p^{21}N^2\frac{\partial x^{21}}{\partial p^{21}} - \frac{\partial C^1}{\partial X^1}N^2\frac{\partial x^{21}}{\partial p^{21}} - \lambda x^{21} = 0,
\tag{A.17}
$$

$$
\frac{\partial S^1}{\partial T^{21}} = N^2 - \lambda = 0.
\tag{A.18}
$$

Rewriting Equation (A.16) using Equations (12) and (13) yields $p^{11} = \frac{\partial C^1}{\partial X^1}$. From Equation (A.18), we have $\lambda = N^2 > 0$, which immediately leads to $T^{21} = \int_{q^{21}=p^{21}}^{\infty} x^{21}(q^{21}, p^{22})dq^{21}$. Substituting $\lambda = N^2$ into Equation (A.17) and rearranging the resulting expression, we obtain $p^{21} = \frac{\partial C^1}{\partial X^1}$. This result demonstrates that the decentralized solution coincides with the centralized solution of Equation (18) under this two-part tariff scheme with the fixed charge of $T^{21} = \int_{q^{21}=p^{21}}^{\infty} x^{21}(q^{21}, p^{22})dq^{21}$.

A.5. *Proof of Proposition 3*

Maximizing Equation (22) with respect to p^{11} and p^{21} yields

$$\frac{\partial S^{1\prime\prime}}{\partial p^{11}} = N^1 \left(-x^{11} - p^{11}\frac{\partial x^{11}}{\partial p^{11}} - p^{12}\frac{\partial x^{12}}{\partial p^{11}} + \frac{\partial u^1}{\partial x^{11}}\frac{\partial x^{11}}{\partial p^{11}} + \frac{\partial u^1}{\partial x^{12}}\frac{\partial x^{12}}{\partial p^{11}} \right)$$

$$+ N^1 x^{11} + p^{11} N^1 \frac{\partial x^{11}}{\partial p^{11}} - \frac{\partial C^1}{\partial X^1} N^1 \frac{\partial x^{11}}{\partial p^{11}} = 0, \tag{A.19}$$

$$\frac{\partial S^{1\prime\prime}}{\partial p^{21}} = N^2 x^{21} + \left(p^{21} + \frac{\partial \phi^{21}}{\partial x^{21}} \right) N^2 \frac{\partial x^{21}}{\partial p^{21}} - \frac{\partial C^1}{\partial X^1} N^2 \frac{\partial x^{21}}{\partial p^{21}} = 0. \tag{A.20}$$

Rearranging Equation (A.19) yields Equation (19). From Equation (A.20), we derive

$$p^{21} = \frac{\partial C^1}{\partial X^1} - \left(\frac{\partial \phi^{21}}{\partial x^{21}} - \left(-\frac{x^{21}}{\frac{\partial x^{21}}{\partial p^{21}}} \right) \right) = \frac{\partial C^1}{\partial X^1} - \left(\frac{\partial \phi^{21}}{\partial x^{21}} - \frac{p^{21}}{\varepsilon^{21}} \right), \tag{A.21}$$

which shows that $p^{21} \lesseqgtr \frac{\partial C^1}{\partial X^1}$ when $\frac{\partial \phi^{21}}{\partial x^{21}} \gtreqless \frac{p^{21}}{\varepsilon^{21}}$.

References

Arnott, R., and Grieson, R.E. (1981). Optimal Fiscal Policy for a State or Local Government. *Journal of Urban Economics*, *9*(1), 23–48.

Besley, T., and Coate, S. (2003). Centralized Versus Decentralized Provision of Local Public Goods: A Political Economy Approach. *Journal of Public Economics*, *87*(12), 2611–2637.

Brueckner, J.K. (2004). Fiscal Decentralization with Distortionary Taxation: Tiebout vs. Tax Competition. *International Tax and Public Finance*, *11*(2), 133–153.

Brueckner, J.K. (2015). Decentralized Road Investment and Pricing in a Congested, Multi-Jurisdictional City: Efficiency with Spillovers. *National Tax Journal*, *68*(35), 839–854.

Cantos, P., Mercedes, G.-A., and J. Maudos, J. (2005). Transport Infrastructures, Spillover Effects and Regional Growth: Evidence of the Spanish Case. *Transport Reviews*, *25*(1), 25–50.

Cohen, J.P., and Morrison Paul, C.J. (2003). Airport Infrastructure Spillovers in a Network System. *Journal of Urban Economics*, *54*(3), 459–473.

Cohen, J.P., and Morrison Paul, C.J. (2004). Public Infrastructure Investment, Inter-State Spatial Spillovers, and Manufacturing Costs. *The Review of Economics and Statistics, 86*(2), 551–560.

Cornes, R., and Sandler, T. (1996). *The Theory of Externalities, Public Goods, and Club Goods* (2nd Edn.). Cambridge University Press, New York.

Czerny, A.I., Shi, Z., and Zhang, A. (2016). Can Market Power be Controlled by Regulation of Core Prices Alone? An Empirical Analysis of Airport Demand and Car Rental Price. *Transportation Research Part A: Policy and Practice, 91*, 260–272.

De Borger, B., and Proost, S. (2016). The Political Economy of Pricing and Capacity Decisions for Congestible Local Public Goods in a Federal State. *International Tax and Public Finance, 23*(5), 934–959.

De Palma, A., and Lindsey, R. (2007). Transport User Charges and Cost Recovery. *Research in Transportation Economics, 19*, 29–57.

Eichner, T., and Runkel, M. (2012). Interjurisdictional Spillovers, Decentralized Policymaking, and the Elasticity of Capital Supply. *American Economic Review, 102*(5), 2349–2357.

Fitzroy, F.R., and Smith, I. (1999). Season Tickets and the Demand for Public Transport. *Kyklos, 52*(2), 219–238.

Kanemoto, Y., and Kiyono, K. (1995). Regulation of Commuter Railways and Spatial Development. *Regional Science and Urban Economics, 25*(4), 377–394.

Kidokoro, Y., Lin, M.H., and Zhang, A. (2016). A General-Equilibrium Analysis of Airport Pricing, Capacity, and Regulation. *Journal of Urban Economics, 96*, 142–155.

Mohring, H., and Harwitz, M. (1962). *Highway Benefits: An Analytical Framework.* Northwestern University Press.

Oates, W.E. (1972). *Fiscal Federalism.* Harcourt Brace Jovanovich, New York.

Ogawa, H., and Wildasin, D.E. (2009). Think Locally, Act Locally: Spillovers, Spillbacks, and Efficient Decentralized Policymaking. *American Economic Review, 99*(4), 1206–1217.

Oi, W.Y. (1971). A Disneyland Dilemma: Two-Part Tariffs for a Mickey Mouse Monopoly. *The Quarterly Journal of Economics, 85*(1), 77–96.

Oum, T.H., Zhang, A., and Zhang, Y. (1996). Optimal Airport Pricing in a Hub-and-Spoke System. *Transportation Research Part B: Methodological, 30*(1), 11–18.

Samuelson, P.A. (1954). The Pure Theory of Public Expenditure. *The Review of Economics and Statistics, 36*(4), 387–389.

Sandler, T., and Tschirhart, J. (1997). Club Theory: Thirty Years Later. *Public Choice, 93*(3–4), 335–355.

Tiebout, C.M. (1956). A Pure Theory of Local Expenditures. *Journal of Political Economy, 64*(5), 416–424.

Ueda, T., Koike, A., Yamaguchi, K., and Tsuchiya, K. (2005). Spatial Benefit Incidence Analysis of Airport Capacity Expansion: Application of SCGE Model to the Haneda Project. *Research in Transportation Economics, 13*, 165–196.

van Vuuren, D., and Rietveld, P. (1999, August 23–24). The Demand for Tickets and Travel Cards of Railway Travellers. 39th Congress of the European Regional Association: "Regional Cohesion and Competitiveness in 21st Century Europe", Dublin, Ireland. https://www.econstor.eu/bitstream/10419/114186/1/ERSA1999_a002.pdf.

Wilson, J.D. (1999). Theories of Tax Competition. *National Tax Journal, 52*(2), 269–304.

Zhang, A. (2012). Airport Improvement Fees, Benefit Spillovers, and Land Value Capture Mechanisms. In Ingram, G.K., and Hong, Y.-H. (Eds.), *Value Capture and Land Policies* (pp. 323–348). Lincoln Institute of Land Policy, Cambridge, MA.

https://doi.org/10.1142/9789811271663_0005

Chapter 5

Why Do COVID-19 Infection Rates Vary Between Neighborhoods in Toronto, ON Canada? The Role of Housing and Transportation

Mike Brown

Transport Strategy Centre, Imperial College, London, UK

This chapter looks at the socio-economic characteristics of neighborhoods in Canada's largest metropolitan area, Toronto, Ontario and correlates them with cumulative Covid-19 case rates. Firstly, we find that, like plagues and pandemics throughout history, less affluent neighborhoods suffer higher rates of Covid-19. More specifically, neighborhoods with a large share of the labor force in what we call "high-touch" industries, that is, involving a high degree of direct client or customer contact and a lower likelihood of working from home, also have higher Covid-19 rates. Neighborhoods with a high incidence of crowded dwellings and a large share of the labor force commuting as a passenger in a car or enduring long or multiple commutes, which we think is surrogate measure for the incidence of multiple job holders, have higher rates of infection. One public policy response would be to requisition some of the many empty hotel rooms and make them available to people living in these neighborhoods.

1. Introduction

This chapter looks at the variation in Covid-19 infection rates between different neighborhoods in Toronto, Canada and offers reasons for the variation. Firstly, we undertake a review of the relevant literature, then provide some context such as the socio-economic characteristics of Toronto and a timeline of Covid-19 infections. We describe our data and the variances in incidence between neighborhoods, which is followed by the results of our analysis and some public policy recommendations. We also include a field study of one neighborhood with a particularly high rate of Covid-19 cases to illustrate the points made in the chapter. To the best of our knowledge, this is the first analysis of neighborhood-level differences in Covid-19 rates in a Canadian city, made possible because of the City of Toronto's consistent databases of infections and socio-economic conditions at a sufficiently granular level to permit meaningful analysis. Other jurisdictions, the province of British Columbia, for example, have not made available such data, or the geographical units are too large.

1.1. *Literature Review*

The impact of the pandemic on cities has always varied by neighborhood. A study by Cummins *et al.* (2016) revealed that in the 16th and 17th centuries, more affluent areas of London, England were less affected by plagues.

> *"We find in particular that the plagues of 1563, 1603, 1625, and 1665 were all of roughly equal relative magnitude, with burials running at 5.5 to 6 times the average level in the previous five years. Assuming a normal mortality rate of around 3.0–3.5 per cent, this implies that one-fifth of the city's population died each time, within the space of a few months. While the relative size of major plagues remained fairly constant, their spatial impact changed markedly. In 1563, mortality was fairly equal across parishes within the walls and surrounding extra-mural parishes, but by 1665 mortality in the central intra-mural parishes was considerably lower than elsewhere, reflecting the marked increase that we find in the concentration of wealthy households in these areas".*

It was similar in the 19th century as shown below in Figure 1. This is a map showing deaths from a cholera outbreak in Liverpool, England in 1866 and demonstrates the areas most affected. Each red dot marks a death, and it is the poorer, most densely populated areas where most deaths occurred.

In terms of the Covid-19 pandemic, three studies of New York City address the neighborhood differences.

A study by Cohen *et al.* (2021) on the effect of the pandemic on property values in New York City found that Covid-19 case rates

Figure 1. Borough of Liverpool: Mortality Map of Cholera 1866.
Source: Old Maps (reddit.com).

were higher in neighborhoods with lower incomes, lower levels of educational attainment, higher density, higher public transit use, share of rental housing, foreign-born population and limited English language skills. The pandemic manifested itself in residential property values in two ways: Through a contagion effect and an income effect. That is, more affluent neighborhoods experienced the former, as residents migrated from the city, while poorer neighborhoods felt the latter due to incomes being adversely affected by the pandemic. The contagion effect was less than the income effect so inequality between neighborhoods increased as a result.

Also, looking at New York City, Lamb *et al.* (2021) found that socio-economic status explained 56 percent of the variance in Covid-19 case rates between neighborhoods.

Finally, Almagro *et al.* (2021) showed that wealthier residents of New York City, with a higher likelihood of being able to work from home, fled the city for second homes, rental properties and to stay with friends. This is consistent with the findings of Cohen *et al.* (2021) noted above. Poorer neighborhoods exhibited more mobility and therefore exposure to Covid-19, and residents were less likely to be able to work from home or afford home delivery, thus having to shop in person. Crowded housings and commuting to front-line jobs were positively correlated with the risk of contracting Covid-19.

Martínez *et al.* (2020) looked at Covid-19 infection rates in Los Angeles County and New York City and found that in both the cities higher rates were associated, inter alia, with reliance on public transit or carpooling to work.

1.2. *Toronto, Canada*

Toronto is Canada's largest metropolitan area and capital city of the Province of Ontario, with a population of 6.6 million people in 2020.[i] The metro area accounts for 17 percent of Canada's population and an estimated 19 percent of GDP. In the US terms, Toronto is approximately the same size as Washington, D.C., Miami, Florida or Philadelphia, Pennsylvania.

The City of Toronto, which is the subject of this analysis, is the largest component part of the metropolitan area with a population of 2.9 million. Its land area is 630 square kilometres, so 20 percent smaller than New York City's 784 square kilometres. Toronto is in many respects a typical global city with all the opportunities and challenges that it brings. For example, residents have higher levels of education than other Canadians: 69.3 percent of Toronto residents aged 25–64 have some post-secondary certificate, diploma, or degree, compared to 65.1 percent across Ontario and 64.8 percent across Canada. The largest industries are high-order services. So, compared to other Canadians, Toronto residents are much more likely to work in finance, insurance, management of companies, IT, culture, professional, scientific and technical services, and real estate. It is also an innovation hub with the US patent award rate of 154 per million[ii] in 2019 and is amongst the top-10 most innovative metro areas in Canada.

On the downside, city residents commute for a longer time than other Canadians, with more than half (59.4 percent) reporting that it takes them over 30 minutes to get to work. Toronto residents are

---

[i] Statistics Canada Table: 17-10-0135-01.
[ii] Figures for Toronto CMA.

much more likely to take transit to work (37.0 percent) than all Canadians (12.4 percent).[iii]

Average housing price in the City of Toronto is $1,025,925 and is 69 percent higher than the national average.[iv] In Canada, if a household spends more than 30 percent of their before-tax income on shelter costs, they experience affordability issues. In 2016, 46.7 percent of all renter households in Toronto and 27.3 percent of owner households fell into this category.

Toronto has the most income inequality in the country. According to a recent report,[v] net worth increased by $2,100 for the bottom 20 percent between 1999 and 2016, versus more than $600,000 for the top 20 percent. Furthermore, Toronto is the working-age poverty capital of Canada and has high poverty rates for seniors and children compared to other cities.

Toronto Pearson International Airport (YYZ) is Canada's largest airport in terms of total passengers (50 million in 2019) and provides scheduled, non-stop daily services to 69 percent of the global economy, pre-pandemic.[vi]

For context, Canada operates a single payer public health care system that is free at the point of use. Delivery of health care services is a mix of the private and public sector, with most physicians operating individually or as private corporations, for example. Health insurance for medical services that are available in the public sector is not permitted.[vii] This is obviously not a factor in comparing Covid-19 case rates within one jurisdiction but to the extent that readers want to compare case rates in Toronto with cities in other countries, it may be pertinent.

[iii]City of Toronto Backgrounder 2016 Census: Education, labor, journey to work, language of work, mobility and migration.
[iv]Toronto Economic Dashboard — City of Toronto.
[v]"Growing Pains and Narrow Gains", Toronto's Vital Signs Report 2019/20, Toronto Foundation.
[vi]Toronto is also served by a smaller airport, Billy Bishop Toronto City Airport (YTZ), is located close to the CBD and connects Toronto with other northeast metropolitan areas such as Montreal and New York.
[vii]Canadian Healthcare System Fact Sheet American Medical Student Association. Prepared by Kao-Ping Chua, AMSA Jack Rutledge Fellow 2005–2006.

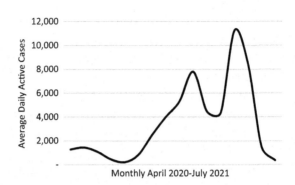

Figure 2. Covid-19 cases in the City of Toronto.
Source: Government of Ontario: Status of COVID-19 cases by Public Health Unit.

Health care is a provincial responsibility in Canada. For further context, the public health measures to contain the pandemic adopted in Ontario were the strictest in Canada, with a Covid-19 Stringency Index (CSI)[viii] of 54.7 compared to the national average, among 10 provinces and three territories, of 44.1 as of July 01, 2021.[ix]

1.2.1. *Timeline of the Covid-19 Pandemic in Toronto*

As shown in Figure 2, Toronto had experienced three waves of Covid-19, with the first case reported on January 23, 2020, to a peak of 11,264 average active daily cases in April 2021. An aggressive vaccination program together with a stay-at-home order issued in the first week of April 2021 have seen the number of Covid-19 cases plummet.

1.2.2. *Incidence of Covid-19 Cases by Neighborhood in the City of Toronto*

For administrative purposes, the City of Toronto is divided into 140 neighborhoods with an average of 21,000 people each. This is reasonably granular and gives us a decent sample size to compare Covid-19 case rates with socio-economic conditions. However, the

---

[viii]COVID-19 Government Response Tracker, Blavatnik School of Government (ox.ac.uk).
[ix]COVID19 Stringency Index, Bank of Canada.

socio-economic data are from the 2016 Census of Canada, but the pandemic hit in 2020 and 2021. Barring a substantial change in the neighborhoods in the last four years, the correlations observed are probably reasonable. Where this may not be the case, for example, due to rapid population growth, it is noted.

The following analyses are of the rate of Covid-19 cases. That is, per capita and not the absolute number. Figure 3 shows the cumulative case rates over the course of the pandemic, from January 2020 to July 2021, with the darker areas representing the higher rates. These are clustered in the north-west quadrant of the city adjacent to Toronto Pearson International Airport (YYZ), with pockets on the eastern side of the city.

The city-wide average was 6,004 cases per 100,000 people while the neighborhoods with the highest rates including Humbermede, Maple Leaf, Black Creek, Downsview-Roding-CFB and Mount Olive-Silverstone-Jamestown recorded rates between 2.0 to 2.3 times

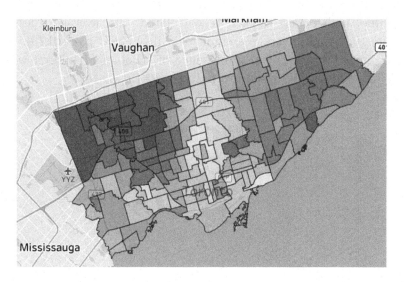

Figure 3. Cumulative of Covid-19 case rates by neighborhood in the City of Toronto as of July 19, 2021 (per 100,000 people). Darker areas indicate high rates of Covid-19. Humbermede, with the highest rate of infection in the City of Toronto, is marked with a red dot.

Source: City of Toronto.

the city average and are all located in the north-west quadrant of the city.

1.2.3. *Income*

Consistent with the history of plagues and pandemics, we find that Toronto in 2020 is no different from Liverpool in the 19th century or London in the 17th century, with the rate of Covid-19 cases declining as after-tax household income increases. Specifically, a 10 percent increase in income resulted in a 9.8 percent decline in the Covid-19 case rates, so almost a one-to-one ratio with income explaining 54 percent of the variation in rates. It is also evident from Figure 4 that neighborhoods with similar after-tax household incomes have very different Covid-19 case rates and, conversely, neighborhoods with similar case rates can have very different income levels. This indicates that there are other factors at work. For example, income is a "flow" measurement that does not include the "stock" of wealth. However, other surrogate measures of low income revealed similar results. For example, higher case rates were correlated with average sales tax credits (0.73) and average amount of child benefit paid (0.73). The latter may also indicate the presence of school-age children which may increase the risk of exposure to Covid-19.

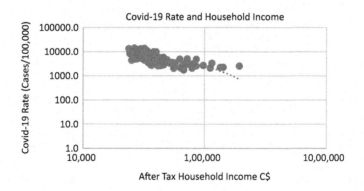

Figure 4. Relation between Covid-19 case rates and after-tax household incomes. *Source*: City of Toronto.

1.2.4. *Employment*

Case rates declined as the employment rate increased, but we found no relationship with the incidence of part-time work.

We did see a correlation between case rates and employment in certain industries, as shown in Figure 5. We introduced the concept of "high-touch" industries in which employees generally cannot work at home and tended to have direct contact with clients and customers. For our purposes, "high-touch" industries are defined to include healthcare and social assistance, transportation, warehousing,[x] accommodation, food services and the retail trade. Obviously, some people working in these industries can work from home, but the majority cannot.

In Ontario as a whole, across all industries in 2016, 23 percent of occupations were classified as sales and service, but 57 percent in retail and 81 percent in accommodation and food services, while health care and social assistance was inherently client- or patient-facing. Only 8 percent of occupations in transportation and warehousing were classified as sales and service but when we added

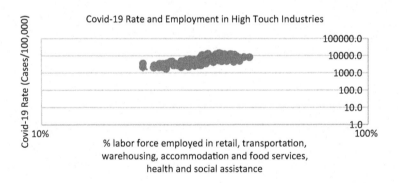

Figure 5. Covid-19 case rates and employment in "high-touch" industries. *Source*: City of Toronto.

---

[x]There is a 'high noise' component to this, for example, in warehouses. When employees work in noisy environments, they have to shout which increases the risk of the virus being transmitted.

in the number of people driving buses, streetcars, taxis and Ubers, flight attendants and airline agents, as well as those delivering mail and parcels, we arrived at 38 percent of employment in transportation and warehousing that could be described as public facing.[xi]

Perhaps unsurprisingly, then, we find that there was a positive correlation (0.70) between the share of the labor force in these "high-touch" industries and Covid-19 case rates such that a 10 percent increase in the share so employed results in a 24 percent increase in case rates. This explains 60 percent of the variation.

1.2.5. *Commuting Patterns*

Having looked at employment, were there any characteristics of how people get to work that are correlated with Covid-19 case rates?

Obviously, the pandemic has changed commuting patterns dramatically. Using Google's Community Mobility Reports, we see how various types of trips have changed compared to a pre-pandemic baseline, which is the median value of the five-week period from January 03 to February 06, 2020, as shown in Figure 6. There is a dramatic reduction in the first weeks of the pandemic in March and April 2020, but then it has stabilized and remained between 40 and 50 percent below baseline levels since then.

When we look at pre-pandemic commuting patterns and case rates, we find a moderate correlation between the incidence of carpooling (0.53) but no correlation with the share commuting by public transit (−0.01). This non-existence of a relationship probably reflects the aggressive cleaning policies implemented by the Toronto Transit Commission (TTC) and the fact that transit vehicles were less crowded during the pandemic as the "nine-to-five" cohort worked from home.

We, however, find a significant positive correlation between case rates and the duration of commute, as shown in Figure 7 below. A 10 percent increase in the share of the labor force reporting commuting times more than one hour was correlates with an

---

[xi]Statistics Canada, 2016 Census of Population, Statistics Canada Catalogue No. 98-400-X2016298.

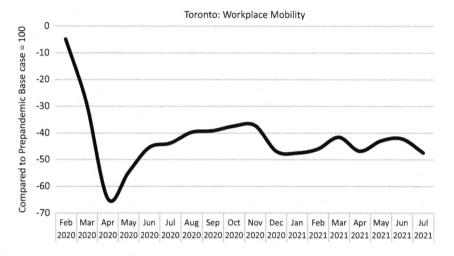

Figure 6.   Toronto's workplace mobility.
Source: Google Community Mobility Reports.

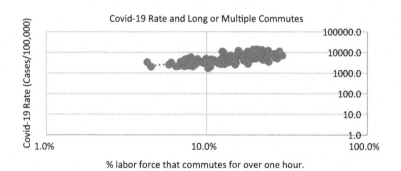

Figure 7.   Covid-19 case rates and long or multiple commutes.
Source: City of Toronto.

8.5 percent increase in Covid-19 case rates, and this explains 52 percent of the variation. There are two possible conclusions: Firstly, it is not the commuting mode that is the issue but vehicle occupancy and secondly, the commuting duration may have been capturing the aggregate duration of several shorter commutes by people holding more than one job. Statistics Canada report that 5.7 percent of

Canadian workers hold more than one job simultaneously but the share was higher in some of the industries that we have described as "high touch". For example, 8.7 percent of workers in the health and social assistance field hold multiple jobs while 6.8 percent in accommodation and food services do so.[xii] This exposes individuals to more customers, colleagues and varying efficacies of Covid-19 workplace prevention measures.

The incidence of people with no fixed workplace is also correlated with higher case rates while the share of people normally commuting between 0600 and 0900 hours are negatively correlated, presumably because a large proportion of these "nine-to-fivers" were working from home.

We also observe a moderate negative correlation (-0.62) between after-tax household income and commuting times, so lower income earners are associated with longer or multiple commutes.

There has been relatively little research on the commuting patterns of multiple job holders. But Hirsch *et al.* (2017) observed that commuting was a fixed cost of employment and hours worked at second jobs were fewer. So, the relative costs of commuting were high in second jobs, leading to riskier options such as a shared vehicle.

1.2.6. *Dwelling Characteristics*

1.2.6.1. Institutional living

We find a relationship between share of the neighborhood population living in institutions, as opposed to private dwellings, during the first wave of Covid-19, approximately from January to June 2020. During this time period, long-term care (LTC) homes were badly affected, but remedial measures since, and priority vaccination for LTC residents, means that more recently there was no longer a correlation.

[xii]Statistics Canada, Labor Force Survey, Tables 14-10-0044-01 and 14-10-0023-01.

1.2.6.2. Overcrowding

We know that Covid-19 spread when people were in close proximity but this has not been an urban density problem. In fact, there was no correlation between case rates and persons per acre (-0.15). Nor was there a relationship with the type of housing stock. For example, the correlation between case rates and the share of dwellings in apartment buildings was -0.04. The latter was surprising given the common facilities such as elevators, laundry rooms and lobbies. However, masks were mandated early in the pandemic and most buildings stepped up their cleaning protocols.

We did find a positive correlation between overcrowded accommodation, measured as the share of households with more than one person per room, as shown in Figure 8. This aligned with the public health advice that prolonged exposure to an infected person in close quarters increased the risk of contracting the virus. A 10 percent increase in the share of households experiencing overcrowding was correlated with a 4.3 percent increase in case rate. This explained 57 percent of the variation between neighborhoods.

In contrast, there was a moderate negative correlation (-0.41) between case rates and the percentage of households living alone.

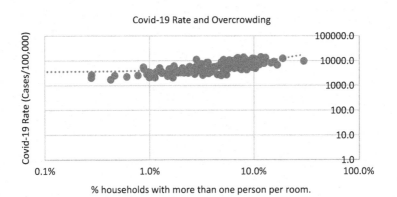

Figure 8. Covid-19 case rates and overcrowding.

Source: City of Toronto.

1.2.6.3. Social housing

Toronto Community Housing Corporation (TCHC) is a municipally owned corporation which serves as the public housing agency in Toronto. It is the largest social housing provider in Canada and the second largest in North America, owning and managing approximately 60,000 rental housing units in over 2,100 buildings.

There is only a weak correlation (0.27) between the incidence of social housing, measured as TCHC units as a share of total dwellings, and Covid-19 case rates,[xiii] as shown in Figure 9. But there is a slight upward trend in neighborhoods where more than 20 percent of the dwelling units were social housing. Also, when we compare incidence of social housing with overcrowding, there is only a weak correlation, so overcrowding would appear to be associated with private dwelling units.

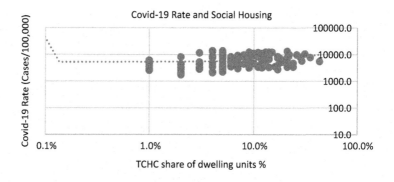

Figure 9.   Covid-19 and social housing.

Source: City of Toronto.

[xiii]This dataset contains unit density profiles of Social Housing in the City of Toronto for the 140 neighborhoods that make up the City of Toronto. For Reference Period 2014: Social housing units including Toronto Community Housing Corporation locations, Housing Connections locations, non-profits and co-op developments participating in the Social Housing Wait List. Social Housing Unit Density by Neighborhoods — City of Toronto Open Data Portal.

1.2.6.4. Specific neighborhoods

Humbermede was the neighborhood with the highest Covid-19 case rate of 13,959 per 100,000, or 2.3 times the city average. While it had above-average scores on the three significant variables that explain differences in case rates, long commutes, overcrowding and employment in high-touch industries, it was not the worst performer in the city in any of those categories. In other words, there may well have been unforeseen interactions between these forces or locally specific characteristics that cause this. For example, one thing this study has not captured is the mobility of neighborhood residents during the pandemic. Based on some of the research by Almagro *et al.* (2021) in New York City, it is possible that residents of Humbermede were more mobile than most.

Visiting the area, there were visual cues to this, including large private apartment complexes and signs at bus stops offering shared accommodation and advertisements for manual labor (see the photographs in Appendix 1).

Looking at some of the other neighborhoods with high Covid-19 rates, one may be struck by how heterogeneous they were. For example, the Maple Leaf neighborhood, bounded by Keele Street, Lawrence Avenue, Culford Road and Highway 401, was a mix of single-family bungalows and some large rental apartment complexes. Likewise, in Humber Heights–Westmount, there were single-family homes along Scarlett Road but a cluster of apartment blocks at Lawrence Avenue and Weston Road. In other words, there were probably significant differences in Covid-19 rates within Toronto's 140 neighborhoods, as well as between them.

2. Summary

In summary, the best multi-variable model combines the share of the labor force in high-touch industries, incidence of overcrowded dwellings and incidence of long-duration commutes. Collectively, these explain 66 percent of the variation in Covid-19 case rates between neighborhoods in Toronto.[xiv] These results are broadly consistent with those found in New York City.

3. Public Policy Implications

Clearly, the largest coefficient is the share of labor force in high-touch industries and, by extension, a higher probability of being a multiple job holder. Public health measures targeted at preventing the spread of Covid-19 in workplaces in these industries was an obvious priority. In terms of ameliorating overcrowding in the short-term, there were about 36,000 hotel rooms in the Greater Toronto Area (GTA)[xv] and at the height of the third wave of the pandemic in April 2021, 64 percent of them were empty.[xvi] So, making these 23,000 hotel rooms available to those living in overcrowded dwellings or undertaking long-duration commutes could help reduce the spread of the virus, as well as support employment in the hotel industry. To put these numbers into some context, approximately 110,000 people lived in the five neighborhoods with the highest Covid-19 rates. So, these empty hotel rooms could provide respite for the 20 percent of those residents who undertook lengthy or multiple commutes or lived in an overcrowded dwelling.[xvii] In long-term, it would appear that greater regulation of overcrowding in private accommodation may be required.

4. Conclusion

Pandemics have a differential impact on neighborhoods in cities goes back thousands of years. In terms of housing and transportation, the key variables explaining differences in Covid-19 case rates between

---

[xiv]See Appendix 2.
[xv]Member Benefits & Resources | Greater Toronto Hotel Association (gtha.com).
[xvi]Current Performance (mtc-currentperformance.com).
[xvii]The incidence of overcrowded dwellings and long duration commuting is 21 percent and 12 percent respectively.

neighborhoods in the City of Toronto are employment in high-touch industries, commuting in a shared car and/or undertaking long-duration or multiple commutes or living in an overcrowded dwelling. Because the demand for travel has evaporated, a public policy response would be to make available some of the thousands of empty hotel rooms to people at higher risk of contracting Covid-19, because of these housing and transportation characteristics.

Appendix 1

Humbermede

Source: Author.

Source: Author.

Source: Author.

Appendix 2

Dependent Variable: LOGCASESPERCAP			
Method: Least Squares			
Sample: 1 140			
Included observations: 139			
Variable	Coefficient	Std. Error	t-Statistic	Prob.
---	---	---	---	---
C	10.82928	0.206922	52.33516	0.0000
LOG(HIGH-TOUCHSHARE)	0.881183	0.317437	2.775929	0.0063
LOGMORE-THAN1PERROOM	0.190001	0.052734	3.603025	0.0004
LOGCOMMU-TINGMORETHAN1HR	0.315080	0.093502	3.369764	0.0010
R-squared	0.664915	Mean dependent var	8.576396
Adjusted R-squared	0.657469	S.D. dependent var	0.514434
S.E. of regression	0.301079	Akaike info criterion	0.465464
Sum squared reside	12.23753	Schwarz criterion	0.549910
Log likelihood	−28.34978	Hannan-Quinn criter.	0.499781
F-statistic	89.29432	Durbin-Watson stat	1.839441
Prob(F-statistic)	0.000000		

References

Almagro, M., Coven, J., Gupta, A., and Orane-Hutchinson, A. (2021). Disparities in COVID-19 Risk Exposure: Evidence from Geolocation Data. *NYU Stern School of Business Forthcoming*.

Cohen, J.P., Friedt, F.L., and Lautier, J.P. (2021). The Impact of the Coronavirus Pandemic on New York City Real Estate: First Evidence. *Journal of Regional Science*, *62*(3), 858–888.

Cummins, N., Kelly, M., and Ó Gráda, C. (2016). Living Standards and Plague in London, 1560–1665. *Economic History Review*, *69*(1), 3–34.

Hirsch, B.T., Husain, M.M., and Winters, J.V. (2017). The Puzzling Pattern of Multiple Job Holding Across U.S. Labor Markets. *Southern Economic Journal*, *84*(1), 26–51.

Lamb, M.R., Kandula, S., and Shaman, J. (2021). Differential COVID-19 Case Positivity in New York City Neighborhoods: Socioeconomic Factors and Mobility. *Influenza Other Respir Viruses*, *15*(2), 209–217.

Martínez, L.E., Bustamante, A., Balderas-Medina Anaya, Y., Domínguez-Villegas, R., Santizo-Greendwood, S., Diaz, S.F.M., and Hayes-Bautista, D. (2020). COVID-19 in Vulnerable Communities: An Examination by Race/Ethnicity in Los Angeles and New York City. *UCLA: Latino Policy & Politics Initiative.*

Chapter 6

Estimation of a Production Function Model of Driving Knowledge

Andrew M. Welki

Department of Economic and Finance,
John Carroll University, USA.

Thomas J. Zlatoper

Department of Economic and Finance,
John Carroll University, USA.

This chapter formulates and estimates a model that explains driving knowledge demonstrated by performance on a written drivers test. The specified model takes the form of an educational production function. Performance measures used in its estimation come from a unique dataset, the GMAC Insurance National Drivers Test. The model is estimated by linear regression on the annual US state-level data for the years 2005 to 2010. Performance on the written drivers test is found to have statistically significant positive relationships with the following: the cumulative effects of three regulations on the driving activities of new motorists (supervision of novice drivers for six months by an adult licensed driver, supervised driving of novice drivers for 30 to 50 hours, and restrictions on the number of teenage passengers); the ratio of rural to urban vehicle-miles; the percentage of high school graduates; the percentage of young male drivers; and the percentage of old female drivers. Exam performance is found to have statistically significant negative associations with the following: the percentage of young female drivers, the percentage of old male drivers, and per capita income. There are statistically significant differences in test performance across years and regions of the country.

1. Introduction

Recent research indicates that greater driving knowledge enhances road safety. Simmons *et al.* (2016) report that such knowledge — as measured by performance on a written US national drivers test — has a statistically significant life-saving effect, controlling for a representative set of other motor vehicle death determinants. This evidence suggests that requiring passage of a written test as a condition for obtaining a driver's license has merit from a safety perspective.[i] It also implies that efforts that improve test performance could lead to fewer highway fatalities.

To our knowledge, there has been no research on factors that influence results on written drivers tests. This chapter attempts to fill that void by formulating and estimating a model that explains performance on such tests. The specified model takes the form of an educational production function. Performance measures used in this estimation come from a unique dataset, the GMAC Insurance National Drivers Test.

This chapter is structured as follows: The second section reviews research pertaining to the general construct known as the educational production function and notes how this formulation can be adapted to explain performance on a written drivers test. A particular model of test performance is specified in the third section. The fourth section describes the data used to estimate the model. Regression estimates of the model are discussed in the fifth section. The final section provides a summary.

2. Literature Review

Learning to drive an automobile is an educational process requiring both a knowledge base of laws and a set of physical operating abilities. The model developed in this chapter includes factors that

---

[i]The Insurance Institute for Highway Safety (2016) notes: "License renewal procedures vary from state to state but tend to follow the same pattern. Initial applicants are generally required to provide proof of identity and take vision, written and road tests."

affect the educational process associated with the knowledge base component. It draws upon the framework of educational production functions.

The Coleman Report (Coleman *et al.* (1966)) initiated the study of the linkage between school resources and achievement. Traditional microeconomic theory provided a conceptual framework, the production function, as a method of analysis. Production functions link outputs to a set of inputs. Bowles (1970) provided a thorough explanation of a production function in an educational setting. His paper, written not long after the Coleman Report, included a statistical analysis and set the stage for a large body of subsequent empirical research. In the educational context, a measure of school output is a function of: variables associated with the school environment; variables associated with environmental factors outside of school that affect learning; and variables specific to a student and her/his initial knowledge level.

Hanushek (1986) summarized much of the early findings associated with the estimation of educational production functions. This research was motivated by a desire to provide better policy prescriptions for educational attainment. Hanushek (2010) updated the body of evidence in developed countries resulting from the estimation of educational production functions. He described what we know about school inputs and educational attainment and concluded the following:

> The existing research suggests inefficiency in the provision of schooling. It does not indicate that schools do not matter. Nor does it indicate that money and resources never impact achievement. The accumulated research surrounding estimation of education production functions simply says there currently is no clear, systematic relationship between resources and student outcomes. At the same time, more modern research into the determinants of student achievement strongly indicates that teacher-quality differences are the most significant part of differences across schools. (Hanushek, 2010, p. 410).

Academic achievement measures take various forms including standardized scores, attendance rates, and student attitudes to name a few. In addition, in the human capital literature (e.g., Becker, 2009), wages and/or income become output measures with schooling, training, socioeconomic characteristics and other variables serving as the inputs in such production processes.

The school-related institutional inputs consist of factors associated with the educational institution and its personnel and often result from policy decisions. They include teacher characteristics, teacher experience levels (e.g., Rivkin *et al.*, 2005; Acuña and Blacklock, 2022), curriculum, teacher/student ratios (e.g., Krueger, 1999; Krueger and Whitmore, 2001) and so forth. These attributes frame and describe the learning environment a student experiences in a school setting. Often, empirical analyses attempt to quantify the effectiveness of institutional inputs in order to make informed policy decisions.

In the educational production function literature, family background and circumstances also impact the student learning environment (e.g., Boonk *et al.*, 2018; Barrera-Osorio *et al.*, 2020). Family members can place different levels of emphasis on educational achievement and serve as role models for a student. Further, family members can support school activities at home by offering homework assistance, study habit development, and positive reinforcement for educational activities. Finally, depending on income level, family members can provide supplemental resources to assist student learning.

As a counterpart to the contribution of the family, an individual's ability to learn is affected by classmates (e.g., Chen *et al.*, 2020; Wilson *et al.*, 2011). A student's classroom peers frame the learning environment in the school. Highly motivated, supportive peers can create spillover benefits to others in the class. The student peers in a school classroom offer positive (or negative) contributions analogous, to some degree, to the family in the home setting.

Students differ in innate abilities. Individuals with greater intellectual capability are better equipped, and more likely, to demonstrate higher levels of academic achievement (e.g., Mammadov, 2022; Costa and Faria, 2018). One anticipates this will happen independent of the other inputs in the production process.

The previously identified inputs — school inputs, student peer attributes, family background, and innate ability — interact at a point in time to create educational output. However, learning is a cumulative process (e.g., Maton, 2009; Ferrante, 2017). In a traditional school setting, the learning that occurs in grade 3, for example, depends on the skill set and knowledge base a student developed in grades 1 and 2. In each school year, students do not arrive as blank slates. Rather, educational achievement is measured at the end of a school year by the sum of what a student knew at the beginning of the year plus what was learned during the year.

This chapter applies the education production approach to the area of highway safety, more specifically the knowledge base associated with the drivers test to acquire a license.[ii] While drivers tests have both written and driving portions, this chapter focuses solely on the written portion. Applicants can be denied a driver's license if they fail either the written or the driving portion of the test.

This chapter specifies a model in which highway law knowledge for the state's driving population depends on — the driver's education process, innate learning abilities, and the influence of family and peers. These three factors interact to produce how well a driver license applicant understands the materials tested on the written driver's exam.

Unlike a traditional K-12 educational setting, students preparing for their driving test have limited institutional structure. License candidates have a variety of preparation choices such as private driving schools, driving courses taught in high schools, or relying upon family members and friends. In addition, the availability of these options changes over time. Drivers currently 65 years of age or older probably learned to drive under different conditions than the conditions of drivers 16–20 years old today.

Each state identifies the conditions under which a driver's license is granted. Prescribed activities and experiences try to ensure that qualified applicants master a variety of skills related to driving

---

[ii]The written portion of a drivers test assesses a prospective driver's understanding of a body of laws and rules. To be judged worthy of a driver's license, applicants must demonstrate mastery of a satisfactory level of this body of information. The written portion of the drivers test is analogous to a statewide test administered to a particular grade level in a K-12 setting.

conditions and also possess the knowledge that promotes safer driving. Both physical skills and knowledge base improve the driver's quality.

One can anticipate the temporary license driving requirements are a supplement to the text and print materials designed to teach the applicant the laws of the road. Supervised driving times, for instance, permit conversations about decision-making, speed limits, and safe driving distances among other things. These actual experiences can reinforce print materials and engage other learning styles of the applicant.

States are at different levels of a graduated driving licensing process (GDL).[iii] This program moves young drivers through three stages before granting a license with full privileges. The first stage (learner's stage) involves a six-month holding period and adult supervised driving. The intermediate stage involves unsupervised driving with nighttime and passenger restrictions. A full privilege license is the final stage. Not all states have laws mandating all parts of all stages.

Any knowledge base effects associated with the driving preparation requirements will take time to manifest themselves in the entire driving population. A policy implemented in 2013, for example, only impacts a small subset of actual drivers trained under that set of requirements. A particular requirement enacted long ago will affect a larger proportion of that state's drivers. The effects of policy changes accumulate over time as more of the driving population become subject to the modified requirements.

The innate abilities of the prospective driver should also affect success on the written portion of the driver's test. One anticipates students with better reading skills, memories, comprehension skills, and disciplined study habits will adapt those traits to the driver's test. Skills that demonstrate a better ability to succeed in the K-12 educational environment should translate to greater mastery of driving laws, rules, and regulations.

[iii]See the Insurance Institute for Highway Safety (2012).

Consistent with the educational production function literature, family and peers can supplement an individual applicant's efforts. Family members may be actively engaged in the on-road experience. Additionally, family may discuss road rules, quiz the applicant about the laws, and also create a positive learning environment for the test taker.

Peers to the applicant can provide support analogous to that offered by the family members. They can motivate, challenge, encourage, study with, and in general reinforce the activities of the family support groups. One can imagine friends pushing each other, in a competitive way, to succeed on both the written and driving portions of the driver's test.

Every state takes ownership of its own driving license process including its test. A part of all driver license tests is a written portion covering knowledge of laws and rules specific to that state. Despite state-to-state variation, a body of knowledge is common to all tests. A test of that common body of laws and rules — the GMAC Insurance National Drivers Test — is utilized in this chapter.

3. Model

As noted previously, the model of this chapter is an educational production function. The output of interest — driving knowledge — is presumed to depend on inputs that influence individuals' mastery of driving laws, rules and regulations. The general functional form of the model is:

Driving Knowledge = f(Driver Education, Driver Abilities,

Driver Influencers)   (1)

where

Driving Knowledge = performance on a written drivers test

Driver Education = driver education process

Driver Abilities = driver innate learning abilities

Driver Influencers = influences of family and peers.

The right-side factors in Equation (1) represent categorical determinants of mastery of driving laws, rules and regulations, as measured by performance on a written drivers test. Driver Education consists of elements that shape the environment in which an individual obtains driving knowledge. Among other things, these include driving regulations and conditions imposed on individuals seeking drivers' licenses. Driver Abilities comprise general learning skills and habits that influence an individual's mastery of knowledge pertaining to driving. Driver Influencers include actions by an individual's family and peers that affect the mastery.

4. Data

This chapter utilizes data that the General Motors Acceptance Corporation (GMAC) collected in an online survey conducted from 2005 to 2011. The survey, known as the GMAC Insurance National Drivers Test, consisted of 20 multiple choice questions on general driving safety rules.[iv] The questions were drawn from actual written drivers tests administered by departments of motor vehicles of each state. State- or region-specific questions were not included, so the GMAC survey results should provide a comparable measure of driving knowledge across the US. Survey results were reported for the 50 individual states and the District of Columbia. This chapter utilizes survey data from 2005 to 2010 because data on some of the non-survey variables were unavailable for 2011. (GMAC Insurance, 2011).

For estimation purposes, the dependent variable Driving Knowledge in Equation (1) is measured by two alternate values. One of the values is TESTAVG, the average score for a state's respondents on the GMAC Insurance National Drivers Test. Each of the 20 questions on the test was worth five points, so an individual respondent could achieve a score ranging from zero to 100. Driving Knowledge is

---

[iv]The sample for the 2011 GMAC Insurance National Drivers Test consisted of 5,130 respondents who were licensed drivers of ages 16–65 years. It included 100 or more respondents from each U.S. state and the District of Columbia and was weighted to be representative of the U.S. population. (GMAC Insurance, 2011).

alternately measured by TESTRANK, the numerical ranking of an individual state's TESTAVG score. These rankings range from one for the state with the highest TESTAVG figure to 51 for the state with the lowest figure. The source for the values of TESTAVG and TESTRANK is GMAC Insurance (2011).

The category Driver Education in Equation (1) includes factors that form the environment in which an individual learns driving laws and rules. Regulations on driving activities of new motorists are examples of such factors. Some states require one or more of the following: that novice drivers be supervised by an adult licensed driver for six months; that novice drivers have 30 to 50 hours of supervised driving; that unsupervised teenage nighttime driving be restricted; and that the number of teenage passengers be restricted. The dummy variables 6MONTH, SUPER, NIGHT, and PASSRES are equal to one when a state has the relevant requirement and are equal to zero in the absence of the requirement. The number of previous years that the relevant requirements were in effect are measured by the variables YRS6MONTH, YRSSUPER, YRSNIGHT, and YRSPASSRES. The source for the information on the four regulations is the Insurance Institute for Highway Safety (2012). Location is another factor that might influence an individual's learning environment. RURURB (the ratio of rural to urban vehicle-miles) accounts for this. The information on vehicle-miles comes from the Federal Highway Administration (n.d.).

The category Driver Abilities in Equation (1) accounts for an individual's innate learning abilities. Several variables control for such abilities. HS (percent of persons 25 years old and over who attained high school graduation or more) is a measure of educational achievement. The source for this information is the *Statistical Abstract of the United States* (U.S. Census Bureau, n.d.). Four variables represent age and gender considerations: PCTYFDR (percent of registered drivers who are females aged 24 years or younger), PCTYMDR (percent of registered drivers who are males aged 24 years or younger), PCTOFDR (percent of registered drivers who are females aged 65 years or older), and PCTOMDR (percent of registered drivers who are males aged 65 years or older).

The source for the gender and age information is the Federal Highway Administration (n.d.).

The category Driver Influencers in Equation (1) represents the influence of family and peers on driver learning. RDSINPC (real disposable income per capita, in US dollars) serves as a proxy for this. This variable is calculated using the Bureau of Economic Analysis (2011) figures on total state nominal disposable income, the US Census Bureau (2011, 2014) state population values, and the Bureau of Labor Statistics' (2014) Consumer Price Index [base period: 1982–84] for all urban consumers.

To account for unobserved factors that are constant across geographical units but vary over time, the following dummy variables were utilized in the estimations: YEAR2005, YEAR2006, YEAR2007, YEAR2008, YEAR2009, and YEAR2010. Each variable equals one for the relevant year and zero for all other years. To account for unobserved factors that vary across geographical areas but are constant over time, the following dummy variables corresponding to the nine US Census Regions were used in the estimations: NEWENGL (New England), MDLATLAN (Middle Atlantic), ENOCNTRL (East North Central), WNOCNTRL (West North Central), SOUTHATL (South Atlantic), ESOCNTRL (East South Central), WSOCNTRL (West South Central), MOUNTAIN (Mountain), and PACIFIC (Pacific). The information used to construct these regional variables comes from the US Census Bureau (2010).

Table 1 provides descriptions and summary statistics for the variables used in this chapter. It is noteworthy that the mean score on the GMAC Insurance National Drivers Test is about 80, while the rank on the test averages around 25. Each of the four regulations on the driving activities of new motorists are effective in at least two-thirds of the cases, from a low of 68 percent of observations for PASSRES to a high of 89 percent for 6MONTH. Regulations requiring that novice drivers be supervised by adult drivers for six months (6MONTH), have 30 to 50 hours of supervised driving (SUPER), limit unsupervised nighttime driving (NIGHT), and limit teenage passengers (PASSRES) were on average in effect

Table 1. Variable descriptions and summary statistics.

Variable	Description	Mean	Std. Dev.
TESTAVG	State average score on GMAC Insurance National Drivers Test	79.61	3.94
TESTRANK	Ranking (from 1 for highest to 51 for lowest) of TESTAVG among the 50 US states and Washington, D.C.	25.11	14.46
6MONTH	Dummy variable for whether state requires novice drivers to be supervised by adult licensed drivers for six months (Yes = 1, No = 0)	0.89	0.31
SUPER	Dummy variable for whether state requires novice drivers to have 30 to 50 hours of supervised driving (Yes = 1, No = 0)	0.81	0.39
NIGHT	Dummy variable for whether state restricts unsupervised teenage nighttime driving (Yes = 1, No = 0)	0.82	0.39
PASSRES	Dummy variable for whether state restricts the number of teenage passengers (Yes = 1, No = 0)	0.68	0.47
YRS6MONTH	Number of previous years state requirement — that novice drivers be supervised by adult licensed drivers for six months — was in effect	6.41	3.92
YRSSUPER	Number of previous years state requirement — that novice drivers have 30 to 50 hours of supervised driving — was in effect	5.11	3.79
YRSNIGHT	Number of previous years state requirement — that restricts unsupervised teenage nighttime driving — was in effect	6.00	5.41
YRSPASSRES	Number of previous years state requirement — that restricts the number of teenage passengers — was in effect	2.85	3.09
RURURB	Ratio of rural vehicle-miles to urban vehicle-miles	0.95	0.78
HS	Percent of persons 25 years old and over who attained high school graduation or more	86.68	3.61

Table 1. (*Continued*)

Variable	Description	Mean	Std. Dev.
PCTYFDR	Percent of registered drivers who are females aged 24 years or younger	6.66	0.98
PCTYMDR	Percent of registered drivers who are males aged 24 years or younger	6.84	0.98
PCTOFDR	Percent of registered drivers who are females aged 65 years or older	8.07	1.16
PCTOMDR	Percent of registered drivers who are males aged 65 years or older	7.53	0.91
RDSINPC	Real disposable income per capita, in US dollars [base period: 1982–84]	16,188.94	2,092.85
YEAR2005	Dummy variable equal to one if year is 2005 and equal to zero otherwise	0.16	0.37
YEAR2006	Dummy variable equal to one if year is 2006 and equal to zero otherwise	0.17	0.37
YEAR2007	Dummy variable equal to one if year is 2007 and equal to zero otherwise	0.17	0.37
YEAR2008	Dummy variable equal to one if year is 2008 and equal to zero otherwise	0.17	0.37
YEAR2009	Dummy variable equal to one if year is 2009 and equal to zero otherwise	0.17	0.37
YEAR2010	Dummy variable equal to one if year is 2010 and equal to zero otherwise	0.17	0.37
NEWENGL	Dummy variable equal to one if state's US Census Region is New England and equal to zero otherwise	0.12	0.33
MDLATLAN	Dummy variable equal to one if state's US Census Region is Middle Atlantic and equal to zero otherwise	0.06	0.24
ENOCNTRL	Dummy variable equal to one if state's US Census Region is East North Central and equal to zero otherwise	0.10	0.30
WNOCNTRL	Dummy variable equal to one if state's US Census Region is West North Central and equal to zero otherwise	0.14	0.35
SOUTHATL	Dummy variable equal to one if state's US Census Region is South Atlantic and equal to zero otherwise	0.16	0.37
ESOCNTRL	Dummy variable equal to one if state's US Census Region is East South Central and equal to zero otherwise	0.08	0.27

Table 1. (*Continued*)

Variable	Description	Mean	Std. Dev.
WSOCNTRL	Dummy variable equal to one if state's US Census Region is West South Central and equal to zero otherwise	0.08	0.27
MOUNTAIN	Dummy variable equal to one if state's US Census Region is Mountain and equal to zero otherwise	0.16	0.37
PACIFIC	Dummy variable equal to one if state's US Census Region is Pacific and equal to zero otherwise	0.09	0.29

for about six years, five years, six years, and three years, respectively. The mean value of RURURB of 0.95 suggests that urban travel tends to slightly exceed rural travel. On average, 87 percent of individuals 25 years old or over have at least graduated from high school. The mean percentages of both young female drivers and young males drivers are about seven; and the mean percentages of both old female drivers and old male drivers are about eight. Real disposable income per capita averages more than $16,000.

5. Estimation Results

Table 2 reports regression estimation results for two models. Both models have linear functional forms and include the same independent variables.[v] Alternate measures are used for the dependent variables — TESTAVG and TESTRANK. The amount of the variation in these dependent variables explained by the independent variables is 86 percent and 67 percent, respectively. Both of the models possess a statistically significant amount of explanatory power as their F-tests are significant at the 1 percent level of significance.

---

[v]The linear functional form in both models is $Y = \beta_0 + \beta_1 X_1 + \beta_2 X_2 + \cdots + \beta_k X_k + \varepsilon$, where Y is the dependent variable; $X_1, X_2, \ldots, X_k$ are independent variables; β_0 is the intercept; $\beta_1, \beta_2, \ldots, \beta_k$ are partial regression coefficients; and ε is the error term. In the regressions, ε is assumed to have a Normal distribution with mean of zero, constant variance, and zero covariance.

Table 2. Regression of driving knowledge production function for US, 2005–2010. The control category for the year variables is YEAR2005. The control category for the Census Divisions is New England (NEWENGL).

Dependent Variable	TESTAVG		TESTRANK	
	(1)		(2)	
Variables	Coefficient	t-stat	Coefficient	t-stat
Constant	56.84**	14.85	169.69**	7.84
6MONTH	−0.70*	−1.78	2.72	1.23
SUPER	0.08	0.22	0.53	0.25
NIGHT	0.10	0.26	−0.55	−0.26
PASSRES	0.25	0.65	−2.96	−1.39
YRS6MONTH	0.10**	2.90	−0.54**	−2.77
YRSSUPER	0.09**	2.30	−0.38*	−1.69
YRSNIGHT	−0.01	−0.38	0.10	0.69
YRSPASSRES	0.09*	1.87	−0.46*	−1.77
RURURB	0.87**	5.14	−5.06**	−5.28
HS	0.29**	6.09	−1.52**	−5.70
PCTYFDR	−1.27**	−2.33	7.86**	2.55
PCTYMDR	1.08**	1.98	−7.02**	−2.27
PCTOFDR	1.04**	3.70	−5.82**	−3.67
PCTOMDR	−0.96**	−3.07	5.81**	3.29
RDSINPC	-1.46×10^{-4}**	−2.12	5.56×10^{-4}	1.42
YEAR2006	0.07	0.21	2.16	1.21
YEAR2007	−6.58**	−19.66	1.73	0.91
YEAR2008	−5.46**	−15.44	3.75*	1.87
YEAR2009	−7.43**	−19.54	5.34**	2.48
YEAR2010	−7.32**	−17.67	6.93**	2.96
MDLATLAN	−0.48	−0.89	−2.51	−0.82
ENOCNTRL	2.88**	5.98	−17.28**	−6.34
WNOCNTRL	3.82**	7.81	−22.86**	−8.26
SOUTHATL	2.48**	5.84	−12.04**	−5.01
ESOCNTRL	3.13**	5.38	−15.62**	−4.75
WSOCNTRL	4.00**	6.81	−19.85**	−5.97
MOUNTAIN	3.95**	8.56	−22.06**	−8.46
PACIFIC	4.34**	8.35	−23.05**	−7.84
Observations	298		298	
R-squared	0.861		0.668	
Adjusted R-squared	0.846		0.634	
Prob (F-statistic)	0.00		0.00	

Notation: **indicates significance at 5 percent level, *indicates significance at 10 percent level.

Changes in the driver education process could influence the knowledge level of the driving population in two ways. A change in the process could immediately affect someone who is preparing for their initial driver's license test. The second way is that any process changes will have a cumulative effect. The longer a particular change is in effect, the larger the proportion of the driving population that experienced that requirement. The impacts of the driver education process on the level of the driver knowledge occur primarily through the cumulative effects of the different components.

Multiple parts of the driver education process demonstrate a cumulative ability to raise driver knowledge levels. The six-month preparation period (YRS6MONTH), the supervised driving component (YRSSUPER), and the passenger restrictions (YRSPASSRES) all reveal statistically significant positive coefficients. The more years that pass from the initial implementation of a process change increases the proportion of drivers who benefit from the changes, raising the overall driver knowledge level on the roads.

For both dependent variables, TESTAVG and TESTRANK, the coefficients associated with those accumulation effect variables display the anticipated signs and are significant at the 10 percent or less level. Under supervision, the aspiring driver benefits from the mentorship, conversation, and guidance of the licensed driver during the road time. Real road conditions can familiarize the potential test taker with speed limits and reinforce other rules and regulations specified in the test preparation materials. The combination of theory and practices deepens one's knowledge base. The six-month period permits time to reinforce the learning process with potentially repeated experiences. The passenger restrictions create minimal distractions in the car while driving, which can permit the pre-full privilege driver to concentrate better and better assimilate the experiential piece of preparation with the subject materials component.

For the immediate impact process variables, all but 6MONTH have the anticipated signs in the TESTAVG model. None are statistically significant. The 6MONTH variable negatively affects TESTAVG and is significant. It is unclear what the length of the process is for states without a specified duration.

The location and diversity of driving conditions a driver learns under should contribute to a better prepared driver. In addition, the necessity to be a licensed driver may be stronger in rural areas than in urban areas. In urban areas, mass transit options are more abundant and provide a reasonable transportation option to driving. The incentive and need for a driving license are probably stronger, other things constant, in a rural area. The coefficient for RURURB, the ratio of rural to urban vehicle-miles is statistically significant in both models at the 5 percent level of significance.

A driver's innate learning abilities contribute to performance on the driving knowledge test. States with higher proportions of high school graduates have higher averages on the drivers knowledge test and those states rank higher. One anticipates a more educated population and a population with stronger academic abilities, especially at the age the drivers test is typically taken, will perform better on the test. The HS variable supports this. Its coefficient is statistically significant in both models.

Both the age distribution and the composition of the driving population by gender affect performance on the drivers knowledge test. While it is reasonable to believe physical driving skills and situational awareness improve with more driving, as more time passes between the age one typically acquires one's driving license and the driver's current age, it is unclear what will happen to the driver's command of the rules and regulations associated with the test.

For males and females, the effect of age on driver knowledge is different. For females, TESTAVG is lower and TESTRANK is higher for young women drivers. That behavior pattern reverses, that is, TESTAVG increases and TESTRANK is lower as the proportion of older women drivers on the road increases. Young male drivers reveal more driver knowledge earlier and the amount decreases as the male drivers age. In the TESTAVG model, the coefficient is positive for PCTYMDR and negative for PCTOMDR. It is unclear why the patterns differ by gender. All of the coefficients for the composition of the driving population by age and gender are statistically significant at the 5 percent level of significance.

It is plausible to believe as drivers age from young to old, they never revisit any of the rules and regulations associated with the original test. In addition, this test knowledge pattern may reflect differences in maturation rates; differences in the amount of driving done by one group relative to the other as stages of life and family circumstances change; who is the primary driver in households; among other possible explanations.

As per capita income rises, TESTAVG falls. The coefficient of RDSINPC is negative and statistically significant. As income levels rise, so does the opportunity cost of time. This may affect the choice of mode of transportation for travel and leisure. Less time spent on driving could diminish the familiarity with that knowledge base as it is used less, other things held constant.

Demonstrated driver knowledge on the drivers test has decreased over time. The coefficients on the year dummy variables (YEAR2007, YEAR2008, YEAR2009, and YEAR2010) are all statistically significant and negative. This suggests the average scores in those years were lower than in the base year of 2005.

Test performance differs dramatically across the regions of the country. Relative to the base region, the New England Census Division, the Mid-Atlantic region performs more poorly, albeit the coefficient is not statistically significant. The seven other census regions, all have average scores higher than New England, and every coefficient is statistically significant. It is clear that driver knowledge varies widely depending upon where the person is driving. This may reflect the importance of driving to meet transportation needs in different parts of the country, among other things.

6. Conclusion

The level of driver knowledge on the roads is influenced by driver education, driver abilities, and driver influencers. States specify the circumstances that prepare aspiring test takers who seek driving privileges. States with Graduated Driving Licenses (GDL) prescribe preparation periods, supervised driving conditions, night driving experiences, and passenger restrictions. The cumulative effects of the six-month driving period, the supervised driving experience, and passenger restrictions all increase the level of driver knowledge. In addition, driver knowledge increases with more driving experience in rural situations as compared to urban situations.

The innate ability of the driver also raises the level of driver knowledge. As the percentage of high school graduates in a state increases, so does the driver knowledge in the state.

The composition of the driving population affects the driving knowledge in a state. Both the age and the gender of the drivers matter. Male driver knowledge appears to decrease over time, while the pattern for females is the opposite.

As of 2021, all states and the District of Columbia currently have some form of GDL system. The systems and conditions vary widely across the states. Policymakers should consider standardizing the systems nationally at the best practice levels associated with the various components. Additionally, it would be beneficial to regularly collect state level data, across all states, on the common body of knowledge expected of every driver. At the present, the level of driver knowledge can vary widely, and one would anticipate it to affect the driving safety.

References

Acuña, K., and Blacklock, P.J. (2022). Mastery Teachers: How to Build Success for Each Student in Today's Classrooms. *Journal of Higher Education Theory and Practice*, *22*(1), 136–140. https://doi.org/10.33423/jhetp.v22i1.4970.

Barrera-Osorio, F., Gertler, P., Nakajima, N., and Patrinos, H. (2020). *Promoting Parental Involvement in Schools: Evidence from Two Randomized Experiments*. National Bureau of Economic Research. https://doi.org/10.3386/w28040.

Becker, G.S. (2009). *Human Capital: A Theoretical and Empirical Analysis, with Special Reference to Education*. The University of Chicago Press, Chicago.

Boonk, L., Gijselaers, H.J., Ritzen, H., and Brand-Gruwel, S. (2018). A Review of the Relationship Between Parental Involvement Indicators and Academic Achievement. *Educational Research Review*, *24*, 10–30. https://doi.org/10.1016/j.edurev.2018.02.001.

Bowles, S. (1970). Towards an Educational Production Function. In Lee, W.H. (Ed.), *Education, Income, and Human Capital* (pp. 11–70). National Bureau of Economic Research, MA.

Chen, X., Saafir, A., and Graham, S. (2020). Ethnicity, Peers, and Academic Achievement: Who Wants to be Friends with the Smart Kids? *Journal of Youth and Adolescence*, *49*(5), 1030–1042. https://doi.org/10.1007/s10964-019-01189-7.

Coleman, J.S., Campbell, E.Q., Hobson, C.J., McPartland, J., Mood, A.M., Weinfeld, F.D., and York, R.L. (1966). *Equality of Educational Opportunity*. US Government Printing Office, Washington, D.C,.

Costa, A., and Faria, L. (2018 June 5). Implicit Theories of Intelligence and Academic Achievement: A Meta-Analytic Review. *Frontiers in Psychology*, *9*, 829. https://doi.org/10.3389/fpsyg.2018.00829.

Federal Highway Administration, U.S. Department of Transportation. (n.d.). *Highway Statistics*. https://www.fhwa.dot.gov/policyinforma statistics.cfm.

Ferrante, F. (2017). Assessing Quality in Higher Education: Some Caveats. *Social Indicators Research*, *131*(2), 727–743. https://doi.org/ 10.1007/s11205-016-1267-8.

GMAC Insurance. (2011). *2011 GMAC Insurance National Drivers Test*. http://www.gmacinsurance.com/SafeDriving/ (accessed March 2014).

Hanushek, E.A. (1986). The Economics of Schooling: Production and Efficiency in Public Schools. *Journal of Economic Literature*, *24*(3), 1141–1177. https://www.jstor.org/stable/2725865.

Hanushek, E.A. (2010). Education Production Functions: Developed Country Evidence. In Peterson, P. (Ed.), *International Encyclopedia of Education* (pp. 407–411). Elsevier, Amsterdam. https://doi.org/10.1 016/B978-0-08-044894-7.01231-8.

Insurance Institute for Highway Safety, Highway Loss Data Institute. (2012). *Effective Dates of Graduated Licensing Laws*. http:// www.iihs.org/laws/pdf_effective_dates.pdf (accessed December 2012).

Insurance Institute for Highway Safety, Highway Loss Data Institute. (2016). Older Drivers. http://www.iihs.org/iihs/topics/laws/older drivers (accessed August 2016).

Krueger, A.B. (1999). Experimental Estimates of Education Production Functions. *The Quarterly Journal of Economics*, *114*(2), 497–532. https://doi.org/10.1162/003355399556052.

Krueger, A.B., and Whitmore, D.M. (2001). The Effect of Attending a Small Class in the Early Grades on College-Test Taking and Middle School Test Results: Evidence from Project STAR. *The Economic Journal*, *111*(468), 1–28. https://doi.org/10.1111/1468-0297.00586.

Mammadov, S. (2022). Big Five Personality Traits and Academic Performance: A Meta-Analysis. *Journal of Personality, 90*(2), 222–255. https://doi.org/10.1111/jopy.12663.

Maton, K. (2009). Cumulative and Segmented Learning: Exploring the Role of Curriculum Structures in Knowledge-Building. *British Journal of Sociology of Education, 30*(1), 43–57. https://doi.org/10.1080/01425690802514342.

Rivkin, S.G., Hanushek, E.A., and Kain, J.F. (2005). Teachers, Schools, and Academic Achievement. *Econometrica, 73*(2), 417–458. https://doi.org/10.1111/j.1468-0262.2005.00584.x.

Simmons, W.O., Welki, A.M., and Zlatoper, T.J. (2016) The Impact of Driving Knowledge on Motor Vehicle Fatalities. *Journal of the Transportation Research Forum, 55*(1), 17–27. https://doi.org/10.5399/osu/jtrf.55.1.4337

U.S. Census Bureau. (n.d.). *Statistical Abstract of the United States.* https://www.census.gov/library/publications/time-series/statistical_abstracts.html (accessed July 2021).

U.S. Census Bureau. (2010). *Geographic Terms and Concepts — Census Divisions and Census Regions.* https://www.census.gov/geo/reference/gtc/gtc_census_divreg.html (accessed July 2014).

U.S. Census Bureau. (2011). *Annual Estimates of the Resident Population for the United States, Regions, States, and Puerto Rico: April 1, 2000 to July 1, 2009* (NST-EST2009–01). http://www.census.gov/popest/data/historical/2000s/vintage_2009/index.html (accessed June 2011).

U.S. Census Bureau. (2014). *2010 Census.* http://www.census.gov/2010census/ (accessed July 2014).

U.S. Department of Commerce, Bureau of Economic Analysis. (2011). *SA51–53 Disposable Personal Income Summary.* http://www.bea.gov/iTable/iTable.cfm?reqid=70&step=1&isuri=1&acrdn=4#reqid=70&step=30&isuri=1&7028=1&7040=1&7083=levels&7031=0&7022=21&7023=0&7024=nonindustry&7025=0&7026=01000&7027=2012&7001=421&7029=23&7090=70&7033=-1 (accessed June 2011).

U.S. Department of Labor, Bureau of Labor Statistics. (2014). *Consumer Price Index — All Urban Consumers.* http://www.bls.gov/ (accessed July 2014).

Wilson, T., Karimpour, R., and Rodkin, P.C. (2011). African American and European American Students' Peer Groups During Early Adolescence: Structure, Status, and Academic Achievement. *The Journal of Early Adolescence, 31*(1), 74–98. https://doi.org/10.1177/0272431610387143.

Chapter 7

Allocative Efficiency in the US Air Cargo Industry

Zoe Laulederkind

*Economics Department,
University of Wisconsin-Milwaukee, USA*

James H. Peoples, Jr.

*Economics Department,
University of Wisconsin-Milwaukee, USA*

Providing affordable service is critical to the success of air cargo companies, especially given the potential in the increase of competition from airline companies in the passenger service sector. Operating efficiently is key to offering an affordable service in this increasingly competitive business environment. This study estimates a cost function specified to include shadow input prices as an approach to examine whether air cargo carriers have been able to satisfy allocative efficiency. Findings suggest that the US all-cargo air companies use an allocatively efficient combination of labor and fuel as well as an allocatively efficient combination of labor and other nonlabor inputs. Findings do uncover that all-cargo air companies use an allocatively inefficient combination of labor and capital. We interpret these findings and suggest that while these companies generally operate in a cost-effective manner, there remains room for improvement by lowering investment in capital (e.g., aircrafts) relative to other inputs. Nonetheless, functioning with a business model that contributes to operating at excess capacity may be justified due to the potential of generating greater revenue by flying frequent flights with lower load factors.

1. Introduction

Arguably some of the most iconic factor inputs are employed by air transportation service companies. For instance, it is not unusual for documentaries and films to feature the accomplishments and tragedies of aircraft pilots.[i] Public attention toward air transportation inputs is not limited to labor as aircraft failures and the roll-out of new aircrafts typically make news headlines.[ii] Operationally, these factor inputs along with jet fuel critically contribute to the success of air transportation service companies. Historically however, success in this industry has been proven quite challenging. Air transportation companies are required to comply with union- and federally imposed work-rules, to manage idle aircrafts due to excess capacity, and to negotiate operations in the presence of volatile fuel prices. These factor market idiosyncrasies contribute to difficulty in satisfying cost minimization and allocative efficiency conditions and thus play a role in preventing air transport companies from generating meaningful profits.

Past research, investigating the allocative efficiency in air transport service sector is bifurcated by examining this market during the years near the 1978 Airline Deregulation Act and the years significantly following the passage of this Act. Findings examining the allocative efficiency immediately preceding and following the Airline Deregulation Act show that the air transport companies employed an inefficiently high level of labor relative to capital and fuel (Kumbhakar, 1992). In contrast to those early results, analysis using more recent data finds that the passenger airline companies use an inefficiently low amount of labor relative to fuel, capital and other inputs (Bitzan and Peoples, 2014). These latter results indicate passenger airlines employ too many nonlabor inputs. While these findings provide valuable insight into the air transport companies' ability to satisfy the condition for cost minimization/allocative efficiency, these studies focus exclusively on the passenger service sector of the air transportation market. The other major sector of this market includes air cargo companies who face similar input market challenges as passenger service companies. Furthermore, cost

---

[i]Famous examples of luminary pilots are Charles Lindbergh, Amelia Earhart, the Tuskegee airmen, and Chesley 'Sully' Sullenberger.

[ii]Aircraft tragedies include Turkish Airline flight 981 (1974), American Airlines flight 191 (1979) and Air India Express flight 812 (2010).

analysis of this sector of the airline service industry is important in part because air cargo services have become an ever increasingly key component to the economy due to their role in the supply chain of product distribution. This chapter contributes to our understanding of the scope of allocative efficiency in the air transport market by testing whether all-cargo air companies are able to operate in a manner that satisfies the condition of cost minimization.

The succeeding section of this chapter presents institutional background on the factor input market of the air cargo transportation sector so as to identify potential sources of allocative inefficiency. Section 3 presents a theoretical and empirical model of firm cost minimization as well as a method for examining allocative efficiency. Specifically, we use the approach developed by Atkinson and Halverson (1984) which assumes that firms minimize "shadow costs" by taking into account the different prices firms pay for labor and nonlabor input services in comparison to their market prices. Section 4 presents the data used for the analysis, and presentation of the empirical results are provided in Section 5. Concluding remarks and a discussion on the results and their implications are reported in the last section.

2. Background

The air transport sector is historically characterized as operating below the capacity and operating within the limits of union negotiated and federally mandated work-rules. Past analysis of excess capacity in the air cargo sector centers around the actual measure of operational outcomes (Baltagi *et al.*, 1998). For instance, research that utilizes the engineering measure of load factor rarely, if ever, finds that the air cargo companies are operating at full capacity, since the industry average for load factors rarely exceeds 70 percent of aircraft freight potential (Baltagi *et al.*, 1998). Thus, from an engineering perspective, air cargo carriers consistently operate below capacity. A shortcoming associated with using load factor as a measure of air cargo capacity is that it does not account for the possibility of rising marginal costs at higher levels of output. An alternative to using load factors is the use of the minimum average cost as the definition of capacity (Klein, 1960; Hickman, 1964). For example, Baltagli *et al.* (1998) reveals the potential for air cargo carriers to operate at capacity when using minimum average cost in place of the load factor. Nonetheless, operating at minimum average cost output levels remains a challenge in this industry given its sensitivity to variations in global and regional demands. Indeed, as recent as March 2020 the International Air Transport Association (IATA) reported a 15.2 percent year-on-year drop in demand for air cargo freight shipped. Furthermore, in the future, air cargo carriers are likely to face greater competition for freight services as more cargo shifts to passenger planes and back onto the seas.[iii] High value goods such as electronics have also become smaller, eliminating the need for transportation via dedicated air freighters and opening up the possibility of transportation via passenger aircrafts. Operating below full capacity contributes to allocative inefficiency because air cargo companies pay (lease) for the services of their aircrafts without receiving commensurate productivity from this factor input (capital). Paying input prices that match marginal productivity is the underpinning of an allocatively efficient use of inputs.

Work-rules intended to provide a healthy work environment could also have unintended consequences which influence allocative efficiency in the all-cargo air industry. This chapter identifies three separate work-rules that can potentially affect air cargo carriers'

[iii]Even though operating at full capacity has historically been a challenge the combination of disrupted supply chains and a drastic decline in air passenger travel has positively impacted cargo-only airlines. Both rates and yields have gone up. In fact, the cargo load factor increased by 11.5 percent year-on-year in April 2020 and reached an all-time high since 1990. This unusual increase suggests that the air cargo market has been currently undersupplied. Hence, it seems that, so far, the pandemic has had a positive impact on some cargo airlines. In fact, revenue ton-miles (RTM) increased by 13.86 percent from 2019 to 2020, as air cargo companies RTM reached $18,687.95 million by for 2020. Normally, about 50 percent of the world's air cargo is carried in the bellies of passenger aircraft, which have been all but idled due to the coronavirus crisis presenting air cargo companies with an unexpected demand for their services. However, post pandemic operations are likely to present passenger carriers the opportunity to compete for cargo service as they increasingly use more of their aircraft fleet.

ability to satisfy the condition of allocative efficiency by using inputs in a cost-minimizing manner.[iv] The three labor practices we focus on are (1) deadheading, (2) hours of service regulation, and (3) scope provisions (clause). Deadheading occurs when employees such as pilots are compensated for non-flight activity. While this provision is intended to compensate employees for the inconvenience associated with commuting to airports where there is an immediate shortage of labor, the labor activity associated with this commute does not contribute to productivity (flying a plane). Hence, compensation does not correspond accurately with wage. On the other hand, the ability to transport workers to a high-need airport helps the air cargo company to avoid the costly effect of paying for idle planes due to an immediate shortage of flight and maintenance personnel. Hours of service regulation are intended to improve flight safety by limiting flight time. However, when flight crews meet the maximum hours limitation, air companies face the immediate shortage of vital personnel, requiring the use of deadheading to avoid grounding some of their fleet. The scope provision, which is negotiated by labor unions prohibits air cargo companies from outsourcing routes to carriers that are presumably using aircrafts better suited for the routes in question. The effect on allocative efficiency is not obvious *a priori* because negotiated fees for this type of code-sharing may not depict cost minimization if the principal (the company outsourcing) doesn't have complete information on the actual productivity associated with the third party's service. Despite the potential challenge satisfying allocative efficiency conditions, in general, it does not appear that air transport companies likely suffered significant efficiency challenges from operating within the guidelines of union negotiated and government mandate work-rules. For example, evidence examining the cost of labor in this sector reveal that worker productivity has increased by 80 percent from 1990 to 2010 (Donatelli, 2012). In addition, Hirsch (2006) reports that labor

---

[iv]The Air Line Pilots Association (ALPA) represents pilots for over 35 airlines including FedEx and UPS, the two major all-cargo air companies.

cost as a percentage of available seat miles fell from 4.7 percent per mile to 3.17 percent per mile from 1990 to 2005.

The potential factor input distortion associated with operating at excess capacity and within the limits of work-rules is captured in the following mathematical representation of the comparison between an optimal input mix and the input mix associated with potential market distortions due to operating with unused capacity and employing workers in a manner that satisfies the conditions of union-negotiated and federally mandated work-rules.

Standard economic theory indicates that cost minimization occurs when companies employ factor inputs efficiently by equating the ratios of factor input marginal productivities with factor input prices across all factor inputs. For example, assume a hypothetical carrier faces no constraints in the labor market and is thereby able to satisfy the condition for cost minimization depicted by Equation (1),

$$\frac{MP_L}{MP_K} = \frac{P_L}{P_K}, \tag{1}$$

where MP_L and MP_K are the marginal product of labor and capital, respectively, and P_L and P_K are input prices. This same cost minimizing condition can be shown graphically as the point of tangency between a firm's isoquant for producing a particular output level and an isocost line based on input prices (Figure 1). Optimization using observed input prices without excess capacity and restrictive work-rules is represented graphically by point A in Figure 1, where the combination of L^* units of labor and K^* units of capital minimize the cost of producing q units of output at a cost of C^* such that $C^* = (P_L)^*L^* + (P_K)^*K^*$ (using an isocost line based on observed input prices).

However, given the possibility that adherence to work-rules can alter the productivity of inputs and/or the costs of employing additional units of each input, air cargo companies may experience difficulty satisfying the aforementioned condition of allocative efficiency. This concept is depicted graphically in Figure 1 by showing that the actual isocost curve of a company adhering to work-rules could prove steeper than the cost-minimizing isocost curve

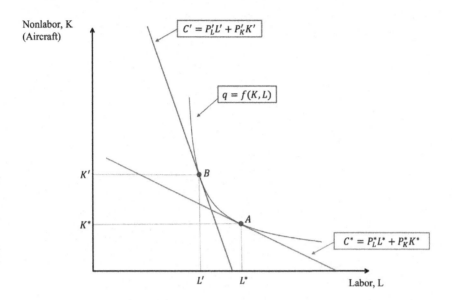

Figure 1. Overinvestment in nonlabor inputs in the presence of restrictive work-rules.

depicted by $C^* = (P_L)^* L^* + (P_K)^* K^*$. For example, if deadheading results in employees such as pilots receiving compensation for non-flight activity, then the shadow price of nonlabor inputs increases, all else equal. The curve $C' = (P_L)' L' + (P_K)' K'$ depicts the steeper isocost curve derived when paying the higher nonlabor shadow price $(P_L)'$. Thus, the actual input combination used by this hypothetical company is depicted by coordinate B in Figure 1, which when compared to coordinate A, indicates that the firm uses an allocatively inefficiently high amount of nonlabor inputs relative to labor.

As mentioned earlier in this chapter, operating in an industry facing restrictive work-rules is not the only potential source of misallocation of factor inputs. Although operating at excess capacity may contribute to a steeper isocost curve, dominant firms such as FedEx and UPS incorporate excess capacity into their business models. Both integrators operate according to consistent, daily schedules which results in increased flight frequency and lower load

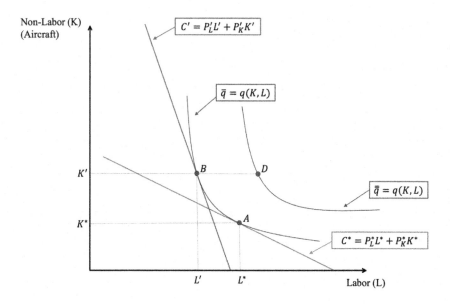

Figure 2. Overinvestment in nonlabor inputs in the presence of excess capacity.

factors. This outcome is depicted in Figure 2, where coordinate D is the allocatively efficient combination of inputs at output capacity Q. This input combination, however, is not efficient if the company is operating at excess capacity and the actual output level is q. This input combination is efficient if the company is operating at excess capacity with lower load factors and greater flight frequency to accommodate express delivery and volatile demand. For ease of comparison with the restrictive work-rule example, we use the cost minimizing equation used to explain overinvestment in capital due to restrictive work-rules. Hence for the cost equation $C^* = (P_L)^*L^* + (P_K)^*K^*$, allocative efficiency for the actual output level q is depicted by point $A(L^*, K^*)$ which is the allocatively efficient combination of inputs used at this output level. In comparison, the combination of inputs used at the higher output level Q is depicted by point D where one may assume efficient output should be in the absence of excess capacity. For this excess capacity example, the hypothetical all-cargo air company over-invests in capital relative to labor as depicted by the amount of nonlabor inputs available at capacity K' compared to the amount of capital K^* which satisfies the condition of allocative efficiency at the lower level of actual demand.

While the graphical depiction of allocative efficiency model's over-investment in nonlabor inputs associated with restrictive work-rules and operating with excess capacity, this chapter also explains that allocative efficiency could arise when air cargo companies adhere to restrictive work-rules. Also, these companies could satisfy allocative efficiency even when using their business model which incorporates greater flight frequency. Operating at excess capacity with greater flight frequency provides the conditions for air cargo companies using an allocatively efficient combination of inputs if these companies experience greater returns to density from flight frequency which compensates for flying with low load factors (Swan, 2002).

Using the graphical representation of allocative efficiency presented above allows for a mathematical examination of an optimal input mix, if restrictive work-rules and operating with excess capacity alter the true unit costs of using inputs. Following the graphical presentation, the ratios of marginal productivities are set equal to the ratios of shadow prices (rather than observed input prices) as in Equation (2). These equations indicate that the marginal product of a dollar's worth of labor is equal to the marginal product of a dollar's worth of nonlabor input at the true unit costs of each (Equation (3)).

$$\frac{MP_L}{MP_K} = \frac{P_L^*}{P_K^*} \tag{2}$$

$$\frac{MP_L}{P_L^*} = \frac{MP_K}{P_K^*} \tag{3}$$

If the shadow price of using nonlabor inputs P_K^* is lower than the observed price of nonlabor inputs P_K' due to the restrictive work-rules, but the shadow price of labor P_L^* is equal to the observed price of labor P_L' then the equality in Equation (3) implies that the marginal product of a dollar's worth of labor is more than the marginal product of a dollar's worth of nonlabor inputs at observed input prices (Equation (4)). This suggests that the firm is using less labor relative to nonlabor inputs than it would if it optimized based on observed input prices.[v]

$$\text{If } \frac{MP_K}{w_{K'}} > \frac{MP_K}{w_K}, \text{ and } \frac{MP_L}{w_{L'}} = \frac{MP_L}{w_L} \text{ then } \frac{MP_L}{w_L} > \frac{MP_K}{w_K}. \quad (4)$$

Alternatively, if operating at excess capacity as depicted by Equations (2) and (3) decreases the cost of using additional nonlabor inputs, but not labor inputs as depicted by Equation (4), then the firm would use more nonlabor inputs relative to labor than it would if it optimized based on observed input prices. Hence, the impact that work-rules and operating at excess capacity have on input prices and consequently on the mix of inputs used is an empirical question.

The preceding graphical and mathematical representations on factor input price distortion provides guidance for empirically examining allocative efficiency of factor inputs by highlighting the need to empirically compute the input factor of proportionality (the factor that shows how much shadow input price deviates from actual input price) to attain information on the magnitude of the price distortion, and consequently the overutilization or underutilization of various inputs.

3. Data

The empirical analysis of allocative efficiency in the US all-cargo industry uses data from individual airline Form 41 Financial Reports and T-100 Traffic Data reported by large, certificated US air carriers to the US Department of Transportation for the years 1993–2014. Information on all-cargo companies' total costs, prices of factor inputs, outputs, and movement characteristics are taken from these reports. Specifically, *Total Cost* is computed by taking the sum of *Operating Expense* and *Opportunity Cost of Capital*. *Operating Expense* is taken from Form 41, Schedule P-6, Line 00360 and *Opportunity Cost of Capital* is computed as the product of *Net*

---

[v]It should be noted that if an employer does not sell their goods and services in a perfectly competitive industry the inequalities presented in Equation (4) can become distorted (Morrison, 2012). It should also be noted that the presentation of Equation (4) assumes firms satisfy the condition of cost minimization with regards to shadow factor input prices.

Property and Equipment and *Before Tax Cost of Capital*. Annual average *Net Property and Equipment* over four quarters is taken from Form 41, Schedule B-1, Line 16750 and *Before Tax Cost of Capital* is computed using data from Aswath Damodaran, New York University, Damodaran Online.[vi] The Damodaran Online data includes historical US Treasury Bond rates, before tax cost of debt for US Airlines, effective tax rates for US Airlines, US Market Risk Premiums, historical betas for US Airlines, historical debt and equity shares for US Airlines from 1999–2014. Since the 1993–1998 data are unavailable, we use the 1999–2014 means as proxies.

Input prices include those for labor, fuel, capital and other nonlabor factor inputs. *Capital Price* is computed as the sum of the *Opportunity Cost of Capital, Rentals, Depreciation* and *Amortization* divided by *Air Hours*. Information on total *Air Hours* for the year is taken from the T-100 Segment, *Air Time Minutes*/60. *Fuel Price* is computed as *Fuel Cost* divided by *Gallons Consumed*. Information on total *Gallons Consumed* for the year is taken from Form T-2, *Aircraft Fuel Gallons*. *Labor Price* is computed as *Salaries and Benefits* divided by *Full Time Equivalent Employees*. Information on annual average *Full Time Equivalent Employees* over 12 months is taken from 41, Schedule P-1(a), *FTE Employees*. Prices for *Other Nonlabor Factor Inputs* is computed as the difference between *Total Cost* and the sum of the *Opportunity Cost of Capital, Rentals, Depreciation, Amortization, Fuel*, and *Salaries and Benefits* divided by *Ramp-to-Ramp Hours*. Information on total *Ramp-to-Ramp Hours* is taken from T-100 Segment, *Ramp-to-Ramp Minutes*/60. *Revenue Ton–Miles* serves as the measure of output for the air cargo industry. Information on total *Revenue Ton–Miles* for the year is taken from T1 Summary Data. These other nonlabor inputs consist primarily of outsourced services such as cargo reservation systems and accounting and management systems (Russell, 2017).

The data sources used for this study also includes information needed to compute the cost shares of these factor inputs. For instance, *Capital Share* is computed as the sum of *Opportunity Cost*

[vi]http://pages.stern.nyu.edu/~adamodar/

of Capital, Rentals, Depreciation, and *Amortization* divided by *Total Cost.* Information on total *Rentals, Depreciation,* and *Amortization* for the year is taken from Form 41, Schedule P-6 on Line 00310, Line 00320, and Line 00330 respectively. *Fuel Share* is computed as *Fuel Cost* divided by *Total Cost.* Information on total *Fuel Cost* for the year is taken from Form 41, Schedule P-5.2, Line 51451. *Labor Share* is computed as *Salaries and Benefits* divided by *Total Cost.* Information on total *Salaries and Benefits* for the year is taken from Form 41, Schedule P-6, Line 00140. Cost share information for these four inputs is critical for estimating cost functions.

Output and movement characteristics are included in this analysis to account for cost changes attributable to non-input price determinants. Revenue Ton–Miles (RTM) is used to measure output levels and captures the potential of economies of scale associated with transporting greater cargo volumes. Movement characteristics include air cargo companies' stage length, load factor and number of airports served. Stage length is the aeronautical distance flown per route. Longer stage lengths contribute to lower costs because they require fewer costly take-offs and landings. Load factor for air cargo transport is defined as Revenue Ton–Miles divided by Available Ton–Miles. These are included to take into account the fact that many costs of operating a flight (e.g., flight crew, maintenance, fuel) do not increase proportionally with the freight volume on a flight. The number of points served is included as a proxy for firm size. This cost determinant is included to account for the potential of companies with more extensive networks to benefit from economies of network size by collecting larger quantities of freight without increasing staff and capital proportionately. Data used to depict these cost determinants are taken from the T-100 Traffic Data reports.

Descriptive statistics for each of these variables are presented in Table 1. Findings reported in Table 1 suggest that air cargo companies spend a relatively large amount on services other than inhouse labor, capital and fuel as, expenditure on other nonlabor inputs accounts for 41.8 percent of total cost. In comparison, labor, fuel and capital's cost share are 20.2, 18.2 and 19.9 percent, respectively. The relatively low share for labor is interesting in part

Table 1. Descriptive statistics.

	Variables	Mean
Factor Input Shares	Labor Share	0.202
	Fuel Share	0.182
	Capital Share	0.198
	Other Share	0.418
Factor Input Prices*	Labor Price	102,843.800
	Fuel Price	1.430
	Capital Price	15,685.880
	Other Price	27,430.840
Output	Revenue Ton–Miles	1,980,000,000
Total Cost		2,660,000,000
Movement Characteristics	Stage Length	2,022.999
	Load Factor	0.564
	Number of Airports Served	160.282
Number of Observations		202
Number of Firms		22

Note: *Computed using 2009 GDP deflator.

because the mean annual salary for air cargo employees is \$102,843.80 in 2009 dollars. Mean pay for these workers is markedly higher than the mean \$54,283 earned nationally by all the US workers in 2009.[vii] The low labor share generated by these high salaries is consistent with the notion that worker compensation in this sector is commensurate with high worker productivity. The relatively low share for fuel is consistent with companies in this industry investing in fuel efficient aircrafts. Results on total cost and output reveal that at the mean, the US air cargo companies transport \$1.98 trillion Revenue Ton–Miles of freight at a cost of \$2,66 trillion dollars. Notable findings on movement characteristics show a mean load factor of 56.4, suggesting that on average air cargo companies do not operate at capacity when using this engineering measure of capacity. Findings on the two remaining movement characteristics indicate a mean stage length of

---

[vii]Source for US annual salary: https://www.reuters.com/article/us-usa-economy
-incomes/u-s-incomes-fell-sharply-in-2009-irs-data-idUSTRE77302W20110804

2022.99 miles and a mean number of airports served of 160.98. Both of these measures significantly exceed findings from past research on stage length and number of airports served by the US passenger airlines for the same observation sample. Those findings report mean values 89.6 aeronautical miles and 89.66 airports served by the US passenger airlines (Bitzan and Peoples, 2014).

4. Empirical Approach

The airline cost function used to analyze allocative efficiency in the US air cargo sector includes the cost determinants presented in the data section as well a time trend. The generalized airline cost function that depicts this cost association is as follows:

$$C = f(P_l, P_f, P_k, P_o, Q, LOAD, Stg\ Length, Pts\ Served, T)$$

where:

$$P_l = \text{price of labor}$$
$$P_f = \text{price of fuel}$$
$$P_k = \text{price of capital}^{viii}$$
$$P_o = \text{price other}^{ix}$$
$$Q = \text{freight output (Revenue Ton–Miles)}$$
$$LOAD = \text{load factor freight (Revenue}$$
$$\text{Ton–Miles/Available Ton–Miles)}$$
$$Stg\ Length = \text{average stage length}$$
$$Pts\ Served = \text{number of airports served}$$
$$T = \text{time trend}$$

As previously shown by Atkinson and Halvorsen (1984) and Oum and Zhang (1955), we can test for allocative efficiency by estimating the firm's cost function with an embedded "shadow cost" function. If adherence to work-rules and operating with excess capacity alter the costs of using various inputs, the effective price of using an input will vary from its market price. Firms are expected to base their input hiring decisions on these unobserved shadow prices, and therefore,

---

[viii]Including P_k in the cost function assumes a long run model, since capital is usually a fixed factor in the short run (Morrison, 2012).

[ix]The price of other includes the price of all inputs other than labor, capital, and fuel. It is calculated as a residual per hour of operation.

minimize total shadow costs. We can specify the firm's shadow cost function as:

$$C^S = (Q, P_i^*, M_g, T), \tag{5}$$

where C^S is the firm's shadow costs, Q is the firm's output as measured by volume of freight shipped[x] (RTM), P_i^* is a vector of shadow prices, M_g is a vector of movement characteristics that include load factors, number of airports served and stage length, and T is a vector of technological characteristics. Input shadow prices (P_i^*) are equal to the market input price multiplied by a factor of proportionality (Yotopoulos and Lau, 1970),

$$P_i^* = k_i \, P_i. \tag{6}$$

This factor of proportionality (k_i) shows the relationship between the true input prices and market prices paid by firms for inputs:

$$k_i = \frac{P_i^*}{P_i}. \tag{7}$$

If k_i is greater that one, it suggests that the firm's shadow price for this input is greater than the market price. This would suggest an underutilization of this input. Alternatively, if k_i is less than one, overutilization of the input is suggested.

Atkinson and Halvorsen (1984) show that applying Shepard's Lemma to the shadow cost function yields input demands:

$$\frac{\partial C^S}{\partial P_i^*} = x_i. \tag{8}$$

---

[x]Inclusion of output in any given cost function invites endogeneity concerns. However, Bitzan and Keeler (2003) report similar output-instrumented and - uninstrumented rail freight cost function estimations as well as inability to reject exogeneity for all variables. While findings for rail and air freight cannot be conflated, price elasticity of demand for air freight services may suggest output cost exogeneity. Chi and Baek (2012) find long-run elastic price and income elasticity of demand for air freight services. In combination with average annual load factors between 0.5 and 0.7, long run elastic demand for air freight services suggests air freight output is more likely influenced by consumers than producers making output exogenous to the producer cost function.

Total actual cost is:

$$C^A = \sum_i P_i x_i = \sum_i P_i \frac{\partial C^S}{\partial P_i^*}. \qquad (9)$$

As shown by Atkinson and Halvorsen (1984) the share of shadow costs accounted for by input i is:

$$S_i^S = \frac{k_i P_i x_i}{C^S}. \qquad (10)$$

This implies that input x_i is:

$$x_i = \frac{S_i^S C^S}{k_i P_i}. \qquad (11)$$

The total actual cost function is:

$$c^A = \sum_i P_i \frac{S_i^S C^S}{k_i P_i} = c^s \sum_i \frac{S_i^S}{k_i}. \qquad (12)$$

Taking the logarithm of Equation (12) gives the following:

$$\ln(C^A) = \ln(C^S) + \sum_i \ln\left(\frac{S_i^S}{k_i}\right). \qquad (13)$$

Thus, the shadow cost function can be estimated as an embedded part of the total cost function.

Using the translog functional form for the shadow cost function:[xi]

$$\ln(C^5) = \alpha_0 + \alpha_1 \ln(Q) + \alpha_2 T + \sum_i \alpha_i \ln(k_i P_i) + \sum_g \alpha_g \ln(M_g)$$

$$+ \frac{1}{2}\phi_1 \ln(Q)^2 + \frac{1}{2}\phi_2 T^2 + \frac{1}{2}\sum_i \phi_i \ln(k_i P_i)^2$$

$$+ \frac{1}{2}\sum_g \phi_g \ln(M_g)^2$$

$$+ \phi_{12} \ln(Q)T + \sum_i \phi_{1i} \ln(Q) \ln(k_i P_i) + \sum_g \phi_{1g} Q \ln(M_g)$$

[xi]One potential challenge with the translog is the inclusion of explanatory variables with values of zero since the log of these values are undefined. Cohen and Morrison Paul (2003) show the generalized Leontiff is a way to circumvent this issue. Nonetheless, all variables used in this study have values greater than zero.

$$+ \sum_i \phi_{2i} T \ln(k_i P_i) + \sum_g \phi_{2g} T \ln(M_g)$$

$$+ \sum_{ij} \phi_{ij} \ln(k_i P_i) \ln(k_j P_j)$$

$$+ \sum_{ig} \phi_{ig} \ln(k_i P_i) \ln(M_g) + \sum_{gh} \phi_{gh} \ln(M_g) \ln(M_h), \qquad (14)$$

where all cost determinants are normalized by their sample mean values. Imposing symmetry and homogeneity conditions yields the following parameter restrictions:

$$\sum_i \alpha_i = 1, \sum_{ij}(\phi_i + \phi_{ij}) = \sum_i(\phi_1 + \phi_{1i}) = \sum_i(\phi_2 + \phi_{2i})$$

$$= \sum_{ig}(\phi_g + \phi_{ig}) = 0. \qquad (15)$$

To get the shadow cost share equations, Shepard's Lemma is used and the translog shadow cost function with respect to shadow prices is differentiated from the actual translog cost function as follows:

$$\frac{\partial \ln(C^s)}{\partial \ln(k_i P_i)} = \frac{\partial \ln(C^s)}{\partial C^s} \frac{\partial C^A}{\partial(k_i P_i)} \frac{\partial(k_i P_i)}{\partial \ln(k_i P_i)} = \frac{x_i(k_i P_i)}{C^s} = s_i^s$$

$$\text{s.t. } s_i^s = a_i + \phi_{1i} \ln(Q) + \phi_{2i} T + \sum_j \phi_{lj} \ln(k_j P_j) + \sum_g \phi_{ig} \ln(M_g).$$

$$(16)$$

Since all cost determinants are normalized by their sample mean values, the input price parameters derived when estimating Equation (14) represent the respective input's share of shadow total cost at the mean. Similarly, the parameter estimates of the actual cost function specified in its translog form present the respective input's share of the actual total cost at the mean. In addition, the parameter estimate on outputs (RTM) of the actual cost equation indicates economies of scale at the mean, such that a parameter estimate less than one depicts increasing returns to scale and an estimate greater than one depicts decreasing returns to scale.

From Equations (13), (14) and (16) we can obtain the following total cost function:

$$\ln(C^4) = \alpha_0 + \alpha_1 \ln(Q) + \alpha_2 T + \sum_i \alpha_i \ln(k_i P_i) + \sum_g \alpha_g \ln(M_g)$$

$$+ \frac{1}{2}\phi_1 \ln(Q)^2 + \frac{1}{2}\phi_2 T^2 + \frac{1}{2}\sum_i \phi_i \ln(k_i P_i)^2 + \frac{1}{2}\sum_g \phi_g \ln(M_g)^2$$

$$+ \phi_{12} \ln(Q)T + \sum_i \phi_{1i} \ln(Q)\ln(k_i P_i) + \sum_g \phi_{1g} Q \ln(M_g)$$

$$+ \sum_i \phi_{2i} T \ln(k_i P_i) + \sum_g \phi_{2g} T \ln(M_g) + \sum_{ij} \phi_{ij} \ln(k_i P_i)\ln(k_j P_j)$$

$$+ \sum_{ig} \phi_{ig} \ln(k_i P_i)\ln(M_g) + \sum_{gh} \phi_{gh} \ln(M_g)\ln(M_h)$$

$$+ \sum_i \ln\left(\frac{\alpha_i + \phi_{1i}\ln(Q) + \phi_{2i}T + \sum_j \phi_{ij}\ln(k_j P_j) + \sum_g \phi_{ig}\ln(M_g)}{k_i}\right)$$

$$(17)$$

As in other applications of the translog cost function, we jointly estimate total costs with factor share equations in a seemingly unrelated system of equations. In order to obtain factor share equations, note that the share of expenditures on factor i is:

$$S_i^A = \frac{P_i x_i}{C^A}. \tag{18}$$

As shown by Atkinson and Halverson (1984) we can put this in terms of shadow share equations by using Equations (7) and (8):

$$S_i^A = \frac{s_i^s/k_i}{\sum_i(s_i^s/k_i)}. \tag{19}$$

Substituting from Equation (12):

$$S_i^A = \frac{\left(\dfrac{\alpha_i + \phi_{1i}\ln(Q) + \phi_{2i}T + \sum_j \phi_{ij}\ln(k_j P_j) + \sum_g \phi_{ig}\ln(M_g)}{k_i}\right)}{\sum_i \left(\dfrac{\alpha_i + \phi_{1i}\ln(Q) + \phi_{2i}T + \sum_j \phi_{ij}\ln(k_j P_j) + \sum_g \phi_{ig}\ln(M_g)}{k_i}\right)}. \tag{20}$$

Since the factor shares sum to 1, one of the cost share equations is deleted to obtain a nonsingular covariance matrix. Because the total cost function is homogeneous of degree zero in factors of proportionality, one of the factors of proportionality (the one for labor) is normalized to one. Thus, all other factors of proportionality are measured relative to that for labor. Any statistically significant factor price distortion value less than one suggests overinvestment in input x_i relative to input x_j and any value statistically significantly greater than one suggests underinvestment in input x_i relative to input x_j. Assuming air cargo companies choose inputs to minimize total costs based on input's shadow prices, the factor of proportionality derived from using the MLE procedure captures deviations from cost minimization based on the actual input price. Thus, empirically the factor of proportionality is a parameter that can be estimated because it is presented in the cost function as a component of the shadow input price (k_i P_i). Therefore, the use of the MLE approach allows estimation of nonlinearity introduced when taking the product of the factor of proportionality and the actual price. It should be noted that the stochastic frontier procedure used to estimate the production function is an alternative estimation approach that can be used to estimate allocative efficiency and addresses the possibility of measurement error that could arise if the error term includes a non-random component depicting technical efficiency. We view the MLE estimation of the shadow cost system of equations over the stochastic frontier estimation of the production function due to the advantages of estimating a cost function over a production function. Past research observes a lower probability of introducing measurement error due to less reliable information on input quantities compared to input prices. In addition, endogeneity between input quantities and output arises when estimating the production function and estimating the production function also faces the presence of multicollinearity between inputs (Al-Hadi *et al.*, 2019). In contrast, Shephard (1970) observes that estimating the cost function can easily avoid endogeneity issues associated with estimating the production function. Moreover, in the event that shadow cost estimation results do not reject the hypothesis of allocative efficiency, by default, the disturbance term also excludes the technical efficiency component.

Additional information on factor inputs is obtained by using parameter estimates from the cost equation to compute factor demand elasticities and elasticities of substitution. Examining these elasticities fills an important void in the analysis of allocative efficiency, in part, because the size of the parameter for factor proportionality does not provide any insight on the magnitude of input price distortion. Alternatively, computing these elasticities contributes to our understanding of allocative efficiency because these measures indicate the potential magnitude of input misallocation due to artificially high input prices and exogenous limitations on the use of inputs, such as restrictions outlined in work-rule agreements. For instance, high elasticity of substitution suggests the potential for significant input misallocation because companies are highly likely to switch to alternative inputs in response to restrictive work-rules.

Own and cross factor price elasticity are calculated using the equations shown below:

$$\varepsilon_i = \frac{\phi_i}{S_i} + s_i - 1, \ \forall i \tag{21}$$

$$\varepsilon_{ij} = \frac{\phi_{ij}}{s_i} + s_j, \ \forall i \neq j, \tag{22}$$

Where the symbols ϕ_i and ϕ_{ij} are the translog cost estimated coefficients on the own and cross second order terms for input prices, and the symbols S_i and S_j are the respective input shares for the ith and jth factor inputs. In addition to computing own and cross price elasticities, the Allen-Uzawa partial elasticity of substitution (AES) is calculated for each input paired combination. Those elasticities are derived using the following equation,

$$AES_{ij} = \frac{\phi_{ij}}{S_i S_j} + 1 = \frac{\varepsilon_{ij}}{S_j}, \ \forall \, i \neq j. \tag{23}$$

5. Results

Results derived from using the NLSUR technique to estimate the translog total cost function, as depicted by Equation (17) are presented in Table 3. The model explains a substantial amount of variation in the cost of providing air freight service as the R-squares are 93.4 and 92.94 for the two specifications reported in this

Table 2. Regularity conditions.

Condition	% of Observations Satisfied
Monotonicity in output	100.00
Concavity in input prices	
Labor	100.00
Capital	94.10
Fuel	96.50
Other	100.00

table. However, before examining the cost results, we analyze the regularity properties needed to satisfy the condition of a well-behaved cost function that are presented in Table 2. The findings reported in this table show the condition for factor input price concavity that is satisfied for labor, capital, fuel and other nonlabor inputs prices for 100, 94.1, 96.5 and 100 percent of the observations. In addition, the condition for monotonicity in output is satisfied for all observations. The condition for homogeneity in input prices is imposed via constraints on the SUR estimation.

The findings in Table 3 are presented such that the estimated coefficients on the input prices are reported in the left column and represent the actual mean cost shares of the cost function estimated without shadow prices. The cost shares of labor, capital, other nonlabor inputs and fuel are 18.9, 21.7, 45.5 and 13.8 percent, respectively. These values for the cost shares of factor inputs closely resemble the raw mean values reported in summary Table 1. The estimated coefficients on the input prices reported in the right column represent the mean shadow input cost shares. These findings show the mean shadow cost shares of labor, capital, other nonlabor inputs and fuel are 19.0, 16.4, 35.3 and 19.4 percent, respectively. When comparing the estimated cost shares in columns 1 and 2, what we find to be the most noticeable is that the substantially smaller cost share for other nonlabor inputs when estimating shadow prices. Conversely, the cost share for fuel is much larger when estimating shadow prices. Excluding output, findings on the remaining first order terms lack

Table 3. Regression results.

Variables	Cost Function SUR (1)		Cost Function NLSUR (2)	
	Coefficient	t-stat	Coefficient	t-stat
intercept	21.559***	179.93	21.517***	159.35
pl	0.189***	13.78	0.190***	5.44
pk	0.217***	25.79	0.164***	3.71
po	0.455***	54.37	0.353***	6.07
pf	0.138***	15.35	0.294***	5.26
rtm	0.789***	9.35	0.696***	8.18
stage	−0.246	−1.35	−0.145	−0.77
load	−0.579	−1.31	−0.387	−0.82
port	0.165	1.19	0.273*	1.84
time	0.082***	3.49	0.062**	2.45
0.5*pl*pl	0.049***	12.33	0.057***	5.03
0.5*pk*pk	0.112***	32.66	0.110***	9.21
0.5*po*po	0.153***	35.3	0.149***	14.94
0.5*pf*pf	0.067***	18.33	0.076***	6.68
0.5*rtm*rtm	0.085*	1.92	0.002	0.04
0.5*stage*stage	−0.044	−0.26	−0.347**	−2
0.5*load*load	−4.668***	−3.22	−4.392***	−2.68
0.5*port*port	0.015	0.14	0.094	0.82
0.5*time*time	−0.007***	−3.5	−0.005**	−2.38
pl*pk	−0.004	−1.32	−0.004	−0.52
pl*po	−0.024***	−7.65	−0.028***	−4.57
pl*pf	−0.022***	−9.07	−0.026***	−3.67
pl*rtm	0.003	0.65	0.002	0.19
pl*stage	−0.073***	−7.26	−0.090***	−3.82
pl*load	−0.045	−1.43	−0.084	−1.17
pl*port	−0.003	−0.39	−0.014	−0.77
pl*time	−0.004***	−3.26	−0.003	−1.24
pf*po	−0.033***	−12.56	−0.032***	−4.75
pf*pk	−0.012***	−5.24	−0.018***	−2.69
pf*rtm	0.001	0.55	0.000	0.02
pf*stage	0.027***	5.66	0.048**	2.5
pf*load	0.086***	3.19	0.068	1.24
pf*port	−0.010	−1.37	−0.005	−0.32
pf*time	0.002***	3.66	0.002	1.17
po*pk	−0.096***	−34.34	−0.089***	−7.97
po*rtm	0.001	0.03	0.002	0.34
po*stage	−0.132**	−2.18	0.017	1.22

(Continued)

Table 3. (*Continued*)

Variables	Cost Function SUR (1)		Cost Function NLSUR (2)	
	Coefficient	t-stat	Coefficient	t-stat
po*load	−0.053**	−2.36	−0.024	−0.55
po*port	0.008	1.44	0.009	0.8
po*time	0.013***	3.8	0.002	1.6
pk*rtm	−0.005	−0.2	−0.005	−0.55
pk*stage	0.178***	2.94	0.025	1.45
pk*load	0.012	0.61	0.040	0.74
pk*port	0.004	0.87	0.010	0.7
pk*time	−0.011***	−3.27	−0.002	−0.88
rtm*stage	−0.221***	−3.05	−0.248***	−3.22
rtm*load	0.321*	1.68	0.470**	2.14
rtm*port	−0.046	−0.83	−0.004	−0.07
rtm*time	0.006	0.97	0.001	0.2
stage*load	2.167***	5.83	2.305***	5.5
stage*port	0.127	0.94	−0.051	−0.42
stage*time	−0.033**	−2.34	−0.050***	−3.54
load*port	0.160	0.56	0.153	0.52
load*time	0.060	1.63	0.070*	1.83
port*time	−0.015	−1.32	−0.007	−0.54
p2			0.927***	4.1
p3			0.999***	4.08
p4			0.699***	4.08
R-squared	93.4		92.94	
Wald Tests			Statistic	P-value
Fuel/Labor = 1			0.10	0.7464
Other/Labor = 1			0.00	0.9952
Capital/Labor = 1			3.08	0.0794

Notation: ***indicates significance at 1% level, **indicates significance at 5% level and *indicates significance at 10% level.

statistical significance when estimating the actual cost function. The estimated coefficient of this variable is less than one suggesting that at the mean, the US air cargo companies produce increasing returns to scale range. This output finding is consistent with the notion that these companies do not operate at full capacity since minimum average costs cannot be achieved when producing in this region of the cost function.

The findings for the estimated coefficients on the cross second-order terms for input prices are mostly statistically significant for both cost functions. The estimates for the actual cost function in column 1 are used to compute the cross-price demand elasticities for capital, labor, fuel and other inputs. A summary of these elasticities is presented in Table 4. Findings on the own demand elasticities suggests that cargo company's demand for workers is price inelastic. Hence, the probability of job loss associated with the high mean salaries reported in Table 1 is very small. The same can be said for capital and other nonlabor inputs as the demand elasticities are also very low. In contrast, the demand elasticity for fuel is relatively high with a value of -1.938. Presumably, price variation

Table 4.   Estimated elasticities.

Own-Price	Average		
E_{LL}	-0.051		
E_{FF}	-1.938		
E_{KK}	-0.084		
E_{OO}	-0.281		

Cross-Price	Average	Allen-Uzawa	Average
E_{LO}	0.208	AES_{LO}	0.410
E_{LK}	0.345	AES_{LK}	1.978
E_{LF}	-0.099	AES_{LF}	-139.971
E_{OL}	0.134	AES_{OK}	-0.883
E_{OK}	-0.111	AES_{OF}	-2.718
E_{OF}	0.084	AES_{KF}	1.481
E_{KL}	0.319		
E_{KO}	-0.339		
E_{KF}	0.198		
E_{FL}	-1.534		
E_{FO}	-1.439		
E_{FK}	0.318		

Note: L = labor, O = other, K = capital, and F = fuel. A negative value for cross-price elasticity = complements whereas positive values = substitutes.

in fuel has a significant influence on carriers' ability to provide transport services. Findings on cross-price elasticities only reveal substantial input price effects for fuel. The cross-price elasticity for fuel suggests that fuel is a complement of labor and other nonlabor, non-capital inputs. The extent of fuel's complementarity with these two inputs is depicted by the findings on the elasticity of substitution presented in the last column of Table 4. These findings show that fuel and labor are very strong complements as the elasticity of substitution is -139.971 for these two inputs. Since an aircraft cannot function without gasoline (fuel) it follows that the two inputs should be complements. In contrast, labor is a relatively strong substitute for capital as the elasticity of substitution for these two inputs is greater than one equaling 1.978. Thus, any labor/capital employment distortions would be magnified by adherence to work-rules or operating with excess capacity as companies would substitute for high levels of capital to achieve allocative efficiency using shadow prices.

A direct test of allocative efficiency is provided at the bottom of Table 3, which is where the estimated factors of proportionality are reported. These findings show that the condition for allocative efficiency is satisfied for labor relative to fuel and other factor inputs as the value of the Wald statistics reveal that their factors of proportionality are not statistically significantly different from one. However, the condition for allocative efficiency is not satisfied for labor relative to capital. Moreover, the factor of proportionality is statistically significantly less than one suggesting that the shadow prices of capital relative to their market prices are low in comparison to labor. Based on our hypothesis that labor rules might inflate the price of labor above its market price, we interpret this to mean that the shadow price of labor is above its market price, under the assumption that all other factors' shadow prices are equal to market prices. Alternatively, it is possible that operating with excess capacity contributes to the over-investment in capital. Nonetheless, as a result of this divergence between the shadow price of capital and its market price, air cargo companies use more capital relative to labor than they otherwise would.

Given the limited evidence of allocative efficiency which is mainly associated with the underutilization of labor relative to capital, an obvious question one might ask is: How much of a difference does this make to air cargo firms? To obtain an insight into this question, a comparison is made of costs that the mean air cargo company would realize with allocative efficiency to what they realize with allocative inefficiency. This comparison is made by simulating costs realized under allocative efficiency using the mean of all independent variables and the fitted cost function with all factors of proportionality set to one.[xii] Costs realized under allocative inefficiency are simulated using the fitted cost function with the estimated factors of proportionality. In a similar way, we simulate the quantity demanded of each input under allocative efficiency and make a comparison to the quantity demanded under allocative inefficiency. As shown previously, actual cost shares of inputs are specified as:

$$S_i^A = \frac{P_i x_i}{C^A}$$

This suggests that:

$$x_i = \frac{S_i^A C^A}{P_i}$$

Quantity of input i demanded under allocative efficiency is simulated using the above equation with factors of proportionality set equal to one. For allocative inefficiency, the same equation is used with the actual estimated factors of proportionality.

Table 5 contains the findings for the simulated percentage changes in costs and inputs employed as a result of operating allocatively inefficiently. These percentage changes are calculated using a simulation that is performed at the means of all independent variables. As the table shows, the simulated allocative inefficiency accounts for a higher cost of 9.01 percent. The contents of Table 5 also show that at the mean the number of full-time employees hired is

---

[xii]This approach mimic what was also done for electric power generation by Atkinson and Halvorsen (1984). and what was done in passenger airlines by Bitzan and Peoples (2014).

Table 5. Simulated impacts of allocative inefficiency on mean costs and quantities of inputs used.

Mean of all Variables	Percent Change
Cost	9.01
Labor (FTE)	−91.09
Fuel (gallons)	−24.95
Capital (USD)	106.72
Other (material)	−20.31

91.09 percent less than with allocative efficiency and the amount of fuel consumed and other nonlabor inputs used are 24.95 and 20.31 percent less than with allocative efficiency. In contrast, the amount of capital used is 106.72 percent higher than they would be with allocative efficiency. Combined with the findings of cost increases from allocative inefficiency, this seems to suggest that relaxing work-rules and operating closer to full capacity could be a win-win situation for labor and management since this cost minimizing behavior would increase the numbers of employees and lower costs.

6. Conclusion

The air transport industry is a critical component of a vibrant economy, especially in an increasingly interconnected world economy. Given the competitiveness of alternative modes of transportation and the expanding role of communications networks as vehicles of information transmission, providing an affordable transport service is vital to the success of air transport companies. Satisfying the condition of allocative efficiency (cost minimization) then is important as an objective for success in this industry. While much of the research on cost minimization and allocative efficiency in the airline industry primarily examines the passenger sector, there is a dearth of research examining allocative efficiency in the all-cargo air transport sector. Increasing demand for this service due in part to the rise of e-commerce indicates a cost analysis of this sector, in particular, seems more than relevant. Indeed, growing demand for air cargo service has facilitated interest from traditional passenger service carriers who are increasingly using the cargo bellies of the aircraft to transport freight and enhance competition in this transportation services sector. This chapter contributes to our understanding of the scope of allocative efficiency in the air transport market by testing whether all-cargo air companies are able operate in a manner that satisfies the condition of cost minimization.

We consider the potential influence of air cargo companies adhering to union-negotiated and federally mandated work-rules and the potential influence of these companies operating with excess capacity. Our analysis indicates that adhering to work-rules can lead to allocative inefficiency by requiring pay for nonlabor work. On the other hand, we note that such nonlabor work provides companies easy access to qualified workers when facing an immediate labor shortage for a given service route. We also argue that the inability to operate at full capacity can create a challenge in achieving allocative efficiency if all-cargo air companies implement a business model that provides shippers with consistent daily flights at high frequency and low load factors. Empirical findings derived by estimating the shadow cost function indicate that the US all-cargo air companies use an allocatively efficient combination of labor and fuel as well as an allocatively efficient combination of labor and other nonlabor inputs. Findings do uncover that all-cargo air companies use an allocatively inefficient combination of labor and capital. We interpret these findings as suggesting that while these companies generally operate in a cost-effective manner, there remains room for improvement. Simulations indicate a movement towards higher employment of workers and greater investment in other nonlabor inputs relative to investment in capital could reduce costs by up to 9 percent. We also interpret these findings as indicating that adherence to work-rules doesn't necessarily promote exorbitant costs given their ability to satisfy the condition of allocative efficiency with respect to the use of labor in combination with fuel and other nonlabor inputs. Further, the cost savings associated with enhanced safety performance due to adhering to hours of safety rules negotiated by labor unions and mandated by the federal government may compensate for higher costs associated with this source of allocative inefficiency.

References

Atkinson, S.E., and Halvorsen, R. (1984). Parametric Efficiency Tests, Economies of Scale, and Input Demand in U.S. Electric Power Generation. *International Economic Review, 25*(3), 647–662. http://dx.doi.org/10.2307/2526224.

Baltagi, B.H., Griffin, J.M., and Vadali, S.R. (1998). Excess Capacity: A Permanent Characteristic of U.S. Airlines? Journal of Applied Economics, *13*(6), 645–657. http://dx.doi.org/10.1002/(sici)1099-125 5(199811/12)13:6⟨645::aid-jae485⟩3.3.co;2-i.

Bitzan, J., and Peoples, J. (2014). U.S. Air Carriers and Work-Rule Constraints — Do Airlines Employ an Allocatively Efficient Mix of Inputs? *Research in Transportation Economics, 45*, 9–17. http://dx.doi. org/10.1016/j.retrec.2014.07.002.

Bitzan, J.D., and Keeler. T.E. (2003). Productivity Growth and Some of Its Determinants in the Deregulated U.S. Railroad Industry. *Southern Economic Journal, 70*(2), 232–253. http://dx.doi.org/10.2307/ 3648967.

Chi, J., and Baek, J. (2012). Price and Income Elasticities of Demand for Air Transportation: Empirical Evidence from US Airfreight Industry. *Journal of Air Transportation Management, 20*, 18–19. http://dx.doi. org/10.1016/j.jairtraman.2011.09.005.

Cohen, J.P., and Morrison Paul, C.J. (2003). Airport Infrastructure Spillovers in a Network System. *Journal of Urban Economics, 54*(3), 459–473. http://dx.doi.org/10.1016/j.jue.2003.06.002 http://dx.doi.or g/10.1016/j.tra.2019.06.006

Donatelli, D.J. (2012). *Evolution of US Air Cargo Productivity.* Massachusetts Institute of Technology, Boston, MA.

Hickman, B.G. (1964). On a New Method of Capacity Estimation. *Journal of American Statistical Association, 59*(306), 529–549. http://dx.doi. org/10.1080/01621459.1964.10482177.

Hirsch, B.T. (2006). Wage Determination in the U.S. Airline Industry: Union Power Under Product Market Constraints. *IZA Discussion Paper No. 2384, SSRN Electron Journal.* http://dx.doi.org/10.2139/ ssrn.941127.

Klein, L.R. (1960). Some Theoretical Issues in the Measurement of Capacity. *Econometrica, 28*(2), 272–286. http://dx.doi.org/10.2307/ 1907721.

Kumbhakar, S.C. (1992). Allocative Distortions, Technical Progress, and Input Demand in U.S. Airlines: 1970–1984. *International Economic Review, 33*(3), 723–737. http://dx.doi.org/10.2307/2527135.

Morrison, C.J. (2012). *A Microeconomic Approach to the Measurement of Economic Performance: Productivity Growth, Capacity Utilization, and Related Performance Indicators* (1993 Edn.). Springer, New York. http://dx.doi.org/10.1007/978-1-4613-9760-1.

Oum, T.H., and Zhang, Y. (1955). Competition and Allocative Efficiency: The Case of the U.S. Telephone Industry. *Review of Economics and Statistics*, 77(1), 82–96. http://dx.doi.org/10.2307/2109994.

Russell, M. (2017). Economic productivity in the air transportation industry: multifactor and labor productivity trends, 1990–2014. *Monthly Labor Review*, U.S. Bureau of Labor Statistics. http://dx.doi.org/10.21916/mlr.2017.9.

Shephard, R.W. (1970). *Theory of Cost and Production Functions*. Princeton University Press, Princeton, NJ.

Swan, W.M. (2002). Airline Route Developments: A Review of History. *Journal of Air Transport Management*, 8(5), 349–353. https://doi.org/10.1016/S0969-6997(02)00015-7.

Yotopoulos, P.A., and Lau, L.J. (1970). A Test for Balanced and Unbalanced Growth. *Review of Economics and Statistics*, 52(4), 376–384. http://dx.doi.org/10.2307/1926314.

Chapter 8

The Effect of Economic Sanctions on Domestic Production, Trade and Transportation of Sanctioned Goods

Misak G. Avetisyan

Department of Economics, Texas Tech University, USA

David Lektzian

Department of Political Science, Texas Tech University, USA

It is well established that free trade generates larger gains. However, various forms of export control such as tariffs, quotas, taxes, etc. applied by developed and developing countries may substantially reduce gains from trade. In this chapter, we apply a unique methodological refinement of the computable general equilibrium (CGE) approach using the modified version of the dynamic Global Trade Analysis Project (GTAP) model to understand the effect of various types and levels of international sanctions on the severity and dissipation of economic losses over time.

Although the costs of international sanctions will mainly be borne by the targeted country,[i] reducing or eliminating the exports of certain goods from sender countries entering the sanctioned market makes them relatively expensive, and spurs imports of such goods from its other trading partners (Hufbauer *et al.*, 2007), thus also having significant impact on the choice of international transport mode. Also, the targeted goods become cheaper in sending countries due to increased domestic supply. Although, this has the effect of initially advantaging sender countries, the long run negative impacts of international sanctions may

---

[i]One estimate is that as of year 2001, sanctions cost targeted countries approximately $27 billion annually (Hufbauer *et al.*, 2007. Economic Sanctions Reconsidered. 3rd Edn. Washington: Peterson Institute).

dissipate and undermine the intended effects in the targeted economy
due to adjustment to sanctions through increased domestic production
of targeted goods and trade substitution with other trading partners.

1. Introduction

In this chapter we apply a methodological refinement of the computable general equilibrium (CGE) approach to understand the effect
of economic sanctions on the severity and dissipation of economic
losses caused by sanctions. Governments around the world have
turned to the use of economic sanctions with increasing frequency
in the 21st century (Felbermayr *et al.*, 2020) and it is essential that
we gain a greater understanding of their effects, not just for the
economy of the targeted country, but also for its trading partners
and the global economic system.

A unique aspect of the model used in this chapter is that it
considers the import and export of restricted goods in targeted
economies and the use of international transport using the modified
version of the dynamic Global Trade Analysis Project (GTAP)
model of global trade. We introduce substitution between different
modes of transport using the approach developed by Avetisyan and
Hertel (2021). GTAP modelling is a novel approach in the sanctions
literature that allows us to explore questions about changing patterns
of trade and domestic production of sanctioned goods that other
forms of statistical modelling have not addressed. A small number
of papers have also used CGE modeling to simulate the effect of
the imposition of sanctions on the Iranian economy (Kitous *et al.*,
2013; Gharibnavaz and Waschik, 2017; Ianchovichina *et al.*, 2016).
However, these papers do not utilize dynamic models, and are limited
to the analysis of the sanctions against Iran.[ii]

This chapter is motivated by a simple analytical framework.
When a country is subjected to sanctions that block its ability to
import goods from foreign markets it has three choices. It can find
alternative countries to trade with, it can produce the blocked goods

---

[ii]At this time, these are the only papers that we could locate that have utilized
CGE modeling to analyze the effects of economic sanctions.

at home (import substitution), or it can learn to do without the goods (Galtung, 1967).[iii] If the sanctions block the target's ability to export its goods, it can find alternatives to blocked export routes, or it can reduce production of the goods to match its domestic demand. GTAP modeling allows us to simulate the responses of sanctioned states and see the extent to which these options are pursued.

The main focus of this chapter is to investigate how the economies of targeted countries and its trading partners adjust to sanctions. Using general equilibrium modeling we explore two important cases of sanctions, the United Nations' sanctions against North Korea over the testing of nuclear weapons and Russia's sanctions against Georgia over the South Ossetia and Abkhazia dispute. Focusing on these two cases allows us to simulate short and long run effects of sanctions, with the goal of observing how well the target's economies adapted to the restriction by increasing trade with other nations and increasing the domestic production of sanctioned goods.

Some key findings of the empirical analysis are that global water transportation is the most affected mode of transport under sanctions, the economies of sender nations tend to be affected less by sanctions than targets, and that sanctions tend to have the greatest bite on targeted economies in their first year. In the second year of sanctions, we see little effect of sanctions on targets, as targeted states are able to make substitution in exports/imports and adjustments in domestic production to compensate for restrictions to their trade.

2. Literature Review

It is well established that countries generate greater economic benefits from engaging in free trade than from pursuing autarky. Various forms of government intervention in trade, such as tariffs, quotas, and taxes, discourage economic interaction between states, and reduce the gains from free trade. Economic sanctions have similar pecuniary effects as other forms of government intervention

---

[iii]Technically, a fourth option is to give in to the sender's demands in order to get the sanctions lifted, but in this chapter, we assume that sanctions are in place.

in international commerce and "involve similar reductions in the general economic welfare of the sender, target and global economies" (Spindler, 1995, p. 206).

In this chapter, we follow the commonly used definition of sanctions as being "essentially government imposed disruptions of economic exchange between the sanctioning, or 'sending' nation(s), and the sanctioned or 'target' nation(s)" (Spindler, 1995, p. 206). One primary difference between economic sanctions and other forms of government intervention in trade is in the motive for imposing the restriction. Rather than imposing tariffs and quotas to protect their domestic economies, states choose economic sanctions as a foreign policy tool meant to coerce a policy change from a foreign government (Hufbauer *et al.*, 2007). By blocking the targeted country's access to the benefits of foreign trade and finance, sender states seek to coerce the targeted state into changing some type of policy in order to have the sanctions removed.

Countries imposing economic sanctions also generally have a broader range of legal tools with which they block trade and finance with the targeted country than they would have under normal relations. For example, the President of the United States can take actions to block trade and finance under the International Emergency Economic Powers Act (IEEPA) that are not available under normal relations. Additionally, under customary international law, when governments take actions that violate internationally accepted norms of behavior, or they have violated international treaty agreements, states and international organizations have the right to proportionately retaliate (Alexander, 2009).

Because the goal of economic sanctions is to impose costs on the targeted country's government, it is imperative that sender states understand the potential economic effects of different types of sanctions. However, the complexities involved in estimating the effect of sanctions on a foreign country can be immense. The availability of alternative suppliers of the sanctioned goods, the ability to produce sanctioned goods domestically, and the differences in transaction costs for obtaining goods from alternate suppliers are difficult to estimate. The CGE model used in this chapter is designed specifically to provide simulated estimates that account for these many complexities.

Existing research has studied the effect of sanctions on trade and financial interactions between the sender and targeted country, as well as between the targeted country and its other trading partners (Caruso, 2003; Early, 2009; Peterson, 2011; Biglaiser and Lektzian, 2011; McLean and Whang, 2010; Lektzian and Biglaiser, 2013). Another important area of consideration for studies of sanctions, is the effect of sanctions on the domestic economy of targets of sanctions (Lektzian and Patterson, 2015; Pond, 2017). Understanding how states respond domestically to offset the costs of sanctions has a long tradition in the study of sanctions and continues to the present (Galtung, 1967; Gholz and Hughes, 2019).

A small number of papers have also used CGE modeling to simulate the effect of the imposition of sanctions on the Iranian economy (Kitous et al., 2013; Gharibnavaz and Waschik, 2017; Ianchovichina *et al.*, 2016). While each of these papers contributes positively to the understanding of the effect of sanctions, we include several innovations that help extend this line of research. First, we utilize a dynamic version of the CGE model that allows the estimation of more than just the initial reaction to sanctions in the first year. Second, we extend our analysis to look at more than just the Iranian sanctions. We simulate the effect of the United Nations' sanctions against North Korea as well as investigating a lesser-known case, Russian sanctions against Georgia over the South Ossetia and Abkhazia dispute.

3. Theoretical Assumptions

In the short term, the overall welfare effect of sanctions is expected to be negative, although not uniformly across all sectors of the economy (Gharibnavaz and Waschik, 2017). Sanctions blocking the import of goods by the target will cause the domestic prices of those goods to rise, simultaneously harming the welfare of domestic consumers and benefitting domestic producers of the goods. Sanctions blocking exports from the target, on the other hand, will create a domestic surplus of those goods, benefitting consumers as the price falls, and hurting producers of the goods (Black and Cooper, 1987).

Rogowski (1987) describes a process where those that are economically advantaged will convert economic strength into political influence. As sanctions shift economic benefits from one group to another, those that had political influence prior to sanctions are likely to pressure their government to make political changes in order to end the sanctions (Lektzian and Patterson, 2015). However, when senders make large demands of targets, the costs of concession may be too great to concede (e.g., give up a nuclear program, regime change) (Drezner, 1998). In this case, sanctions are likely to persist and the targeted state's economy will have to adapt to new conditions brought about by government intervention.

If sanctions remain in place, countries are likely to attempt to find other sources for imported goods and other markets for exportable goods in an effort to counter the effects of sanctions. Even though economic conditions are likely to shift to accommodate sanction's restrictions, there is still a loss in terms of efficiency. This produces an inward shift in the production possibility curve (Haberler, 1968), as "the dynamic losses amount to a reduction in the quantity and/or productivity of resources used in the production of both exportable goods and import-competing commodities" (Black and Cooper, 1987).

Two specific measures taken by targeted states to counter the effect of sanctions are, developing alternative trade partners, and increasing levels of domestic production of restricted goods. Alternate markets for the supply of sanctioned goods are likely to arise because of the effect of sanctions on local prices for sanctioned goods in targeted countries. Countries that use sanctions attempt to design them in a way that the costs will mainly be borne by the targeted country[iv] with relatively smaller costs to the sender

---

[iv]Hufbauer *et al.* (2007) estimate that as of year 2001, sanctions cost targeted countries approximately $27 billion annually. Our model also allows us to look at the effect of sanctions on sender state economies. Thus, rather than taking on assumption that target economies are hurt more than sender economies, we are able to use our model to compare the effects on senders and targets.

economy. A dilemma faced by states seeking to coerce with sanctions is that, on one hand, sanctions need to restrict access to goods in the targeted country to be effective. On the other hand, if sanctions successfully restrict imports to the target, without decreasing demand, prices of those goods will continue to rise above world prices. For essential goods to the target's economy, where demand is minimally responsive to changes in price, the development of alternate trade routes that replace supply from the sanctioning country should be expected. Thus, sanctions that disrupt essential goods also generate the greatest incentive for third-party countries to step in and replace the supply of those goods.

As trade routes change, from initial preferred routes under free trade, to alternative routes necessitated by government intervention in the form of economic sanctions, the choice of international transport mode will also change. If the initial, pre-sanctions, routes were determined based on profit motivation, then the new routes that emerge to circumvent sanctions are likely to be less efficient. The largest impact of trade sanctions will be on sea transport, since about 73 percent of the world trade (by value) is carried by water transport, 14 percent by land transport, and 13 percent by air transport (Rodrigue *et al.*, 2017).

If alternative markets are not found for sanctioned goods and they are consumed at home, transportation costs are likely to be reduced. One result of restricting trade between the sender and target nations can be an increased use of domestic transportation as more goods are consumed at home. When imports are restricted to the target, the goods that are restricted will become cheaper in the sender as supply increases due to a reduction in available markets. When exports are restricted from the target, the price of those goods will decrease in the targeted country as producers will be left with a surplus of goods once destined for international markets.

Initially these changing patterns of trade and consumption are expected to advantage sender countries. Eventually, as new patterns of trade are routinized, and domestic capacity for production is established, the sanctioned economy is likely to transform so that pre-sanction patterns of trade are no longer preferred to those that develop under sanctions. The long run negative impacts, however, may dissipate over time and undermine their intended effects.

Another way that adjustment to sanctions is expected to take place is through the increased domestic production of targeted goods. The longer that sanctions are in place, the more fully the targeted state's economy will change. Sanctions may result in an increase in the quantity or productivity of import competing resources in the targeted state's domestic economy, producing import-competing biased growth (Black and Cooper, 1987). Over the long term, this can result in a growth in domestic employment opportunities that raise the level of income and, at least partially, offset losses in the export sector. Under these conditions, the net welfare loss is expected to be smaller than when sanctions do not induce an increase in domestic production (Black and Cooper, 1987). However, sanctioned countries with large foreign trade sectors are more likely to experience losses from sanctions that exceed any gains from increased domestic production. This is specifically true for countries that have developed significant specialization in the export sector because it requires a greater amount of change to meet increasing demand for domestic production.

Both measures that states can take to counter the effects of sanctions will entail short term costs as the target adjusts its economy to accommodate for sanctions. Long term effects of sanctions may be less significant if the target's economy benefits from increased domestic production of restricted goods.

One anticipated effect of sanctions is that domestic producers of import-competing goods will gain rents from the reduced lack of competition with foreign goods. These producer groups are expected to convert their economic gains to political strength (Rogowski, 1987; Lektzian and Patterson, 2015). These groups will use their political strength to lobby for trade protection even after sanctions have been lifted. Thus, a long-term effect of sanctions may be an increase in tariff rates in the targeted country (Pond, 2017).

A third possible outcome is that resources may not be efficiently transferable from other sectors of the economy to produce goods that were previously imported. Additionally, the sanctioned sector may be unable to expand production of previously imported goods due to a shortage of critical raw materials, technology, or foreign capital (Black and Cooper, 1987).

Export sanctions will affect trade volumes, while an export tax or quota will increase the export price of the sanctioned product resulting in lower exports. Export restrictions will generally reduce the domestic price of the sanctioned product in the targeted state due to increased supply in the local market. Also, the market prices will be distorted resulting in welfare losses in domestic and foreign markets. The intermediate and final consumption of the sanctioned product is expected to rise locally and thereby reduce the prices of other domestically produced commodities. In addition to the direct impact, the reduction in export volumes is expected to generate spillover effects in various sectors of the targeted state's economy in the short run. Export sanctions can also curtail imports by reducing foreign capital inflows that would have resulted from the sale of goods to foreign markets. However, in the long run these negative impacts may dissipate and undermine the intended sanction effects in the targeted foreign economy due to adjustment to sanctions. More specifically, in this chapter we concentrate on the tradeoff between changes in domestic production and trade patterns and whether such impacts dissipate over time by testing the following hypotheses:

For sanctions that block imports from the sender to the target:

Hypothesis 1: *Substituting increased domestic production for sender country imports will reduce the direct and indirect economic effects associated with import sanctions.*

Hypothesis 2: *Substituting increased imports from other countries for sender country imports will reduce the direct and indirect economic effects associated with import sanctions.*

For sanctions that block exports from the target to the sender:

Hypothesis 3: *Substituting other country export markets for ending country export markets will reduce the direct and indirect economic effects ASSOCIATED with export sanctions.*

The effect of sanctions over time:

Hypothesis 4: *The negative economic effects of economic sanctions will dissipate over time.*

4. Macroeconomic Analysis: Implications of Sanctions for the North Korean and Georgian Economies

The first case that we look at involves the United Nations' sanctions against North Korea in 2006 over issues related to its nuclear weapons program. The fall of the Soviet Union in 1991 eliminated most of North Korea's trading partners and contributed to the country's isolation in the world. In 1991, a number of factories were closed driven by fuel shortages further worsening the North Korean economy.

In 1992, North Korea's last major ally and trading partner, China, established diplomatic and trade relations with South Korea. Due to the worsening economy, North Korea started looking for financial aid, trade relations, and foreign investment from Western countries by developing and approving new legislation to promote foreign investment in the country. This, along with the signing of the Joint Declaration on the Denuclearization of the Korean Peninsula (December 1991), which forbid the manufacture, possession, or use of nuclear weapons or fuel reprocessing facilities, was a major step toward North Korea's increasing openness with the world.

However, at the same time as North Korea was taking these initial steps toward openness, it was also suspected of clandestinely working toward developing a nuclear weapons program, which would eventually attract economic sanctions from the United Nations. Despite repeated attempts at bilateral and multilateral negotiations aimed at restricting North Korea's nuclear program, cooperation began to unravel. The "Agreed Framework" of 1994, which promised sanctions relief and the construction of two light water reactors in exchange for the eventual elimination of North Korea's nuclear program, eventually collapsed, culminating with North Korea announcing its withdrawal from the Nuclear Non-Proliferation Treaty (NPT) in January 2003.

Not long after, on October 9, 2006, North Korea conducted its first military test of its nuclear weapons capability. Five days later the United Nations took action by passing Resolution 1718, prohibiting the export of luxury goods, conventional weapons, weapon of mass destruction (WMD) and missile-related goods, freezing assets, and prohibiting the travel of designated individuals (Bierstecker *et al.*, 2018).[v] Our analysis in this chapter focuses on the initial set of the United Nations' sanctions in 2006. However, this sanction case remains active, as of January 2018. Over the years, the United Nations has followed this initial action with numerous additional resolutions extending the sanctions and calling for tightened enforcement. This explains why North Korea is trading mostly with its largest trading partner, China, via rail transport, and only 10 percent of its trade is carried with other trading partners using other modes of transportation.

Our other case focuses on Russia's attempt to coerce Georgia through the use of import sanctions. In April 2006, Russia imposed an import ban on Georgia's key agricultural exports (wine, water, and fruits) in response to the dispute over South Ossetia and Abkhazia

---

[v]According to Bierstecker *et al.* (2018), the full list of sanctions imposed in this initial stage included: "Arms imports and exports embargo on specific weapons (high end military equipment: battle tanks, armored combat vehicles, large caliber artillery systems, combat aircraft, attack helicopters, warships, missiles or missile systems defined by UN Registry on Conventional Arms), proliferation sensitive goods and technology imports and exports ban (specific items), luxury goods imports ban, and asset freeze on individuals/entities and travel ban on individuals (and their family members) contributing to nuclear proliferation." Additionally, member states were called upon to inspect cargo transiting to and from the DPRK, as necessary.

(Hufbauer *et al.*, 2012).[vi] By October 2006, Russia expanded the sanctions to halt all air, sea, rail and road transport to and from Georgia, and in November, Gazprom doubled Georgia's price for natural gas resulting in a 40 percent reduction in the volume of gas supplied. To cope with these losses, Georgia turned to Azerbaijan for alternative oil and gas supplies (Hufbauer *et al.*, 2007). It is estimated that prior to the sanctions, Georgia sent as much as 80 percent of its wine exports to Russia (BBC News, 2013), and accounted for approximately 10 percent of the Russian wine market. After the sanctions, Georgia's export potential fell and the main importer of Georgian wine shifted to Ukraine (Samofalova, 2013).

Even though Georgia has been an active member of the World Trade Organization (WTO) and attained permanent normal trade relations with other member countries in 2000, the Russian economic sanctions had a negative impact on its trade and economic development. The free trade agreement with the rest of the Commonwealth of Independent States (CIS FTA) and the Association Agreement (AA DCFTA) with the European Union eliminating various trade duties and restrictions, helped mitigate these negative consequences by redirecting exports of sanctioned goods to other countries using air, water, land and pipeline modes of transportation.

4.1. *The Model and Methodology*

Our empirical analysis estimates the impacts of international sanctions on the economies of North Korea and Georgia as well as sender countries using a dynamic CGE model. This is a multi-market model of behavioral responses of producers and consumers to price changes within the limits of labor, capital, and natural resource endowments (Dixon and Rimmer, 2002). CGE is a state-of-the-art approach to economic consequence analysis, which overcomes the

---

[vi]As it frequently does with its former republics (Gutterman, 2013), Russia officially suspended imports on health and sanitation grounds, but independent analysts agree that the actions were taken for political reasons (BBC Monitoring Former Soviet Union, 22 November 2006). Similar sanctions were imposed against Moldova, in the year prior, for scheming against Russia.

major limitations of the Input-Output analysis (Rose, 1995). CGE models incorporate input substitution, behavioral changes, provide information on prices and markets, and can differentiate between goods used for intermediate and final consumption.

CGE models have been extensively used in trade and transport-related analysis. Lloyd and MacLaren (2010) use a "semi-general equilibrium" approach, including non-tariff measures, to capture general-equilibrium impacts ignored in partial-equilibrium forms of the Trade Restrictiveness Index and the Mercantilist Trade Restrictiveness Index. Sandoval et al. (2009) analyze the economic feasibility of hydrogen trade and transportation with different carbon stabilization and tax policy scenarios using a CGE model of the global economy. In a recent study, Winchester et al. (2013) apply a recursive dynamic CGE model to analyze the impacts of a representative carbon policy on the US aviation operation and emissions. In this chapter, we apply a unique methodological refinement of the CGE approach to understand the effect of various types and levels of international sanctions on the severity and dissipation of economic losses over time.

Trade sanctions translate into changes in trade and transportation costs, which, in turn, translate into changes in relative competitiveness of target country imports and exports. By design, the costs of international sanctions will mainly be borne by the target country. They are generally designed to reduce or eliminate the exports of certain goods from sender countries entering the target market, making them relatively expensive, and spurring target country imports of such goods from its other trading partners. Additionally, the targeted goods will become cheaper in sending countries due to increased supply in domestic economics. This has the effect of initially advantaging sender countries. In some cases, sanctions may prevent the imports of certain goods from entering the sender country economy, inducing the target country to adjust domestic production and redirect their exports to other destinations. However, in the long run the negative impacts of international sanctions may dissipate and undermine the intended effects in the target country economy due to adjustment to sanctions through increased domestic production of targeted goods and trade substitution with other trading partners. The extent to which the negative effect of increased international sanctions is offset by the effect of increased domestic production and import/export substitution requires a sophisticated general equilibrium economic modeling approach.

We estimate the direct and indirect effects of differing types and levels of sanctions on the export of restricted goods in targeted economies using the modified version of the dynamic GTAP model called GDyn.[vii] This version of the model incorporates GDP and factor endowment growth rate projections within 2004–2020 for each country or region in the GTAP database (Walmsley, 2006). The GDyn model takes both real GDP and factor input growth as exogenous, and it allows a Hicks neutral technological change variable to balance these changes with other values in the model. We introduce the substitution between different modes of transport into the dynamic version of the GTAP model using the elasticities and approach developed by Avetisyan et al. (2021). The latter is a modified version of the GTAP computable general equilibrium model described in Hertel (1997).

In the GTAP model, the goods are produced by combining labor, capital, land, and intermediate inputs (including the energy substitution nest) using the Leontief functional form. First, the electricity and non-electricity goods are joined to form the energy nest governed by a constant elasticity of substitution (CES). The model then combines the energy sub-product with capital to form the capital-energy sub-product, which is later joined with other factors in a CES production function to generate the value-added nest. At the final level of the production structure, the value added is combined with intermediate inputs to produce the final output. The household forms its preferences over savings, consumption, and government spending based on the Cobb-Douglas assumption, while its consumption is administered by a constant-difference of elasticities (CDE) functional form.

International trade and transport in the GTAP model are represented by merchandise goods and "margin" services (shipping

---

[vii]https://www.gtap.agecon.purdue.edu/models/Dynamic/model.asp

services, or transport costs). These data are included in a "trade matrix," which describes bilateral flows of merchandise commodities, while the transport margins maintain the balance between global exports and imports.

We modify the dynamic version of the GTAP model by incorporating transport mode substitution, similar to that used for assessing the direct and indirect impacts of improved logistics and transport mode substitution in the global economy by Avetisyan and Hertel (2021). The latter estimates the modal substitution elasticities for land-air and water-air transport pairs, which are then modified using transport cost weighted aggregation to generate modal substitution elasticities by commodity, source, and destination. The estimated CES elasticities of substitution between 0.6 and 2.2 govern modal choice decisions in response to changes in the relative cost of various modes of transport. Also, in most sectors the water-air substitution elasticities dominate the land-air modal substitution elasticities.

In the modified version of the GTAP model, the modal use is governed by a CES elasticity of substitution as in the following equation:

$$TRANS_{m,i,r,s} = X_{i,r,s} * \tau_{m,i,r,s}^{(\sigma_{i,r,s}-1)} * \left(\frac{PTRANS_{i,r,s}}{PT_m} \right)^{\sigma_{i,r,s}} \quad (1)$$

where

$TRANS_{m,i,r,s}$ is the international usage of transport mode m to ship good i from region r to s;

$\tau_{m,i,r,s}$ is the transportation technology of mode m to ship good i from region r to s;

$X_{i,r,s}$ is the export sales of commodity i from region r to s;

$\sigma_{i,r,s}$ is the elasticity of modal substitution to ship good i from region r to s;

PT_m is the price of composite transportation services;

$PTRANS_{i,r,s}$ is the cost index for international transport shipping good i from region r to s.

Using the modified version of the dynamic GTAP model we look at how the GDP, local production and trade patterns are expected to change in response to different types of sanctions. Evidence from international sanctions imposed against North Korea over the testing of nuclear weapons and Russian sanctions against Georgia over the South Ossetia and Abkhazia dispute provide additional case study insights on how trade patterns with target countries and its production of different types of goods were altered as a result of the sanctions. In this chapter, we look at how export and import sanctions would have affected the GDP, domestic production, trade and transport patterns in target countries as well as in sender countries, and how these negative effects are likely to dissipate due to adjustment to sanctions over time. Additionally, we are able to provide a more generalized look at the effect of sanctions on different types of countries.

4.2. *Experimental Design*

For both the cases of sanctions, we look at the 2006–2008 period and observe the changes in the main macroeconomic variables and international trade and transport services. We then develop two scenarios for each economic sanction. The first scenario (a) examines only the direct and indirect impacts of economic sanctions for each target country within 2006–2008 (all other things held constant), while the second scenario; (b) replicates the first one and additionally assumes economic growth in all countries and regions of the world within 2006–2008. This enables better understanding of the negative impacts of international sanctions and how those effects dissipate over time.

Given the information about each of these sanctions, we begin there, and develop the analysis in great detail, before moving on to a summary of the results. For consistency, we use the GTAP version 8.1 data base for our economic sanctions experiments in North Korea and Georgia. The data base incorporates 134 regional economies with 57 industry/commodity groupings and includes the bilateral import and export trade linkages between these regions. In each sanctions experiment, we aggregate the GTAP version 8.1 data base to 17 regions and 29 sectors by maintaining the top 15 trading partner countries of North Korea and Georgia based on their trade data available from the International Trade Centre,[viii,ix] and then combining the remaining countries and regions to the 'Rest of World' region. With these sectoral and regional emphases, we begin by implementing two CGE experiments: NKSANCTIONS (a) and (b), in which we ban the export of luxury goods, arms and related material to North Korea, and GEOSANCTIONS (a) and (b), in which we apply an import ban on Georgia's key agricultural exports (wine, water and fruits). Following the detailed examination of total economic and transportation services impacts of these two international sanctions, we move on to a short summary and general conclusions.

5. Results

We first analyze the changes in GDP, domestic production, trade and transport services under scenarios NKSANCTIONS (a) and (b). Firstly, we focus on the effect of the sanctions on macroeconomic indicators of GDP and trade. As shown in Table 1a, under scenario NKSANCTIONS (a), the United Nations sanctions prohibiting exports of luxury goods, arms and related material to North Korea result in GDP, export, and import sales reductions across most countries with the largest reductions found in North Korea, at −1.1 percent, −36 percent, and −83 percent respectively. This result shows that the impact of international sanctions on trade and GDP is negative on both sender and target country economies, although much larger for the target. The major trading partner of North Korea, the China and Hong Kong region, also experiences significant negative impacts from these international sanctions.

Within the 2006–2007 period (Table 1a), we can see changes in imports and transport services use in all regions, with North Korea experiencing the largest reduction. Due to these sanctions, global air,

---

[viii]https://www.trademap.org/Country_SelProductCountry.aspx?nvpm=1%7c408
%7c%7c%7c%7cTOTAL%7c%7c%7c%7c2%7c1%7c2%7c2%7c1%7c1%7c2%7c1%7c1
[ix]https://www.trademap.org/Country_SelProductCountry.aspx?nvpm=1%7c268
%7c%7c%7c%7cTOTAL%7c%7c%7c%7c2%7c1%7c1%7c2%7c1%7c1%7c2%7c1%7c1

Table 1a. Scenario NKSANCTIONS (a) — GDP, trade and transportation impacts in 2006–2007 (no economic growth within 2006–2008) in percent change.

				Year 2006–2007		
					Transport	
Region	GDP	Exports	Imports	Other	Water	Air
China	−0.064	−0.220	−0.064	0.024	0.014	0.088
Hong Kong	−0.166	−0.251	−0.077	0.083	0.047	0.162
North Korea	−1.113	−35.972	−83.108	−17.831	−26.272	−27.173
India	−0.010	−0.099	−0.035	0.014	0.018	0.072
Pakistan	−0.002	−0.037	0.002	0.009	0.053	0.079
Brazil	−0.004	−0.071	−0.011	0.011	0.032	0.023
Colombia	−0.001	−0.034	0.001	0.013	0.011	0.051
Honduras	−0.003	−0.010	−0.004	0.068	0.069	0.080
Germany	−0.011	−0.042	−0.013	0.042	−0.007	0.100
Poland	−0.005	−0.030	−0.001	0.019	−0.076	0.076
Switzerland	−0.025	−0.058	−0.009	0.064	0.006	0.110
Russian Federation	−0.004	−0.028	−0.009	0.019	0.031	0.064
Saudi Arabia	−0.007	−0.023	−0.019	0.101	−0.049	0.203
Senegal	−0.006	−0.046	0.000	0.069	0.049	0.121
Mozambique	−0.003	−0.011	0.001	0.035	0.055	0.078
Zambia	−0.001	−0.017	0.000	0.005	0.012	0.040
Rest of World	−0.009	−0.056	−0.007	0.032	0.010	0.077
Total	—	−0.115	—	−0.055	−0.025	−0.036

water, and land transportation services[x] decline by −0.036 percent, −0.025 percent, and −0.055 percent, respectively. Since North Korea is trading primarily through rail transport, the reduced exports to the country mainly affect the global use of other (land/rail) transportation during the initial year of economic sanctions. Following the first year of international sanctions, during the 2007–2008 period (Table 1a and b) both North Korea and the rest of the countries of the world see improvements in main macroeconomic variables driven predominantly by export and import substitution, changes in domestic production patterns, and transport mode substitution.

---

[x] "Other" transportation services are primarily rail and other land transportation.

Table 1b. Scenario NKSANCTIONS (a) — GDP, trade and transportation impacts in 2007–2008 (no economic growth within 2006–2008) in percent change.

			Year 2007–2008			
				Transport		
Region	**GDP**	**Exports**	**Imports**	**Other**	**Water**	**Air**
China	−0.006	−0.015	−0.003	0.002	0.002	0.008
Hong Kong	−0.052	−0.048	−0.017	0.008	0.005	0.015
North Korea	−1.106	−6.177	−27.679	−2.664	−5.112	−3.759
India	−0.003	−0.014	−0.004	0.001	0.004	0.007
Pakistan	−0.001	−0.004	−0.001	0.001	0.008	0.008
Brazil	−0.001	−0.008	−0.002	0.001	0.006	0.003
Colombia	−0.001	−0.004	0.000	0.002	0.003	0.005
Honduras	−0.001	−0.001	0.000	0.008	0.011	0.008
Germany	−0.004	−0.006	−0.002	0.005	0.002	0.010
Poland	−0.001	−0.002	0.000	0.004	−0.007	0.006
Switzerland	−0.008	−0.008	−0.002	0.007	0.002	0.011
Russian Federation	−0.001	−0.004	−0.002	0.002	0.005	0.007
Saudi Arabia	−0.001	−0.002	−0.002	0.013	−0.005	0.021
Senegal	−0.002	−0.006	−0.001	0.009	0.008	0.013
Mozambique	0.000	−0.001	0.000	0.005	0.009	0.008
Zambia	0.000	−0.001	0.000	0.002	0.002	0.004
Rest of World	−0.003	−0.007	−0.002	0.004	0.003	0.008
Total	—	−0.013	—	0.0009	−0.002	0.0006

This result supports Hypothesis 4, which expects that the negative impacts of economic sanctions dissipate over time. We also observe improvement in global exports. As expected, at the global level, the use of air and other (land/rail) transport services increases, while the sea transport services experience reduction during the two-year period of international sanctions. This is in line with our assumption that economic sanctions will have the largest negative impact on the use of sea transport, since about 70 percent of the world trade is carried by water.

Under scenario NKSANCTIONS (b), shown in Tables 2a and 2b, we consider economic growth along with the United Nations' sanctions banning exports of luxury goods, arms and related material to North Korea. Their trade levels still decline but at a lower rate.

Table 2a. Scenario NKSANCTIONS (b) — GDP, trade and transportation impacts in 2006–2007 (assuming economic growth within 2006–2007) in percent change.

				Year 2006–2007		
				Transport		
Region	GDP	Exports	Imports	Other	Water	Air
China	6.992	8.435	4.847	7.247	6.309	6.809
Hong Kong	4.342	4.012	4.633	4.432	4.182	4.403
North Korea	3.150	−34.697	−82.418	−15.223	−23.610	−25.234
India	5.962	7.819	4.285	6.083	5.487	6.157
Pakistan	5.823	4.507	5.556	6.288	5.730	5.683
Brazil	3.830	0.013	5.266	3.696	2.942	3.616
Colombia	3.470	4.881	2.052	3.460	3.845	3.913
Honduras	2.904	3.033	2.581	3.115	3.131	3.051
Germany	1.979	2.088	2.148	2.277	3.576	2.643
Poland	4.493	3.049	4.273	4.213	3.739	3.901
Switzerland	2.200	1.768	2.408	2.382	2.774	2.576
Russian Federation	4.411	5.386	2.853	4.494	4.700	4.656
Saudi Arabia	3.372	3.516	3.245	3.258	3.357	3.287
Senegal	5.341	4.452	4.680	5.579	5.425	5.152
Mozambique	3.134	3.000	3.212	3.837	3.639	3.737
Zambia	3.700	3.515	3.551	3.716	3.778	3.815
Rest of World	2.973	2.567	3.111	3.037	3.405	3.101
Total	—	3.109	—	3.060	3.881	3.432

In all other regions, economic growth effects dominate the negative direct and indirect impacts of international sanctions imposed on their trade with North Korea.

As illustrated in Tables 2a and 2b, the North Korean economy still experiences some of the negative impacts of international sanctions, but these are declining at the end of the 2006–2008 period, supporting the assumption that the negative effects of international sanctions dissipate over time. Since rail transportation is the main mode of transport for the trade between North Korea and its major trading partner China, increased use of rail transportation (0.003 percent) contributes to the economic growth in North Korea. Global exports and use of all transport services are also increasing due to assumed global economic growth within the 2006–2008 interval.

Table 2b. Scenario NKSANCTIONS (b) — GDP, trade and transportation impacts in 2007–2008 (assuming economic growth within 2007–2008) in percent change.

				Year 2007–2008		
					Transport	
Region	GDP	Exports	Imports	Other	Water	Air
China	6.839	8.491	4.750	7.003	6.158	6.566
Hong Kong	4.495	4.264	4.699	4.382	4.152	4.292
North Korea	3.122	−5.069	−23.811	0.003	−1.778	−1.833
India	5.828	7.861	4.205	5.905	5.426	5.971
Pakistan	5.626	4.757	5.262	6.031	5.600	5.507
Brazil	3.758	0.303	5.073	3.614	2.936	3.534
Colombia	3.572	4.854	2.231	3.530	3.848	3.907
Honduras	3.074	3.102	2.753	3.170	3.110	3.085
Germany	1.922	2.044	2.118	2.173	3.560	2.475
Poland	4.045	3.027	3.785	3.848	3.786	3.608
Switzerland	2.136	1.795	2.329	2.255	2.722	2.421
Russian Federation	3.852	4.777	2.584	3.922	4.192	4.083
Saudi Arabia	3.570	3.670	3.505	3.322	3.484	3.230
Senegal	4.988	4.477	4.326	5.202	5.079	4.830
Mozambique	3.132	2.997	3.224	3.787	3.563	3.653
Zambia	3.722	3.547	3.572	3.724	3.782	3.798
Rest of World	2.965	2.586	3.110	2.989	3.380	3.010
Total	—	3.184	—	3.091	3.887	3.444

In Tables 3a and 3b, we look specifically at the production, export and import of goods restricted by sanctions. According to Tables 3a and 3b, the United Nations' sanctions significantly affect the domestic production of sanctioned goods in North Korea, increasing it by 15.7 percent and 1.7 percent during the first and second years of sanctions and by 21.1 percent and 6.4 percent during the first and second years of sanctions under scenarios NKSANCTIONS (a) and NKSANCTIONS (b), respectively. Under the scenario NKSANC-TIONS (a), majority of the countries reduce their production of sanctioned goods due to decline in exports to North Korea and other regions. However, with scenario NKSANCTIONS (b), North Korean imports of these goods are again eliminated, but other countries

Table 3a. Scenario NKSANCTIONS (a and b) — Domestic production and trade of sanctioned goods in percent change.

Region	No economic growth within 2006–2008 (a)					
	Year 2006–2007			Year 2007–2008		
	Output	Exports	Imports	Output	Exports	Imports
China	−0.0120	−0.318	−0.067	0.0008	−0.020	−0.002
Hong Kong	−0.0229	−0.426	−0.108	0.0022	−0.077	−0.021
North Korea	15.7261	−59.522	−100.000	1.6906	−14.538	−100.000
India	−0.0010	−0.134	−0.022	0.0008	−0.021	−0.003
Pakistan	−0.0026	−0.064	0.008	0.0001	−0.008	0.000
Brazil	0.0000	−0.171	−0.008	0.0004	−0.022	−0.002
Colombia	0.0004	−0.120	0.006	0.0001	−0.016	0.000
Honduras	0.0027	−0.023	−0.007	0.0001	−0.005	−0.001
Germany	−0.0017	−0.070	−0.013	0.0005	−0.011	−0.002
Poland	0.0003	−0.049	0.002	0.0002	−0.003	0.001
Switzerland	−0.0086	−0.141	−0.014	0.0013	−0.020	−0.003
Russian Federation	−0.0030	−0.239	−0.003	0.0000	−0.035	−0.001
Saudi Arabia	−0.0102	−0.364	−0.016	0.0004	−0.020	−0.001
Senegal	−0.0075	−0.199	−0.001	0.0001	−0.027	−0.001
Mozambique	−0.0056	−0.270	0.007	0.0002	−0.013	0.001
Zambia	0.0017	−0.121	0.004	0.0002	−0.006	0.001
Rest of World	−0.0023	−0.121	−0.007	0.0006	−0.017	−0.002

increase both their exports and imports of sanctioned goods to and from the rest of the world regions.

We now turn to the Russian import sanctions against Georgia. As in the previous example of the United Nations' sanctions against North Korea, we analyze changes in GDP, domestic production, trade and transport services under scenarios GEOSANCTIONS (a) and (b). As shown in Tables 4a and 4b, under scenario GEOSANCTIONS (a), the Russian sanctions banning Georgian imports of wine, water and fruits in response to the dispute over South Ossetia and Abkhazia result in GDP, export, and import reduction in several countries with the largest reduction happening in Georgia, −0.0247 percent, −0.0958 percent, and −0.068 percent, respectively. Because we use CGE modelling, we can uncover some of the complex natures of the effect of sanctions. Despite the Russian sanctions being focused on Georgian exports, Georgian imports are also seen to decline because

Table 3b. Scenario NKSANCTIONS (a and b) — Domestic production and trade of sanctioned goods in percent change.

| | No economic growth within 2006–2008 (b) | | | | | |
| | Year 2006–2007 | | | Year 2007–2008 | | |
Region	Output	Exports	Imports	Output	Exports	Imports
China	7.073	8.662	4.375	6.876	8.800	4.282
Hong Kong	4.469	3.876	4.768	4.530	4.291	4.859
North Korea	21.055	−59.251	−100.000	6.430	−14.939	−100.000
India	6.069	8.919	3.454	5.935	8.968	3.351
Pakistan	5.842	4.772	5.219	5.668	5.066	4.857
Brazil	3.869	−1.838	6.046	3.787	−1.381	5.771
Colombia	3.438	5.670	1.476	3.552	5.570	1.704
Honduras	2.793	3.182	2.422	2.963	3.246	2.624
Germany	1.823	1.872	2.098	1.766	1.844	2.085
Poland	4.439	2.834	4.438	3.971	2.856	3.866
Switzerland	2.034	1.355	2.531	1.963	1.451	2.440
Russian Federation	4.182	5.868	2.670	3.627	5.374	2.407
Saudi Arabia	2.803	2.827	3.373	3.069	3.030	3.644
Senegal	5.468	4.626	4.277	5.102	4.799	3.887
Mozambique	3.136	2.727	3.192	3.149	2.920	3.237
Zambia	3.611	3.425	3.467	3.635	3.513	3.495
Rest of World	2.824	2.251	3.168	2.818	2.315	3.180

reduced exports are translated to reduced production, which now requires fewer inputs including imported intermediate goods.

Although the export and import sales as well as the use of all transportation services in Russia decline due the import sanctions, its GDP increases by 0.000011 percent. This result shows that the impact of international sanctions is not always negative on sending country economies. Due to these sanctions, we observe substitution between other (land/rail) and air/water transportation at the global level. Specifically, within the 2006–2007 period, the decline in the global use of other (land/rail) transportation services by 0.001082 percent is compensated by increased use of sea and air transport services by 0.000123 percent, and 0.000526 percent, respectively.

During the 2007–2008 period, both Georgia and the rest of the countries see improvements in main macroeconomic variables driven predominantly by export and import substitution as well

Table 4a. Scenario GEOSANCTIONS (a) — GDP, trade and transportation impacts (no economic growth within 2006–2007) in 10^{-3} percent change.

| | | | Year 2006–2007 | | | |
| | | | | Transport | | |
Region	GDP	Exports	Imports	Other	Water	Air
China	−0.011	−0.019	−0.005	−0.026	0.028	0.079
United States	0.000	−0.039	0.025	−0.016	0.014	0.030
Belgium	−0.005	−0.028	−0.004	−0.159	0.063	0.069
France	−0.002	−0.027	0.005	−0.074	0.072	0.049
Germany	−0.001	−0.015	0.009	−0.027	0.099	0.041
Italy	−0.002	−0.023	0.012	−0.034	0.059	−0.004
Switzerland	−0.001	−0.018	−0.025	−0.037	0.025	0.013
Bulgaria	0.009	−0.059	0.061	−0.238	0.065	−0.059
Russian Federation	0.011	−0.265	−1.319	−0.156	−0.055	−0.052
Ukraine	−0.023	−0.037	−0.044	−0.232	0.209	0.253
Kazakhstan	−0.001	0.175	0.172	−0.099	−0.029	−0.051
Armenia	−0.064	0.731	1.703	0.353	0.534	1.245
Azerbaijan	−0.030	0.205	0.502	−0.314	0.026	0.001
Georgia	−24.701	−95.837	−68.063	41.016	76.123	72.496
Iran	0.000	0.037	0.037	−0.070	0.070	0.046
Turkey	−0.006	0.032	0.175	−0.039	−0.051	−0.082
Rest of World	−0.002	−0.008	0.012	−0.079	0.043	0.027
Total	—	−0.035	—	−1.082	0.123	0.526

as changes in domestic production patterns. This result again supports Hypothesis 4 about the negative impacts of economic sanctions dissipating over time. At the end of the two-year period of Russian sanctions, global exports and the use of all transport services are growing and reducing the global negative impacts of sanctions. However, we observe larger increase in the use of air and other (land/rail) transport services (0.000023 percent and 0.000009 percent, respectively) relative to the use of sea transportation (0.000005 percent), which again supports our initial assumption that international economic sanctions will have the largest negative impact on the use of sea transport, which is the most widely used mode of transportation in international trade.

Under scenario GEOSANCTIONS (b), shown in Tables 5a and 5b, we consider global economic growth along with the Russian sanctions

Table 4b. Scenario GEOSANCTIONS (a) — GDP, trade and transportation impacts (no economic growth within 2007–2008) in 10^{-3} percent change.

| Region | Year 2007–2008 | | | | | |
| | GDP | Exports | Imports | Transport | | |
				Other	Water	Air
China	0.000	−0.001	0.000	−0.001	0.001	0.003
United States	0.000	−0.003	0.002	0.000	0.000	0.001
Belgium	0.000	−0.001	0.000	−0.001	0.002	0.003
France	0.000	−0.002	0.001	−0.001	0.002	0.001
Germany	0.000	−0.001	0.001	0.000	0.004	0.001
Italy	0.000	−0.002	0.001	−0.001	0.002	−0.001
Switzerland	0.000	−0.001	−0.001	−0.001	0.001	0.000
Bulgaria	0.000	−0.006	0.006	−0.003	0.000	−0.008
Russian Federation	0.000	−0.010	−0.047	−0.004	−0.002	−0.001
Ukraine	−0.001	−0.003	−0.006	0.004	0.014	0.016
Kazakhstan	0.000	0.006	0.008	−0.001	−0.001	−0.002
Armenia	−0.002	0.047	0.038	0.052	0.037	0.102
Azerbaijan	−0.002	0.001	0.013	−0.006	0.013	0.023
Georgia	−4.445	−2.109	−5.635	1.447	5.061	4.176
Iran	0.000	0.001	0.002	−0.001	0.002	0.002
Turkey	0.000	0.000	0.005	0.000	−0.001	0.000
Rest of World	0.000	−0.001	0.001	−0.001	0.001	0.000
Total	—	−0.002	—	0.009	0.005	0.023

prohibiting Georgian imports of wine, water and fruits in response to the dispute over South Ossetia and Abkhazia. In all regions, economic growth effects dominate the negative direct and indirect impacts of Russian sanctions imposed on Georgian imports.

As illustrated in Tables 4a, 4b, 5a and 5b, the negative impacts of Russian sanctions on the Georgian economy are declining at the end of the 2006–2008 period, again revealing how the negative effects of sanctions dissipate over time. Georgian exports and imports are carried via air, water, land and pipeline modes of transport, and therefore increased use of all transportation services contributes to the economic growth in the country. Moreover, global exports and international use of all transport services are also increasing due to assumed global economic growth within the 2006–2008 period.

Table 5a. Scenario GEOSANCTIONS (b) — GDP, trade and transportation impacts (assuming economic growth within 2006–2007).

| | | | | | Year 2006–2007 | |
| | | | | Transport | | |
Region	GDP	Exports	Imports	Other	Water	Air
China	6.991	8.624	4.918	7.144	6.235	6.579
United States	3.134	1.468	3.901	3.056	3.127	2.999
Belgium	2.097	2.298	2.098	2.593	3.519	2.752
France	2.531	2.566	2.580	2.736	3.722	3.039
Germany	1.979	2.133	2.149	2.276	3.606	2.667
Italy	2.352	2.750	2.346	2.553	3.438	2.748
Switzerland	2.200	1.822	2.364	2.297	2.764	2.374
Bulgaria	4.194	2.150	4.562	3.595	3.654	2.711
Russian Federation	4.411	5.536	2.814	4.487	4.653	4.595
Ukraine	4.279	4.367	3.798	4.099	4.119	4.085
Kazakhstan	5.736	5.301	5.610	5.577	5.677	5.492
Armenia	5.165	6.599	4.501	5.356	5.527	5.699
Azerbaijan	15.103	14.000	14.756	14.390	10.687	11.079
Georgia	7.751	3.089	8.347	6.202	4.712	5.825
Iran	5.056	5.782	3.738	4.855	4.444	4.909
Turkey	4.910	2.905	5.143	4.970	4.530	3.949
Rest of World	3.092	2.899	3.128	3.170	3.525	3.214
Total	—	3.233	—	3.249	3.933	3.452

The Russian sanctions have significant impact on the domestic production and trade of sanctioned goods in Georgia, as shown in Tables 6a and 6b.

Under scenario GEOSANCTIONS (a), the domestic production of sanctioned goods in Georgia changed by −0.2 percent and 0.001 percent in the first and second years of sanctions, respectively. These results, again, support the expectation presented in Hypothesis 4, of a dissipating effect of sanctions over time. Also, due to export substitution the reduction in Georgian exports of these goods became less severe during the 2006–2008 period.

It is also interesting that we observed an increase in the domestic production of fruits and vegetables, wine, water and preserved fruit in Russia along with reduced total exports and imports of these goods even though its sanctions restricted only the import of such

Table 5b. Scenario GEOSANCTIONS (b) — GDP, trade and transportation impacts (assuming economic growth within 2007–2008).

| | | | | Year 2007–2008 | | |
| | | | | | Transport | |
Region	GDP	Exports	Imports	Other	Water	Air
China	6.839	8.515	4.783	6.988	6.143	6.487
United States	3.179	1.489	3.916	3.089	3.167	3.026
Belgium	2.094	2.260	2.096	2.572	3.497	2.721
France	2.447	2.500	2.503	2.632	3.628	2.943
Germany	1.922	2.057	2.111	2.203	3.579	2.557
Italy	2.314	2.636	2.328	2.491	3.395	2.676
Switzerland	2.136	1.804	2.296	2.238	2.721	2.335
Bulgaria	4.066	2.272	4.312	3.536	3.646	2.814
Russian Federation	3.852	4.878	2.546	3.932	4.182	4.086
Ukraine	3.630	3.888	3.217	3.623	3.812	3.727
Kazakhstan	4.861	4.795	4.604	4.733	4.830	4.773
Armenia	4.969	6.608	4.229	5.231	5.344	5.628
Azerbaijan	11.346	10.956	10.252	10.799	8.710	9.026
Georgia	6.193	3.519	6.386	5.252	4.356	5.066
Iran	5.039	5.704	3.808	4.754	4.294	4.689
Turkey	4.722	3.078	4.819	4.759	4.405	4.010
Rest of World	3.058	2.858	3.100	3.124	3.494	3.169
Total	—	3.190	—	3.183	3.905	3.419

goods from Georgia. This is mostly due to the time required for import substitution. However, in addition to the growing domestic production of these goods, Russia increased their imports from other regions during the second year of economic sanctions to partially substitute for the reduced importation of Georgian goods.

Under the scenario GEOSANCTIONS (b), the domestic production of sanctioned goods in Georgia continues to experience positive growth throughout the first and second years of sanctions. Also, due to export substitution, Georgian exports of fresh and preserved fruits, wine, and water increase by 2.6 percent at the end of the 2006–2008 period. This evidence indicates that Georgia may have had an easier time finding substitute markets for its goods than Russia anticipated when imposing its sanctions and provides general support for Hypothesis 3. Moreover, as can be seen in this quote

Table 6a. Scenario GEOSANCTIONS (a and b) — Domestic production and trade of sanctioned goods in percent change.

| | No economic growth within 2006–2008 (a) (10^{-3}percent) | | | | | |
| | Year 2006–2007 | | | Year 2007–2008 | | |
Region	Output	Exports	Imports	Output	Exports	Imports
China	0.087	1.614	−0.323	0.003	0.055	−0.012
United States	0.097	0.508	−0.065	0.001	0.020	−0.002
Belgium	1.215	0.852	0.147	0.011	0.030	0.005
France	0.116	0.237	−0.054	0.002	0.008	−0.002
Germany	0.234	0.607	0.073	0.003	0.017	0.001
Italy	0.168	0.660	0.093	0.003	0.025	0.001
Switzerland	0.093	0.253	−0.007	0.001	0.004	−0.001
Bulgaria	0.112	0.583	0.378	0.000	0.002	0.013
Russian Federation	2.099	−9.743	−20.353	0.060	−0.393	−0.719
Ukraine	−0.347	−0.922	2.081	−0.051	−0.191	0.073
Kazakhstan	2.050	20.709	−0.322	0.077	0.753	−0.005
Armenia	−0.349	1.578	7.621	−0.025	0.097	0.266
Azerbaijan	−0.637	20.945	2.053	0.002	0.566	0.041
Georgia	−197.815	−3030.96	−164.611	1.138	−151.462	−7.529
Iran	0.605	6.051	0.025	0.027	0.237	0.001
Turkey	0.448	6.289	0.367	0.018	0.246	0.009
Rest of World	0.196	1.036	0.068	0.005	0.038	0.002

from the Daily Telegraph, conditions were observed, at the time, as turning against the perceived Russian advantage, "Worse still for the Kremlin, Georgia increasingly began to show that its dependence on Russia was actually shrinking. Exporters found new markets, while the Georgian government looked to buy its gas from Azerbaijan and encouraged other countries in the region to band together against Russian bullying" (Blomfield, 2007).

During the same period the Russian economy also increased its production and imports of sanctioned goods from other countries to substitute for reduced imports of such goods from Georgia. This is further evidence that the Russian economy was also able to adjust relatively quickly to the effects of its own sanctions. We also see that, while the primary objective of the sanctions was to hurt Georgia, one of their main effects was to dramatically increase all levels of economic activity in Azerbaijan. This was due primarily to the fact that Azerbaijan was the main alternative supplier of gas to Georgia

Table 6b. Scenario GEOSANCTIONS (a and b) — Domestic production and trade of sanctioned goods in percent change.

| Region | No economic growth within 2006–2008 (b) (percent) | | | | | |
| | Year 2006–2007 | | | Year 2007–2008 | | |
	Output	Exports	Imports	Output	Exports	Imports
China	6.113	7.976	3.464	5.968	7.812	3.343
United States	2.813	1.637	3.171	2.845	1.622	3.185
Belgium	2.036	1.959	1.978	2.009	1.918	1.960
France	2.284	2.144	2.279	2.212	2.104	2.210
Germany	1.899	1.849	2.007	1.839	1.794	1.955
Italy	2.141	1.984	2.247	2.097	1.919	2.218
Switzerland	2.114	2.071	2.436	2.051	2.022	2.359
Bulgaria	2.938	2.178	3.297	2.870	2.263	3.092
Russian Federation	3.559	6.169	2.158	3.091	5.387	2.021
Ukraine	3.431	4.231	3.048	2.898	3.605	2.639
Kazakhstan	4.004	3.020	4.747	3.368	2.826	3.948
Armenia	4.357	5.695	3.377	4.175	5.519	3.076
Azerbaijan	12.146	12.382	9.516	9.128	9.955	6.985
Georgia	5.407	−0.355	7.142	4.593	2.606	5.659
Iran	3.517	4.149	2.893	3.461	3.853	2.941
Turkey	3.636	1.942	3.755	3.484	2.012	3.511
Rest of World	2.618	2.514	2.679	2.579	2.469	2.642

after Gazprom doubled the price and cut the volume of gas shipments in December of 2006.

6. Conclusions

The severity of international sanctions and the choice of target countries and sectors have important implications for the economic effects of such sanctions. In the case of international sanctions imposed against North Korea, both the target and sending economies experience negative direct and indirect impacts. However, we can clearly see that the Russian sanctions imposed against Georgian imports positively affect the Russian economy, while having a negative impact on Georgia during the initial period of sanctions. These results illustrate the sending country's ability to design sanctions that negatively affect the target country economy more than the sending country.

We also find that sanctions have significant impacts on the domestic production of sanctioned goods in senders and targets. Our results indicate that sanctions significantly increase the domestic production of sanctioned goods in North Korea during the first and second years of sanctions. The majority of other countries reduce their production of sanctioned goods due to a decline in exports to North Korea and other regions. However, the economic growth during the sanctions period induces other countries to increase their trade of sanctioned goods with the rest of the world.

The simulation of Russia's sanctions against Georgia also provides evidence that sanctions have a dissipating impact on the domestic production of sanctioned goods. Economic growth in Georgia during the simulation induces Georgia to increase the domestic production of sanctioned goods driven by increased exports to other countries. This may seem counter-intuitive, but Georgia is a relatively small country, and the rest of the world is able to absorb the surplus of Georgian goods rather easily. Thus, due to economic growth and export substitution, Georgian exports of sanctioned goods actually increase within the economic sanctions period. These results help in understanding why Russia was unable to compel a meaningful shift in Georgian policy and is generally considered to have failed in its coercion attempt despite economic conditions appearing to favor the use of sanctions (Hufbauer et al., 2007).

We also observe that economic growth in Russia during the sanctions' period induces an increase in production and imports of the sanctioned goods in Russia to substitute for reduced imports from Georgia. Specifically, the CGE results reveal that Russia increases its production of fresh fruits, while substituting reduced imports of wine, water and preserved fruits from Georgia with imports of these goods from other countries during the period of economic sanctions.

Regarding the effect of sanctions on modes of transportation, sea transport is the most cost-effective mode of transportation to move goods and raw materials between countries, with over

90 percent of the world's trade being carried by sea.[xi] Therefore, any international trade sanction will have the largest negative impact on sea transportation, as shown in our analysis. Tables 1 and 4 illustrate that at the end of the two-year period of international sanctions, global water transportation is the most affected mode of transport under both the United Nations–North Korea and Russia–Georgia sanctions.

The results of this study have some limitations and because of compositional variations in the sanctioned goods across regions, these cannot be generalized to all countries. We can state that both direct and indirect negative impacts of international sanctions on target economies dissipate over time due to export and import substitution, changes in domestic production patterns, and transport mode substitution.

References

Alexander, K. (2009). *Economic Sanctions: Law and Public Policy.* Palgrave Macmillan, London.

Avetisyan, M., and Hertel, T. (2021). Impacts of Trade Facilitation on Modal Choice in International Trade. *Economics of Transportation, 28*, 100236.

Bierstecker, T., Tourinho, M., and Hudakova, Z. (2018). Sanctions App. https://unsanctionsapp.com/ (accessed January 24, 2018).

Biglaiser, G., and Lektzian, D. (2011). The Effect of Sanctions on U.S. Foreign Direct Investment. *International Organization, 65*(3), 531–551.

Black, P.A., and Cooper, J.H. (1987). On the Welfare and Employment Effects of Economic Sanctions. *The South African Journal of Economics, 55*(1), 1–15.

Blomfield, A. (2007, January 20). *Russia Backs Down in Spat With Georgia.* The Daily Telegraph,London. .

British Broadcasting Company Monitoring Former Soviet Union. (2006, November 22). Referenced in Hufbauer, Gary, Jeffrey J. Schott, Kimberly Ann Elliott, and Barbara Oegg. 2007. Economic Sanctions Reconsidered. 3rd ed. Washington: Peterson Institute.

[xi]https://business.un.org/en/entities/13

British Broadcasting Company. (2013). *Russian Wine Move Draws Protests*. http://news.bbc.co.uk/go/pr/fr/-/2/hi/europe/4860454.stm (accessed January 24, 2018).

Caruso, R. (2003). The Impact of International Economic Sanctions on Trade: An Empirical Analysis. *Peace Economics, Peace Science and Public Policy, 9*(2), 1–34.

Dixon, P.B., and Rimmer, M.T. (2002). Dynamic General Equilibrium Modeling for Forecasting and Policy: A Practical Guide and Documentation of MONASH. *Contributions to Economic Analysis, 256*. North-Holland, Amsterdam.

Drezner, D. (1998). Conflict Expectations and the Paradox of Economic Coercion. *International Studies Quarterly, 42*(4), 709–731.

Early, B.R. (2009). Sleeping With Your Friends' Enemies: An Explanation of Sanctions-Busting Trade. *International Studies Quarterly, 53*(1), 49–71.

Felbermayr, G., Aleksandra, K., Syropoulos, C., Yalcin, E., and Yotov, Y. (2020). The Global Sanctions Data Base. *European Economic Review*.

Galtung, J. (1967). On the Effects of International Economic Sanctions: With Examples from the Case of Rhodesia. *World Politics, 19*(3), 378–416.

Gharibnavaz, M.R., and Waschik, R. (2017). A Computable General Equilibrium Model of International Sanctions in Iran. *The World Economy, 41*, (1), 287–307.

Gholz, E., and Hughes, L. (2019). Market Structure and Economic Sanctions: The 2010 Rare Earth Elements Episode as a Pathway Case of Market Adjustment. *Review of International Political Economy*, Online First. DOI: 10.1080/09692290.2019.1693411.

Global Trade Analysis Project. (2015). Available from: https://www.gtap.agecon.purdue.edu/models/current.asp

Gutterman, S. (2013, October 7). Russia Halts Lithuanian Dairy Imports Before EU Summit. *Reuters*. https://www.reuters.com/article/us-russia-lithuania-dairy/russia-halts-lithuanian-dairy-imports-us-russia-lithuania-dairy/russia-halts-lithuanian-dairy-imports-before-eu-summit-idUSBRE99604Y20131007. Last Accessed: January 24, 2018.

Haberler, G. (1968). International Trade and Economic Development. In Theberge, J.D. (Ed.), *Economics of Trade and Development* (pp. 103–112). John Wiley, New York.

Hertel, T. (1997). *Global Trade Analysis: Modeling and Applications*. Cambridge University Press, Cambridge.

Hufbauer, G.C., Elliott, K.A., Cyrus, T., and Winston, E. (1997). US Economic Sanctions: Their Impact on Trade, Jobs, and Wages. *Peterson*

Institute for International Economics. https://www.piie.com/publica tions/working-papers/us-economic-sanctions-their-impact-trade-jobs-and-wages.

Hufbauer, G.C., Schott, J.J., Elliot, K.A., and Muir, J. (2012). Case Studies in Economic Sanctions and Terrorism: Post-2000 Sanctions Episodes. *Peterson Institute for International Economics.* https://piie.com/sites/ default/files/publications/papers/sanctions-timeline-post-2000.pdf (accessed January 24, 2018).

Hufbauer, G.C., Schott, J.J., Elliott, K.A., and Oegg, B. (2007). *Economic Sanctions Reconsidered* (3rd Edn.). Peterson Institute, Washington.

Ianchovichina, E., Devarajan, S., and Lakatos, C. (2016). Lifting Economic Sanctions on Iran: Global Effects and Strategic Responses. *World Bank Group* (Policy Research Working Paper 7549).

Kim, J. (2010). Recent Trends in Export Restrictions. *OECD Trade Policy Papers*, No. 101, OECD Publishing, Paris. http://dx.doi.org/10.1787/ 5kmbjx63sl27-en.

Kitous, A., Saveyn, B., Gervais, S., Wiesenthal, T., and Soria, A. (2013). Analysis of the Iran Oil Embargo. *Joint Research Centre Scientific and Policy Reports*, European Commission. file:///C:/Users/User/ Downloads/lfna25691enn.pdf

Lektzian, D., and Biglaiser, G. (2013). Investment, Opportunity, and Risk: Do US Sanctions Deter or Encourage Global Investment? *International Studies Quarterly, 57*(4), 65–78.

Lektzian, D., and Patterson, D. (2015). Political Cleavages and Economic Sanctions: The Economic and Political Winners and Losers of Sanctions. *International Studies Quarterly, 59*(1), 46–58.

Lloyd, P., and MacLaren, D. (2010). Partial-and General-Equilibrium Measures of Trade Restrictiveness. *Review of International Economics, 18*(5), 1044–1057.

McLean, E.V., and Whang, T. (2010). Friends or Foes? Major Trading Partners and the Success of Economic Sanctions. *International Studies Quarterly, 54*(2), 427–47.

Peterson, T. (2011). Third-Party Trade, Political Similarity, and Dyadic Conflict. *Journal of Peace Research, 48*(2), 185–200.

Pond, A. (2017). Economic Sanctions and Demand for Protection. *Journal of Conflict Resolution, 61*(5), 1073–1094.

Rodrigue, J.-P., Comtois, C., and Slack, B. (2017). *The Geography of Transport Systems.* Routledge.

Rogowski, R. (1987). Political Cleavages and Changing Exposure to Trade. *American Political Science Review, 81*(4), 1121–1137.

Rose, A. (1995). Input-Output Economics and Computable General Equilibrium Models. *Structural Change and Economic Dynamics*, *6*(3), 295–304.

Samofalova, O. (2013). *Cheaper than in Ukraine*. https://vz.ru/economy/2013/2/4/618877.html (accessed January 24, 2018).

Sandoval, R., Karplus, V.J., Paltsev, S., and Reilly, J.M. (2009). Modelling Prospects for Hydrogen-Powered Transportation Until 2100. *Journal of Transport Economics and Policy*, *43*(3), 291–316.

Spindler, Z. 1995. The Public Choice of "Superior" Sanctions. *Public Choice*, *85*, 205–226.

Walmsley, T. (2006). A Baseline Scenario for the Dynamic GTAP Model. GTAP Working Paper 2854.

Winchester, N., Wollersheim, C., Clewlow, R., Jost, N.C., Paltsev, S., Reilly, J.M., and Waitz, I.A. (2013). The Impact of Climate Policy on US Aviation. *Journal of Transport Economics and Policy*, *47*(1), 1–15.

Chapter 9

Highway Project and Residential Property Quality: The Case of Vías Nuevas De Lima

T. Edward Yu

Department of Agricultural and Resource Economics, University of Tennessee, USA

Pedro Rojas

Research Center, Universidad del Pacífico, Peru

Yohnny Campana

Macroconsult, Peru

David Hughes

Department of Agricultural and Resource Economics, University of Tennessee, USA

Julio Aguirre

Department of Economics, Universidad del Pacífico, Peru

The impacts of a highway renovation and expansion project, Vías Nuevas de Lima (VNL) (starting in 2013 in Lima, Peru), on the number of residents in nearby higher-quality property is examined in this study. A regression model is applied to block-level residential data near the North Panamericana section of the VNL in 2007 and 2017. The model includes linear and quadratic terms measuring proximity to the renovated highway as well as other (control) variables. Model results suggest that, before the project, proximity to the highway did not affect the number of people residing in higher-quality properties. However, after renovation, proximity to the VNL has a non-monotonic type of impact, suggesting that the expanded and renovated highway attracts more residents to settle in nearby "middle-buffer" higher-quality properties. A similar pattern is also found in terms of the formal education levels of residents. However, proximity to the highway does not affect the number of residents in lower-quality housing regardless of the status of the project. Findings imply that renovated highway project may affect the composition of nearby neighborhoods and increase the demand for higher quality, more valuable property in proximate areas.

1. Introduction

A large body of research has been conducted to evaluate the impact of public transportation infrastructure investment on urban and/or regional development. Transportation infrastructure investments in a region may trigger population decentralization and influence levels of congestion and vehicle emissions (Baum-Snow, 2007; Brueckner, 2000). Enhanced transport infrastructure plays a major role in the process of structural transformation and suburbanization by creating more efficient connection between business activities and the labor force (Berg *et al.*, 2017). The scale of resulting residential reallocation and population redistribution is varied, subject to the land development policies and restrictions (Levkovich *et al.*, 2020).

Reductions in the cost of commuting to work and enhanced accessibility in peripheral areas through road and highway infrastructure can considerably impact regional housing markets (Levkovich *et al.*, 2020; Bourassa *et al.*, 2021). New and improving transportation infrastructure can lead to changes in residential composition and property quality of neighborhoods, thus, reshaping the residential environment in the long-term (Won *et al.*, 2015; Gonzalez-Navarro and Quintana-Domeque, 2016). Empirical analyses of the impacts of transportation infrastructure on housing prices or rents in the United States and Europe have generally found positive impact on housing values (Martínez and Viegas, 2009). However, most of the studies in the relevant literature evaluate the impact of new road infrastructure rather than the impact of improvements in existing road infrastructure (Liang *et al.*, 2021). In particular, research regarding the impact of renovating and expanding a road system on the quality of nearby residential property and the composition of property residents is especially lacking.

The Vías Nuevas de Lima (VNL) project in Lima, Peru provides an interesting case study regarding the impact of renovation and expansion of an existing highway system on nearby residential property's quality and its occupants. In 2013, the Metropolitan Municipality of Lima (MML) granted to Rutas de Lima S.A.C. Consortium the VNL project with an estimated investment of nearly US $500 million and a self-sustaining toll concession for 30 years. Based on a Private–Public Partnership (PPP), the project includes the designing, construction, operation, and maintenance of new urban roads, as well as the operation and conservation of existing urban roads over 20 urban districts. The project extends nearly 115 kilometers (km) and expects to benefit the residents and businesses in those districts with a more modern and secure highway system providing improved connections with each other and the capital.

Since the project's inception, the share of single-family dwellings in the 20 affected districts has decreased while the number of the multi-family (apartments) units have continued to increase. As shown in a case study of Da Nang city in Vietnam, road construction led to changes in the composition of nearby residents, and the quality and nature of nearby properties. In particular, residential density increased in proximate areas (Won *et al.*, 2015). Thus, the objective of this study is to examine the impact of proximity to the highway on the number of residents in higher-quality housing. In this sense, we are more interested in exploring the longer-term impacts of the highway improvement on resident behavior and property decision instead of the short-term impact that is usually observed by real estate values (Cervero and Kang, 2011).

The remaining of the chapter is organized as follows. Section 2 discusses the VNL project and the related study area in our analysis. Section 3 describes the methodology and data, and the model estimates are presented in Section 4. Discussion and conclusion comprise Section 5.

2. Study Area

2.1. *The Vías Nuevas de Lima (VNL) Project*

The VNL project extends from the Santa Rosa district in northern Lima Province to Pucusana in the south of the province, covering 20 of the province's districts[i] and the Constitutional Province of Callao. The project of highway expansion and renovation aims to improve the efficiency and safety of the road infrastructure, thus, resulting in better quality of the operation and maintenance of the roads for the residents in the province. Furthermore, the renovated highway system is expected to increase districts' connectivity with each other and with the capital, thus, promoting their development.

Based on a PPP framework, the project utilizes a Build–Operate–Transfer (BOT) scheme to construct and renovate the North Panamericana highway (31.5 km), South Panamericana highway (54.1 km), and Ramiro Prialé highway (29 km). The project involves the design, construction, and operation of the new roads as well as the renovation of the existing roads. For the North Panamericana section (Panamericana Norte in Figure 1), the project includes: (i) Construction of the Óvalo Habich–Puente Chillón road, and intersections of Los Alisos, Naranjal, 25 de Enero and Canta Callao avenues with North Panamericana highway, and (ii) Improved operation and maintenance of the Eduardo de Habich–Ancón connection. For the South Panamericana section (Panamericana Sur in Figure 1), the project considers: (i) Construction of connections at El Derby–San Borja Norte avenues, Vivanco–Buganvillas avenues, and Benavides Avenue–South Panamericana highway. In the Ramiro Prialé section (Ramiro Prialé in Figure 1), the project covers the renovation of the Las Torres bridge section and 19 km expansion of Ramiro Prialé highway.

As of 2017, 92 percent of the proposed renovation of the North Panamericana section has been completed; while the progress of

---

[i]The 20 districts include Santa Rosa, Ventanilla, Puente Piedra, Los Olivos, Comas, Independencia, Santa Anita, Ate, Lurigancho-Chosica, Chaclacayo, San Borja, Santiago de Surco, San Juan de Miraflores, Villa el Salvador, Lurín, Punta Hermosa, Punta Negra, San Bartolo, Santa María del Mar, and Pucusana.

Figure 1. Vías Nuevas de Lima project.
Source: https://rutasdelima.pe/sobre-nosotros/

the South Panamericana and the Ramiro Prialé sections have been delayed with only 54.5 and 18.4 percent completed. Thus, this study is associated with the North Panamericana highway section (the solid black line in Figure 2) that connects four districts, including San Martín de Porres, Los Olivos, Independencia and Comas. These four

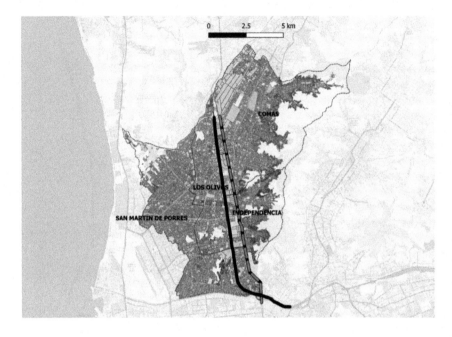

Figure 2. Map of the study area.
Note: The black solid line represents Via Nueva de Lima (VNL), and the dashed line is the Metropolitano bus rapid transit system.

districts are suburban areas of Lima. The population in these four districts increased from 1.59 million people to 1.71 million between 2007 and 2017, with an average of 7 percent growth per year.

2.2. *Residential Characteristics in the Study Area*

Prior to 2000, residential properties were primarily owned by high-income families that build their house independently. However, the share of single-family property has gradually reduced since 2000 as higher and middle-income families have also focused on the reuse of already developed land for other types of property (Wiese *et al.*, 2016). The top panel in Table 1 presents the share of single-family, multi-family and other dwelling type in the study area in 2007 and 2017. It is clearly seen that the share of single-family type of dwelling has declined between 2 and 13 percent points among the four districts

Table 1. Percent of dwelling type and property characteristics by district in 2007 and 2017.

	Comas		Independencia		Los Olivos		San Martín de Porres	
	2007	2017	2007	2017	2007	2017	2007	2017
Single-family	92.60	85.90	91.17	89.09	83.69	70.69	84.05	74.43
Multi-family	5.10	12.50	6.28	9.32	13.33	28.15	12.46	23.64
Other	2.30	1.60	2.55	1.59	2.98	1.16	3.49	1.93
Cement as the main material in floor	89.44	93.00	22.51	35.49	35.36	53.07	85.53	88.50
Cement as the main material in walls	89.00	89.15	52.07	87.60	88.21	94.85	88.43	87.35

over the 10 years. Meanwhile, the multi-family dwelling has expanded by 3 to nearly 15 percent point.

The bottom panel in Table 1 presents a general context of the change in housing quality among the four districts in 2007 and 2017. An improvement in the quality of houses is observed across the study area, given an increased share of residential properties with cement as predominant material in floor and walls over the 10 years. Independencia has the greatest improvement in residential property quality with the share of the property using cement as the main material in floor and walls both increasing by more than 50 percent.

3.   Methodology and Data

3.1.   *Econometric Specification*

To estimate the effect of the VNL project on household's residential property quality and number of residents, we form an econometric model that considers the proximity between households in residential block and the renovated highway. As suggested in the literature, the effects of highway infrastructures on residency could be positive because of increased accessibility to transportation network but also unfavorable due to negative externalities, such as noise or pollution (Levkovich *et al.*, 2020; Tillema *et al.*, 2012; Iacono and Levinson, 2011). These effects imply a non-monotonic relation between residential choice and the highway. We thus propose the following specification:

$$y_{ij} = \alpha + \beta_1 ln(Distance_{ij}) + \beta_2 (ln(Distance_{ij}))^2$$
$$+ X'_{ij}\gamma + \phi_j + \varepsilon_{ij} \tag{1}$$

where y_{ij} is the dependent variable representing the number of households in higher-quality property at residential block i in district j; $ln(Distance_{ij})$ is the natural logarithm of shortest Euclidean distance between the household at block i in district j and the VNL highway; X_{ij} is a matrix with some covariates as control variables and ϕ_j represents district fixed effects. The squared term in $ln(Distance)$ is included to capture the potential non-linear effects of proximity to the highway. A concave relationship is anticipated as the effect of proximity to the highway could be null or even negative due to externalities, if a household is located very close to the renovated highway. However, the effects could become positive when the distance to the highway gradually extends given reductions in negative externalities and reasonable accessibility. The positive effect is likely to decay and eventually disappear along with the increasing proximity from the household location to the highway (Iacono and Levinson, 2011).

The dependent variable in our model is the number of people living in "higher-quality property". The variable is generated by multiplying the number of people living in a residential block with the proportion of residents living in the property with floors and walls made by good construction materials (e.g., cement). We hypothesize that the VNL renovation project will affect the number of residents living in higher-quality housing nearby; that is, parameters β_1 and β_2 are statistically null in year 2007, while different from zero in year 2017. Also, the impact is hypothesized to be non-monotonic along with the distance to the highway.

In addition to the VNL, there is a bus rapid transit (BRT) system of Lima, the Metropolitano, in the study area. The route of this BRT is parallel to VNL (the dashed line in Figure 2) and could act as a confounder. Thus, we include the proximity from residential block to the Metropolitano in the model to control its impact on the dependent variable.

Several other control variables are also considered in the model, including three distance variables from the household's residential block (proximity to pre-school, secondary-school, higher education institutes) and two demographic variables of households in the block (percent of household's native language and percent of higher education). The district fixed effect is also incorporated. Some proximity variables, such as proximity to park, to supermarket, are excluded because of their high correlation with the proximity to schools or institutes.

Equation (1) is estimated using Ordinary Least Squares with the robust standard errors for each year. Based on the estimates, the semi-elasticity of the distance to the renovated highway is calculated.

3.2. *Data*

The dependent variable and the demographic variable of household in residential block are derived from National Census of People and Houses (in Spanish, Censos Nacionales de Población y Vivienda, CPV). This census is conducted every decade by the National Institute of Statistics and Informatics (in Spanish, El Instituto Nacional de Estadística e Informática, INEI) and collects information of, among others, the number of the household members, physical characteristics of the houses, and socioeconomic characteristics of residents.[ii] We use the census data in 2007 and 2017, which corresponds to the pre- and post-VNL project periods. The individual household data in 2007 is available to us; however, only aggregate information at a block level is accessible in 2017. Thus, we compile and aggregate the 2007 individual data into a block level to maintain the consistency in our estimates.

The georeferenced data for distance variables is collected from different sources. Firstly, polygons of districts in Lima are taken from the Spatial Data Infrastructure website.[iii] This information allows us to select districts of Lima where the VNL is located. From this

---

[ii]The data is available from http://censos2017.inei.gob.pe/pubinei/index.asp
[iii]https://www.geoidep.gob.pe/servicios-idep/catalogo-nacional-de-servicios-web/servicios-de-publicacion-de-objetos-wfs

source, we also gather the lines of the VNL, as well as the lines of the Metropolitano. Secondly, we collect the polygons of the residential blocks in the districts of the study from INEI. Finally, we gather the location information of schools and higher education institutes in 2007 and 2017 from the National Education Census of the Ministry of Education of Peru.[iv] The Euclidean distance from each residential block to VNL, and other referential points, like the Metropolitano, schools, and higher education institutes, is then calculated with Geographic Information System (GIS software).

For our estimations, we only use blocks within 500 meters from the VNL because they are the most exposed to the improvements in the highway. Table 2 presents descriptive statistics of the dataset. Note that the mean in the number of people living in higher-quality properties remain similar between the two periods, but the dispersion increases in the second period thus resulting in a higher standard deviation. Also, the mean of households per block increases from 47.24 to 56.42 between two periods, indicating increasing residential density after the highway improvement.

4. Results

Model results (i.e., Equation (1)) for 2007 and 2017 are presented in Table 3. Our main variable of interest are the linear and quadratics distances to VNL. In 2007, neither the linear nor quadratic term of this variable is statistically significant at the 5 percent level, whereas both variables become significant after the highway renovation in 2017. This confirms our hypothesis regarding the impact of the VNL project on the quality of residential housing. Also, the positive sign of its linear term in logarithm and negative sign of its quadratic term in logarithm indicate a concave relation between the proximity to the VNL and the number of people living in higher-quality houses. This result confirms our hypothesis of the non-monotonic relationship and suggests that people intend to choose good quality houses with a

---

[iv]http://escale.minedu.gob.pe/

Table 2. Descriptive statistics of the variables per residential block in 2007 and 2017.

Year	Variable	Mean	Std. Dev.	Min	Max	N
2007	# People living in good quality houses	176.01	121.01	0	817.10	905
	ln(distance to the road VNL)	5.47	0.61	2.93	6.22	905
	Number of households	47.24	33.04	1	219	905
	Number of people	192.86	128.78	1	884	905
	Percent of people whose native language is Spanish	0.95	0.06	0	1	905
	Percent of people with higher education	0.42	0.13	0	1	905
	ln(distance to pre-school)	0.08	0.05	0.00	0.24	905
	ln(distance to secondary school)	0.10	0.05	0.01	0.28	905
	ln(distance to institutes)	0.43	0.20	0.02	0.87	905
2017	# People living in good quality houses	176.80	160.19	10.29	2,442.1	894
	ln(distance to the road VNL)	5.47	0.62	2.93	6.22	894
	Number of households	56.42	60.72	6	1,207	894
	Number of people	194.02	183.64	30	3,197	894
	Percent of people whose native language is Spanish	0.94	0.05	0.59	1	894
	Percent of people with higher education	0.45	0.12	0.10	0.82	894
	ln(distance to pre-school)	0.06	0.04	0.00	0.23	894
	ln(distance to secondary school)	0.09	0.05	0.01	0.24	894
	ln(distance to institutes)	0.40	0.20	0.02	0.79	894

Source: National Census of People and Houses of 2007 and 2017, INEI; Spatial Data Infrastructure of the Government of Peru; National Education Census, MINEDU.

reasonable access to the VNL after its renovation, but not too close to the highway to avoid negative externalities (Tillema *et al.*, 2012).

The semi-elasticities of the distance to the highway further illustrates this relationship are presented in Figure 3. Prior to the

Table 3. Parameter estimates for Equation (1) with the number of people living in higher-quality housing as dependent variable.

	2007	2017
ln(distance to VNL)	101.7	231.3*
	[0.281]	[0.017]
ln(distance to VNL)^2	−10.97	−22.49*
	[0.220]	[0.016]
ln(distance to the Metropolitano)	35.37***	31.36***
	[0.000]	[0.000]
ln(distance to pre-school)	−113.3	−358.7*
	[0.251]	[0.042]
ln(distance to secondary-school)	−400.4***	−249.5*
	[0.000]	[0.038]
ln(distance to institutes)	117.3***	81.23*
	[0.000]	[0.012]
Percentage of residents with Spanish as native language	231.3***	274.2***
	[0.000]	[0.000]
Percentage of residents with higher education	33.61	−70.41
	[0.306]	[0.104]
District = Independencia	74.51**	33.47
	[0.002]	[0.232]
District = Los Olivos	−26.59	−38.49
	[0.179]	[0.095]
District = San Martín de Porres	7.784	−3.567
	[0.692]	[0.860]
Constant	−510.9	−809.3**
	[0.053]	[0.002]
Observations	905	894

Note: p-values in brackets. $^*p < 0.05$, $^{**}p < 0.01$, $^{***}p < 0.001$. Comas is the reference district.

VNL project (the left panel), proximity to the highway did not affect the number of people residing in good quality housing at any point within 500 meters from the highway. However, after the renovation (the right panel), the impact of the proximity to the highway on residents in good quality residential property become positive and statistically significant in the same 500 meters area. The positive impact initially increases and diminishes after passing 13.5 meters ($e^{2.6} = 13.46$), and ultimately becomes statistically insignificant

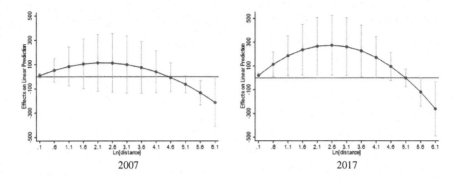

Figure 3. Marginal effects of distance to the VNL on the number of people living in the higher-quality housing before and after the renovation project.

when the proximity is beyond 60 meters ($e^{4.1} = 60.34$). Results in both Table 3 and Figure 3 confirm that the renovated highway affects the number of people living in a good quality house in a "middle buffer" range.

Among other distance variables in Table 3, the impact of proximity to another important public transit (Metropolitano) on the number of people in higher-quality housing is statistically significant in both 2007 and 2017. The positive sign for the distance to the Metropolitano suggests that people in higher-quality housing prefer not to live too close to the transportation facility to avoid the negative externalities. A negative and statistically significant impact of the proximity to the pre- or secondary-schools on the number of people in good quality housing is found, suggesting more people prefer to live closer to those school areas. The positive sign of distance to higher education institutes could be related to more traffic and noises around colleges, so, more people may choose to live further away. The percent of people with Spanish as native language has positive impact on the number of people living in a higher-quality housing. The district fixed effect is generally not statistically significant in both the periods.

To further examine if the proximity to the VNL only affects the number of people living in higher-quality residential property,

Table 4. Parameter estimates for Equation (1) with number of people living in lower- quality housing as dependent variable.

	2007	2017
ln(distance to road VNL)	8.164	15.67
	[0.558]	[0.420]
ln(distance to road VNL)^2	−0.929	−1.552
	[0.558]	[0.419]
ln(distance to the Metropolitano)	3.536**	−1.261
	[0.001]	[0.400]
ln(distance to pre-school)	6.292	−23.05
	[0.675]	[0.615]
ln(distance to secondary-school)	−18.31	−26.40
	[0.136]	[0.309]
ln(distance to higher education institutes)	8.247**	21.03**
	[0.009]	[0.003]
Percentage of people with Spanish as native language	2.339	−27.09*
	[0.832]	[0.036]
Percentage of people with higher education	−34.02***	−3.428
	[0.000]	[0.622]
District = Independencia	−2.652	13.51*
	[0.455]	[0.028]
District = Los Olivos	−5.997	7.568
	[0.060]	[0.181]
District = San Martín de Porres	−1.089	6.981
	[0.723]	[0.140]
Constant	−9.710	2.100
	[0.790]	[0.967]
Observations	905	894

Note: p-values in brackets. $^*p < 0.05$, $^{**}p < 0.01$, $^{***}p < 0.001$. Comas is the reference district.

we also estimate the impact of the proximity to the highway on the number of people living in lower-quality housing. As presented in Table 4, the coefficients for the linear and quadratic terms of the distance variables are not statistically significant regardless of the VNL project implementation. Similarly, Figure 4 shows that the marginal effect of the proximity to the highway is not statistically significant at any point along the distance to the highway. Thus, along with the results in Figure 3 and Figure 4, the findings suggest that the highway renovation affects the number of residents in

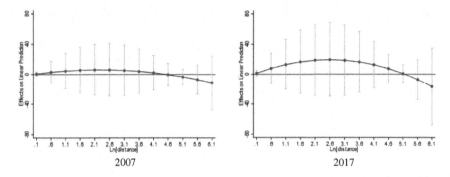

2007   2017

Figure 4. Marginal effects of distance to the VNL on the number of people living in the lower-quality housing before and after the renovation project.

the higher-quality housing only, instead of the overall number of residential units. Also, the renovated highway attracts more people to move to higher-quality housing and likely increases the demand for high-quality residential property within a range of the highway.

To check the robustness of the proxy variable used for the number of people living in higher-quality housing, we compare the estimates of Equation (1) using the proposed proxy for 2007 with the actual data in the same year. As stated in the method section, individual level data for households and persons is only available for 2007. Results in Table 5 suggest that the parameters obtained using the proxy as dependent variable are similar to those using actual data in terms of magnitude and statistical significance. Thus, the performance of the proposed proxy in the estimates is deemed to be validated.

The literature indicates that the improvement of the highway may also change the composition of people that live near the transportation infrastructure (Chapple, 2014). Thus, we further explore the impact of proximity to the highway on the percent of residents with higher levels of formal education in a residential block, which is a typical proxy variable for high-skilled workers. As shown in Table 6, the estimates also suggest that the impact of proximity to the highway on the percent of people holding a higher

Table 5. Parameter estimates using the proxy and actual data for the dependent variable in 2007.

	Proxy	Data
ln(distance to road VNL)	101.7	123.2
	[0.281]	[0.174]
ln(distance to road VNL)^2	−10.97	−13.17
	[0.220]	[0.126]
ln(distance to the Metropolitano)	35.37***	32.69***
	[0.000]	[0.000]
ln(distance to pre-school)	−113.3	−141.7
	[0.251]	[0.148]
ln(distance to secondary-school)	−400.4***	−374.2***
	[0.000]	[0.000]
ln(distance to institutes)	117.3***	109.8***
	[0.000]	[0.000]
Percentage of people with Spanish as native language	231.3***	222.5***
	[0.000]	[0.000]
Percentage of people with higher education	33.61	30.91
	[0.306]	[0.335]
District = Independencia	74.51**	81.77***
	[0.002]	[0.000]
District = Los Olivos	−26.59	−12.25
	[0.179]	[0.517]
District = San Martín de Porres	7.784	14.72
	[0.692]	[0.431]
Constant	−510.9	−547.8*
	[0.053]	[0.030]
Observations	905	905

Note: p-values in brackets. *$p < 0.05$, **$p < 0.01$, ***$p < 0.001$. Comas is the reference district.

education degree in a block is only statistically significant in the post-renovation period (year 2017). Figure 5 depicts a similar pattern as observed for the number of people living in good quality houses in Figure 3; that is, a concave relation between the share of people with higher education with the distance to the VNL after highway renovation. The renovated highway affects the share of people with higher education up to 13.5 meters ($e^{2.6} = 13.46$), the same distance as found for the largest increase in the number of residents in higher-quality property in 2017 as presented in Figure 3.

Table 6. Parameter estimates for Equation (1) using percent of people with higher education in a block as dependent variable.

	2007	2017
ln(distance to road VNL)	0.0796	0.215*
	[0.343]	[0.030]
ln(distance to road VNL)^2	−0.00967	−0.0221*
	[0.236]	[0.020]
ln(distance to pre-school)	−0.472***	−0.173
	[0.000]	[0.125]
ln(distance to secondary-school)	−0.284**	−0.415***
	[0.001]	[0.000]
ln(distance to institutes)	−0.0603**	−0.0279
	[0.006]	[0.180]
ln(distance to the Metropolitano)	0.00697	0.00765
	[0.473]	[0.358]
District = Independencia	0.0520*	0.106***
	[0.041]	[0.000]
District = Los Olivos	0.0339	0.139***
	[0.135]	[0.000]
District = San Martín de Porres	0.00445	0.0742***
	[0.842]	[0.000]
Constant	0.297	−0.151
	[0.189]	[0.564]
Observations	905	894

Note: p-values in brackets. $^*p < 0.05$, $^{**}p < 0.01$, $^{***}p < 0.001$. Comas is the reference district.

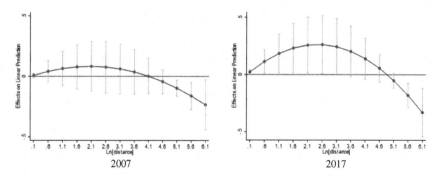

2007   2017

Figure 5. Margin effects of the proximity to the highway on the percent of people with higher education in each block before and after the VNL project.

5. Discussion and Conclusion

In this study we have examined the impact of a road infrastructure renovation project, Vías Nuevas de Lima project, in the north suburban area of Lima, the capital of Peru and the most populated city of the country, on indicators of housing quality and resident education level. The VNL project primarily aims to improve existing highways that transversely connects various parts of the region and the city. Our results suggest that after the renovation project, the relation between proximity and the number of people living in higher-quality houses is concave in nature, suggesting that people move to higher-quality houses in the middle buffer zones around the highway system. Households prefer to keep a certain distance away from the highway to avoid possible negative externalities that may appear (such as noise) but stay sufficiently close to benefit from improved access. This relation in the pre-renovation period, however, is not statistically significant. The results, along with the statistics of households in a residential block, appear to suggest that a number of households chose to move to higher-quality properties with access to the renovated highway system in the north suburban area of Lima after the VNL project. This finding may also imply population redistribution from city central points, which is consistent with the related literature (Baum-Snow, 2007; Levkovich *et al.*, 2020). These households benefit from higher-quality housing in the suburban area while maintaining the connection with the city center through the improved highway system. The impact of proximity to the highway on the share of person with higher education in a block follows the similar pattern, suggesting that these residents were also high-skilled workers.

Our results also suggest that such impact of proximity to the highway during the post-VNL period is only found for the number of residents in higher-quality property and not for lower-quality housing. The findings imply that the improvement of the major transport corridor seems to have attracted an increasing number of new communities from outside (likely reallocated from center cities) into the north suburban area, which is consistent with the findings from Won *et al.* (2015). The migrants are able to afford a higher-quality (and likely expensive) residential property and might have major influence in the development of urban space in the neighborhood in the longer-term and may lead to the change of residential composition, which could result in a gentrification (Bockarjovaa *et al.*, 2020). However, our study does not have sufficient information to shed light regarding a gentrification hypothesis. More analysis will be needed, mainly with other longitudinal databases that allow to track movements of people between locations in different periods.

References

Baum-Snow, N. (2007). Did Highways Cause Suburbanization. *The Quarterly Journal of Economics, 122*(2), 775–805.

Berg, C.N., Deichmann, U., Liu, Y., and Selod, H. (2017). Transport Policies and Development. *The Journal of Development Studies, 53*(4), 465–480.

Bockarjovaa, I.M., Botzenab, W.J.W., van Schiec, M.H., and Koetse, M.J. (2020). Property Price Effects of Green Interventions in Cities: A Meta-Analysis and Implications for Gentrification. *Environmental Science and Policy, 112*(10), 293–304.

Bourassa, S.C., Hoesli, M., Merlin, L., and Renne, J. (2021). Big Data, Accessibility and Urban House Prices. *Urban Studies, 58*(15), 3176–3195.

Brueckner, J. (2000). Urban Sprawl: Diagnosis and Remedies. *International Regional Science Review, 23*(2), 160–171.

Cervero, R., and Kang, C.D. (2011). Bus Rapid Transit Impacts on Land Uses and Land Values in Seoul, Korea *Transport Policy, 18*(1), 102–116.

Chapple, K. (2014). *Planning Sustainable Cities and Regions: Towards More Equitable Development*. Routledge.

Gonzalez-Navarro, M., and Quintana-Domeque, C. (2016). Paving Streets for the Poor: Experimental Analysis of Infrastructure Effects. *Review of Economics and Statistics, 98*(2), 254–267.

Iacono, M., and Levinson, D. (2011). Location, Regional Accessibility, and Price Effects: Evidence from Home Sales in Hennepin County, Minnesota. *Transportation Research Record, 2245*(1), 87–94.

Levkovich, O., Rouwendal, J., and van Ommeren, J. (2020). The Impact of Highways on Population Redistribution: The Role of Land Development Restrictions. *Journal of Economic Geography, 20*(3), 783–808.

Liang, J., Koo, K.M., and Lee, C.L. (2021). Transportation Infrastructure Improvement and Real Estate Value: Impact of Level Crossing Removal Project on Housing Prices. *Transportation, 48*(6), 2969–93011.

Martínez, L.M., and Viegas, J.M. (2009). Effects of Transportation Accessibility on Residential Property Values: Hedonic Price Model in the Lisbon, Portugal, Metropolitan Area. *Transportation Research Record, 2115*(1), 127–137.

Tillema, T., Hamersma, M., Sussman, J.M., and Arts, J. (2012). Extending the Scope of Highway Planning: Accessibility, Negative Externalities and the Residential Context. *Transport Reviews, 32*(6), 745–759.

Wiese, C., Miyahiro, J., and Marcés, R. (2016). Desigualdad urbana en Lima Metropolitana. In Jungbluth, W.M. (Ed.), *Perú hoy: Desigualdad y Desarrollo* (pp. 333–368). Desco: Centro de Estudios y Promoción del Desarrollo, Perú.

Won, S., Cho, S.E., and Kim, S. (2015). The Neighborhood Effects of New Road Infrastructure: Transformation of Urban Settlements and Resident's Socioeconomic Characteristics in Danang, Vietnam. *Habitat International, 50*, 169–179.

Index

Printed in the United States
by Baker & Taylor Publisher Services